CW00968075

The Dangerously Truthful Diary of a Sicilian Housewife

VERONICA DI GRIGOLI

DISCLAIMER

This is a work of fiction. Names, characters, businesses, places, events and incidents are either the products of the author's imagination or used in a fictitious manner. Any resemblance to actual persons, living or dead, or actual events is purely coincidental.

FIRST EDITION

Copyright © 2015 Veronica Hughes
All rights reserved.
ISBN-10: 1514802252
ISBN-13: 978-1514802250

DEDICATION

This book is dedicated to my beloved husband.
Everything in it is his fault.

PROLOGUE

A SICILIAN FISHING VILLAGE

A few years ago, I plucked up the courage to leave my family and friends in London, give up my well paid job as a business consultant, sell my house, car and collection of seventies disco albums, and move to a fishing village in northern Sicily with a population of about seven hundred people (several of whom do still have their own teeth).

When I go for a walk here in the village, I greet almost everyone I see and stop for a chat along the way. Sometimes buying a loaf of bread can take two hours, but I am never in a rush. Nowadays I have time to stop and play with people's babies, to help an old lady who has dropped her keys, or to ask people how they are and really listen to the answer. In this village everyone is watching and everyone cares.

The fishermen go out at night or early in the morning in tiny wooden rowing boats with room for just four people, or one fisherman and a net. In the morning, they sell whatever they have caught - octopus, squid, prawns, rock and cuttlefish - directly on the seafront. In stormy weather they drag their little boats from the beach right up onto the main road, to avoid the risk of never seeing them again, and the heart of the village is brightened up by their orange and royal-blue paint.

Those too old to go fishing bring a kitchen chair outside and sit on the pavement chatting to each other across the narrow streets, among the laundry strung up from one lamppost to the next. Having been examined and discussed in depth by all of them, I am now accepted as benign and, as I stroll past, I am sometimes offered a guest chair to join them for a chat.

"How did you meet your husband, and come to live in our little village?" they ask me.

And I always answer them,

"Well, it all started with a wedding."

Veronica Di Grigoli

1

A WEDDING

"Fancy going to a Mafia wedding in Sicily?" my sister asked, one drizzly English afternoon.

Who could turn down an invitation like that? Certainly not me. I logged onto Europe's rudest low-cost airline and bought a plane ticket before you could say "horse head."

The bride was a German friend of my sister's, but the groom was Sicilian. Obviously, a Sicilian wedding with wine, women and song would be immeasurably more entertaining than a German one with speeches and sausages. I gleefully fantasised about cramming into a medieval Italian church full of men in sharp black suits and dark sunglasses, and settling on a pew amongst magnificently rotund little women dressed in black.

"No more Mafia jokes from now on," ordered my sister Josephine when we landed at Palermo airport. "Sicilians do NOT find it funny."

We took a coach past the turquoise sea and the cloudless, azure sky. In Palermo, showy magnificence stood cheek-by-jowl with filth and dereliction. We passed streets adorned with stone carvings, fancy iron balconies, and baroque statues of naked women cavorting together in fantastical orgies of cellulite. A minute later we were squeezing down litter-strewn back streets which looked like the rubble of war-torn Aleppo or Sarajevo, festooned with tatty laundry. A couple of toddlers sitting in a doorway, beneath a purple bra large enough to use for camping, looked up and waved as we drove past.

The next day, Josephine and I naively turned up outside the church at ten o'clock in the morning, the time printed on the invitations. Since my sister had insisted there is no such thing as being "overdressed" for a Sicilian wedding, I wore a full-length beaded, satin scarlet evening dress with a train, two diamanté necklaces and one choker, and a feather boa. My sister Josephine was dressed similarly, though her gown was black as she always frets that she might look plump: how she actually looks is blonde and voluptuous enough to make Italian men's eyes pop out of their sockets.

I paced nervously around the flagstone courtyard, looking up at the ornate baroque entrance and the statues of two medieval popes staring down at me, stonily. Ten-thirty passed and we were still the only people outside the church.

"We must have come to the wrong place," I panicked.

Josephine phoned the bride.

"Oh," she said after a moment. "I see. Never mind."

The bride, Michaela, had apparently forgotten to let us know that the time printed on invitations to Sicilian weddings is an hour earlier than the actual wedding is going to take place, because everyone is bound to be late. Sure enough the Sicilians, who knew the correct protocol, began drifting along in dribs and drabs at about a quarter to eleven. The men all wore the smartest black suits and black ties I had ever seen, while the women wore black evening dresses, every last one of them, and dripped with jewellery.

"Hmmm," said my sister. "I didn't know they really do all dress in black. Sorry about that."

"But you were right about the spangles," I said.

"It still looks a bit funereal."

"Like a funeral for a chorus dancer from the Moulin Rouge," I answered.

The Sicilians apparently thought my burlesque cabaret outfit was spot on, and were soon greeting me like a long lost relative. The women were, anyway. The men were greeting me with such enticing enquiries as "Avva you gotta one boyfriend?" and "You wont one ice-cream with me?" and romantic compliments like "You avva gotta two very beautifuls blue eyes."

While talking to some of the groom's cousins I tried to revive my rusty Italian, but eventually I had to fish a mini Italian-English dictionary out of my rhinestone-encrusted clutch bag.

"My goodness, stop looking so nerdy!" hissed Josephine. "Put that away!"

"But I want to talk to people," I protested. "And anyway, I just *am* a nerd. I can live with that."

"Yes, you are," said Josephine, affectionately. "I'd go mad if I had to do your job. I couldn't spend twelve hours a day in the bank doing maths."

"I know," I answered.

"You haven't got a calculator in there too, have you?" she asked suspiciously, pointing at my bag with her ostrich-feather fan.

I didn't answer.

Suddenly everyone fell silent. The bride had arrived, exuding classic Hollywood glamour. The female guests devoutly covered their bare shoulders with delicate black lace shawls and crossed themselves before entering the Catholic Church. I modestly wound my red feather boa around my shoulders five times and stalked up the aisle feeling a little like an ostrich.

After three and a half hours, I realised Catholic wedding services take a long time.

"I've heard they last anything up to four days," whispered my sister behind her tickly feather fan.

I tried to keep up while the priest read through Genesis and Exodus; I studied the murals in detail while he was on Deuteronomy; somewhere in the book of Obadiah I realised I had lost the use of my legs. A famous Italian soprano sang *Ave Maria* towards the end of the service, and more than one pair of eyes sparkled with tears as the bride and groom kissed before the altar: perhaps they were tears of relief that we were getting near the beginning of the end.

After the service, the wedding photographers went into such a frenzy of shutter-clicking that the bride emerged from the church like a film star being mobbed by the paparazzi. White doves were released at the church door to represent the couple's joyous future together. Fluttering rose petals filled the air. And, as a single thirty-something, a knot tightened in my stomach as I wondered for the millionth time when it would be my turn.

I had just got out of a relationship with a slob who sometimes left half-eaten slices of pizza on top of the toilet tank. He never paid any household bills, and left his bicycle in the dining room because he was too lazy to unlock the garage door. He also insisted on brewing his own beer *in the bedroom*. Homebrew beer-making kits smell of mushrooms and piddle, for those of you who have never stood near one. When he took to coming home at two or three in the morning blind drunk, I realised that spinsterhood has its benefits, and kicked him out.

The foreign guests without cars were driven by coach to the reception, held in the gardens of a sprawling eighteenth century villa. The lawn was bordered with jasmine and pink roses, and a string quartet played background music. My sister and I sat down as soon as we found our table, since we were finding our six inch heels a little challenging by that point. A group of young men came and sat with us, all of them cousins of the groom. I was starting to feel dazed by the sheer number of gorgeous-looking men who had been introduced to me as cousins of the groom. Once the tally had gone past three hundred, I had just given up trying to keep track, despite the fact that most of them wanted my phone number. My phone memory was full of hastily tapped in entries such as 'Giovanni big eyes', 'Giovanni nice teeth', 'Giovanni deep suntan', 'Giuseppe tall one', 'Giuseppe with the hair', and so on.

Yet the cousin sitting opposite me had an indefinable quality that made him stand out from all the rest. He was so full of happiness it radiated from him like heat from a stove, and yet all the exuberance rested on a bedrock of serenity. He told me his name was Valentino.

"So, how did you meet Michaela?" he asked.

"She's really a friend of my sister's," I answered. "This is actually the first time I've met her."

"No it isn't!" exclaimed Josephine. "She works in the bank with me. Don't you remember? You walked past us once when I was having lunch with her outside a café near work. You stopped and chatted to us for several minutes."

My sister worked in Human Resources in a bank around the corner from mine, and we often bumped into each other like this. I am a tiny bit scared of my sister sometimes. She sometimes spends days at a time telling lists of people they are fired.

"Oh, I don't remember," I mumbled, feeling a little embarrassed.

"Well, she *certainly* remembers you," Josephine declared emphatically. "That's why she invited you to the wedding."

Josephine has a degree in modern languages, and she went on to tell the anecdote to the whole table in her flawless Italian. I had apparently made an unforgettable impression on the bride during the mere five minutes we had ever spent together. In fact, Josephine insisted, I had made her laugh until tea came out of her nostrils by describing an attempted shopping trip in Indonesia.

While on holiday Bali, I had noticed that my clothes had all developed perma-B.O. as a result of the tropical climate. Intent on remedying the situation, I had entered a department store which seemed to contain nothing but children's clothes.

A helpful shop assistant looked anxiously at my boobs - his diminutive stature made it impossible to avoid them - and politely suggested I searched for something larger in the men's section. I browsed through their vast selection of counterfeit trendy tops. A twinkly one by "Dolce & Banana" particularly caught my eye. After splitting three of their fake designer garments in the changing cubicle, although I was only a size ten, I eventually left with a T-shirt that I could just about stretch around myself as a bikini top, groaning at every stitch. The imitation logo, pulled out until the silver letters were three times wider than they were tall, labelled my bust as "CHANNEL."

After this I had ventured back to the women's department, sought out the same diddy sales assistant, and asked if they had any bras.

"For *you*, Madam?" he asked my breasts, his eyes gaping wide.

"Nooooooo."

Having broken the ice with this polite small-talk, Josephine started to chat to one of the groom's cousins beside her, so I turned back to Valentino, the enchanting cousin opposite me.

"What were you doing in Indonesia?" he asked as the first course was served. It was a prawn risotto, which I ate with relish.

"Just on holiday," I explained. "I love travelling as much as I can. I work in a bank, which can get monotonous. I save up my money till I have enough, then go abroad."

"So do you go to a different country every year?"

"More than one a year, usually," I said. "My personal speciality is getting made redundant with a generous pay-off, so I get plenty of free time. In fact I've built myself a lucrative and fulfilling career out of getting repeatedly made redundant."

As I told Valentino about some of my travels, the waiter brought each of us a new glass, and filled it with a different type of wine. Then we were served plates of spaghetti.

"Pasta? But we've already had rice," I said to Josephine, under my breath.

"Just go with it," she answered, gulping down some wine. "The booze helps."

"By the way, they're not really in the Mafia, are they?" I asked, as quietly as possible.

"Of course not, you nitwit!" she answered "I was only joking!"

"Just checking," I told her. Those were the days when I knew no more about the Mafia than one can glean from watching *The Godfather* trilogy.

I managed to eat about two strands of spaghetti. After this we were served a seafood salad with a third glass of wine, and then a plate of roast beef and vegetables with yet another type of wine. I tasted a forkful of each, just for the sake of politeness. When we were served a whole fish with its head still on I could not even manage to do that; my red, beaded bodice was starting to remind me of Indonesia all over again. The poor deceased fish stared up at me reproachfully from the plate with its white googly eye.

"How many courses are there going to be?" I asked, feeling a little alarmed.

"About eight," answered Josephine.

"Oh no," said one of the other cousins. "Certainly not less than fourteen."

I cannot remember most of Valentino's questions or how I answered them. I just remember feeling an overpowering compulsion to lay my soul bare to him. I think it was his eyes that did it. They were a warm reddish brown, and when I looked into them I saw so much kindness I almost felt like crying. Despite my terribly rusty Italian, I talked to him with an ingenuous honesty I had never managed before in my life. Somehow I ended up telling him about my relationship with my ex. Instead of listing his annoying habits in comedic style, as I would usually have done, I talked about how bleak and hurt he had made me feel inside, and how truly desolate it is to stay with the wrong man just because you are in your thirties and afraid you may never meet the right one. I felt he was gazing into my eyes and seeing right into my soul, and it did not even scare me.

"Shall we dance?" Valentino suddenly asked. His eyes sparkled, and I wanted to laugh, just because I was so excited to have met him.

He was a very good dancer, and he twirled me around and made me laugh. Nobody else was dancing. It was not a dancing wedding. We just tangoed between all the tables while everyone else sat politely in their black clothes, eating the umpteenth course of their meal.

"Don't worry," he assured me. "It's completely dark now. Nobody can see us."

"Yes we can!" the people around us laughed.

"It's your blue eyes lighting up the garden," said Valentino into my ear. "They're like two stars fallen down from heaven."

Valentino flung me backwards till my head was six inches from the lawn, and I wound my leg around his waist as he deftly lifted me upright again and changed direction, leading me towards the string quartet. When we were close enough he said something to them in Sicilian.

"What did you ask them?" I whispered.

"I asked if they would play something a bit more lively," he answered. "I'm finding it difficult to dance the tango to this Strauss waltz."

The musicians did change their tune, and other couples gradually stood up too, abandoning their food and dancing with us. Valentino's brother grabbed my sister Josephine and twirled her around so energetically that she became completely dizzy, lost her balance and allowed herself to be guided right into the bridegroom's table. The merry groom sloshed a glass of red wine into his own face and down his shirt.

Suddenly a little old lady appeared at his side, as if by magic. Her mission was to sanitise her nephew, who was also, bystanders told me with amused smiles, one of her godsons.

"Zia Crocifissa!" the groom protested mildly as she produced some kind of product from her handbag and sprayed it at his shirt. He was hardly putting his heart into the protests; it was clear he knew they were all in vain.

"This is my *Mamma*," said Valentino.

"You can call me Crocifissa," said the little lady, smiling.

My brain short-circuited. I have no idea what my face was doing, but it made everyone laugh: Crocifissa is the Italian word for *crucifix*.

She had a maternal, cuddly appearance yet I saw something in her eyes that made me think it would be a grave mistake to do anything naughty in her presence. Her hands looked as if they could probably spank even a decent-sized adult man into low-earth orbit.

If only I had known it, this woman would be my mother in law before a year was up. I look back on those early days of blissful ignorance with a kind of dreamy nostalgia.

My mother-in-law has a big nose, big hands and a big bottom. When her mansize hands are not busy flaying and massacring vegetables or scrubbing household objects to the brink of oblivion, they fiddle with rosary beads. She goes to church twice on Sundays and is godmother to seven children: The Godmother. She likes to feed children portions of food which weigh more than they do, indoctrinate them in the ways of the Lord and scrub their faces by a method plastic surgeons call 'dermabrasion.' You might think children would be afraid of my mother-in-law but, in fact, quite the opposite is true. Children adore her. They cling to her like iron filings to a magnet, all of them.

Valentino suddenly whisked me away, leading me across the lawn in a Viennese waltz, and I gazed into those magical eyes of his again. Everyone else at the wedding gradually became a blur. The toasts to the bride and groom seemed like a dream. I was only vaguely aware of the Sicilians following their ancient wedding tradition of assembling *en masse* to stampede the pudding buffet and consume slightly more than their body weight in refined carbohydrates. I did not even bother to join the scrum for the bride's bouquet. I was just thinking, thank goodness I bought that microscopic T-shirt in Indonesia so that I could meet this wonderful Sicilian.

2

A DATE WITH VALENTINO

The morning after the wedding, I received eleven phone calls before nine-thirty, from various cousins and friends wanting to invite me out on dates. Ice-cream was a recurring theme. After the fifth caller, I realised my hangover was making it impossible for me to speak Italian, so I just let the phone ring after that.

"Turn that ruddy thing off or I'll drop it down the toilet," groaned Josephine, burying her throbbing head under a pillow in desperation.

When I was authorised to turn it on again, at about two in the afternoon, I realised that I had missed a call from Valentino. Dictionary in hand, I phoned him back. He invited me to dinner that evening, so we went.

"Only one course, I promise," he reassured me. "And no desert, if you don't want it."

I spent every afternoon and every evening with him for the next four days. Sometimes we went on sightseeing trips with Josephine and other friends, but sometimes we had dates alone.

"I want to take you out to sample real Sicilian food tonight," said Valentino on the fifth day. "Not the usual pasta and all that stuff. Sicilian food has more substance. I want to reveal all our secrets."

That sounded ominous, and I put on my tight jeans and high-heeled strappy sandals with some trepidation.

"You might want to wear something looser," said Valentino. "And some good weight-bearing footwear."

"Exactly what are you planning to make me eat?" I asked.

"Everything," he answered.

"Yes?" I responded. I noticed my own voice quavering a little.

"You have to know that we Sicilians invented fast food. Many classic Sicilian foods are greasy takeaway snacks dating back to before Christ."

He was probably not exaggerating. As I changed into looser clothing I grew alarmed and demanded a detailed menu.

"I'll tell you in the car," said Valentino.

We climbed into his battered grey Fiat Punto.

"So, the first thing on the menu is a *frittola*," he told me. His eyes glazed over as he reminisced, perhaps, about great frittolas he had eaten in the past, and he then proceeded to describe the frittola in terrifying detail.

"A frittola is made from a hand-picked blend of chunks of animal fat from which any trace of meat has been carefully trimmed away. The Sicilians were the first people in the world to realise that fat is delicious. These flavoursome morsels are deep fried in sizzling oil until they turn golden and crispy and then crammed to overflowing into a bread roll steeped in lashings of melted lard."

Eating one of these had once made a friend of Valentino's gain three stone in a single evening and, by the time he got home, he was so tightly wedged behind the steering wheel that the only way his wife could get him out of the car was to buy another frittola and use it to lubricate his belly and breasts.

We drove just a short distance before hopping out of the car. We entered a café-style restaurant where everyone ate at the bar, while a few of the heavier, presumably regular, clients gave their overworked feet a brief respite by perching one buttock on the solid steel bar stools. The floor and walls were made of gleaming black marble and everyone's voices echoed deafeningly against the hard surfaces until my ears rang with the incomprehensible hubbub of shouted Sicilian.

I was only able to manage about three mouthfuls of my frittola. Valentino had already finished his by the time I gave up, and he polished mine off gratefully. Several other men looked at him enviously as their voluptuous wives chomped through their own frittolas to the last oily crumb. They batted their husbands' marauding hands away defensively each time the men dared reach out in cheeky attempts to break off some small morsel.

Could the frittola be regarded as the zenith of Sicilian cuisine? When it comes to serving saturated fat and refined sugar in concentrations denser than a black hole, no nation on earth can rival the flair and imagination of the Sicilians.

The Sicilians invented fast food long before a mad Armenian genius named Roland McDoughnut™ realised he could become a billionaire if he tipped his entire chemistry set into a sizzling chip pan, dressed up as a clown and sold the resulting cuisine to everyone cursed with an appetite so powerful they could not wait more than four minutes for a cholesterol sandwich with a side order of deep-fried diabetes.

I am not unwilling to give credit where credit is due. I take my hat off to the Scots for inventing the deep-fried, battered Mars Bar. I award an honourable mention to the Navaho tribe of America whose 'Navaho fry-bread' soaks up so much oil it can even turn a farmer's pick-up truck see-through if you swipe it along the side. I acknowledge that Yorkshire lardy cake, that sugared delicacy with a solid plug of lard at the centre, is a creditworthy effort. Yet the gold medal, without dispute, goes to the citizens of Palermo for inventing the frittola.

After this initial foray into the world of Sicilian fast food, Valentino took me to meet an old school friend of his. His friend was a *stigghiolaro*, a Sicilian word I can only translate as 'Small intestine kebab chef.' *Stigghiola* is a flame-grilled small-intestine kebab, made by winding a length of ileum tightly around the whole length of a spring onion. As Valentino slowed down in the car by a street corner, I began to wheeze amid the smell of chokingly acrid smoke.

"Ahh, lovely!" exclaimed Valentino. "That's the sweet smell of Palermo!"

Through the haze, Valentino greeted his old friend. Valentino called him Gianfortuna, which was his surname, but apparently everyone called him that. Gianfortuna was a cheerful and spherical fellow who lived inside an impenetrable column of smoke which rendered him invisible and rose to the stratosphere, where it spread out into an atomic mushroom shape, visible across the whole bay of Palermo. On a good day it could be seen as far away as Sardinia, Valentino assured me.

"What's making so much smoke?" I gasped.

"He's grilling the small intestines," said Valentino. "It's the fat that drips off them and burns under the grill."

I tried a little piece of Valentino's oniony ileum kebab, and found it just as revolting as I had expected. He loved it. A *stigghiolaro* may seem to have a humble profession but they are esteemed as folk heroes in Palermo, for their ability to spend twelve-hour working shifts inhaling smoke so thick and pungent it would make mere mortals need artificial resuscitation and maybe an oxygen mask. They tolerate a constant dousing by droplets of animal fat hotter than the core of the sun and, not least, they stay alive despite dining on small intestines for lunch and dinner almost every day of their lives.

"My wife has to wash all my clothes three times to get the greasy smell out of them when I get home from work," Gianfortuna told me.

As this particular delicacy was not really to my taste, Valentino decided to move along to buy the next item on the menu, '*U pane cu meusa.*'

"It's a subtle blend of stir-friend spleen, Parmesan cheese and lemon juice, served in a bun," said Valentino.

Palermo's most highly esteemed spleen sandwich chef is known as Nino Ballerino, or Nino The Dancer, for the elegance with which he assembles lunch for several hundred customers a day on a pavement outside his café, near the Supreme Court of Palermo. Valentino often joins the throngs of health-conscious enforcers of justice who flock to his café in their lunch hours, because of his unique knack of wringing about half a pint of surplus oil out of the spleen before tossing it into the bread roll.

When we arrived, Nino Ballerino was on the pavement, under a deep blue sky teeming with stars, prancing around a wok so large he could have taken a bath in it. He stirred the sizzling strips of spleen with a wooden spoon longer than himself, and sprang back a couple of times as he got flicked with burning fat.

I timed Nino assembling five spleen sandwiches in twenty five seconds. He can hold three bread rolls in one hand at a time, and flip spleen into all three at once with the other. Then he deftly squeezed fresh lemons over them and finally threw handfuls of stringy Parmesan cheese in arcs, catching it in each open bun as it flew through the air. He told me he had done a five-year apprenticeship in a chippie in South End before gaining his Doctorate in Cholesterology. He managed to speak fairly fluent cockney when I pressed him.

"You enjoy da bun, innit?" asked Nino.

"Yeah, triffick," I answered.

I found the spleen sandwich remarkably palatable but I declined to sample further delicacies that night, saying I wanted to save some treats for a future evening.

"Good idea," said Valentino in English, inspired by Nino Ballerino's efforts in cockney. "Now izza time to being in barrrrr with Josephine, and others friends."

I found his ridiculously strong Italian accent very sexy when he spoke English.

"It's *to be*, not being," I corrected him.

"To be, or not to be, that is a problem," said Valentino, looking thoughtful.

3

A PILGRIMAGE

The next day I suggested I would like to climb to the top of Monte Pellegrino. I had heard that it was a mountain on the outskirts of Palermo with a church at the top carved out of the solid rock of the mountain, and that inside the church were the remains of Santa Rosalia, patron saint of Palermo, and troglodyte.

I wanted to go partly because I thought the church would be interesting, and partly because I had consumed over 999,000 calories the day before which I needed to start burning off, but mainly because I love climbing up mountains. I love the clean, oxygen-rich air. The exertion of walking uphill makes me feel invigorated. The vast open views, from above the mess of city life, make me feel free. I always come back down from a mountain feeling uplifted and inspired. What I did not know was that Sicilians only climb up Monte Pellegrino for one reason; to make a religious pilgrimage. Of course, there could be no other reason why an Italian would risk scuffing his shoes.

The next morning I suffered a holiday-wardrobe crisis. I had been working such long hours before this trip that I had not had time to glance at a travel guide and plan what I wanted do. Associating Italy with shopping for shoes and flirting in nightclubs, I had packed nothing but low-cut tops, skin-tight jeans and sandals with six-inch spiky heels. And a red feather boa, of course. How could I assemble this into a suitable outfit for a pilgrimage? And what could I wear on my feet for the two-hour climb? My sister had one pair of lilac tennis shoes with her which she generously offered to lend me for my excursion.

I do not wish to seem ungrateful, but my sister does suffer from such severe foot cheese that her Odour-eater insoles frequently develop indigestion. When she removes her shoes she always puts them out for the night, like a cat. I discharged almost half a bottle of

Chanel no. 5 into them and hoped for the best. With no heels to occupy the ends of the legs, I had to give my jeans turn-ups almost five inches deep and, yanking my tiny top both upwards and downwards at the same time, I felt as prepared for a pilgrimage as I could make myself, under the circumstances.

By the time Valentino and I were ready to set off, word had spread around his entire extended family that I was not only beautiful, educated, spoke good Italian and had blue eyes, all of which are highly commendable qualities to Italians in equal measure, but that I was also so exceptionally devout that I had insisted on making a pilgrimage to their very own saint, the *Santuzza* of Palermo. *Santuzza* means "cute little saint" and it is the nickname the people of Palermo give Saint Rosalia.

Several uncles and aunts, and Valentino's sister, came to see us off at the foot of the mountain and to bless my holy endeavour. The leader of the devout delegation was Crocifissa, Valentino's spherical little mother. Her big strong hands were holding out a string of red plastic rosary beads for me. Valentino had already told me that she led groups from her local church on pilgrimages to Naples.

"Valentino has never made this pilgrimage before," The Godmother told me, her eyes sparkling excitedly. She was bouncing up and down on her bunions with happiness. "Who would have thought that a girl would come all the way from England and inspire him to such an act of devotion!"

She squeezed my hand tightly, and then pulled my head down so she could kiss me firmly on both cheeks.

"Go!" said The Godmother. "Go, and may God bless you!"

We set off, and the family stood watching us till we turned around a rocky outcrop and could no longer see them.

"So," I said, "I gather making pilgrimages to Santa Rosalia is very important in Palermo."

"Oh yes," said Valentino. "When people have a sick relative, or some other problem, and they want to ask the saint for help, they sometimes climb up here barefoot, or on their knees."

"Gosh," I said. We walked in silence for a while.

The mountain looked almost too perfect in every detail to have been left to nature. Artistically placed stones lay all around me, and succulent plants grew between them. There were thickets of prickly pears, those tree-sized cactuses with leaves like spiky green dinner plates adorned with red, orange and yellow fruits sticking off the edges like the spokes of a wheel. It was still the cool early morning so, when a lizard walked across a rock, he was sluggish enough for me to get a good look at his sparkling emerald scales.

After rounding a few bends in the twisting stone path, we were overtaken by a middle-aged couple carrying long sticks like shepherds in a nativity play. They were wearing those outward-bounder trousers with legs you can unzip and remove, when you suddenly decide you would like to be wearing the world's unsexiest shorts instead. They had no-nonsense hiking boots and floppy cotton sun hats. Were they pilgrims? Mountaineers?

"Guten morgen!" they both called out cheerfully as they strode past.

So that was it! They were Germans.

"Guten morgen!" called Valentino.

I asked Valentino to tell me the story of Santa Rosalia as we walked. Born in 1130, she was a descendant of Charlemagne and a relative of King Roger, the Norman King of Sicily, and she lived in his palace. Before being conquered by the Normans, or Norsemen, Sicily had been ruled by caliphs, sultans and emirs of partially Arabic descent from North Africa. Their date- and walnut-filled luxurious lifestyle impressed the horned helmets off the blonde Vikings, who decided to copy them by keeping their own women in harems, where they presumably sat about weaving their Faroe Islands sheep's wool wimples, wishing they knew how to belly dance, or had some opium to help their eventless Viking lives feel a little less tedious.

King Roger loved hunting on Monte Pellegrino which, in those days, was full of hares, deer, rabbits and mountain lions. One day, Roger was out hunting with a group of his rugged friends when he was attacked by a lion. A visitor to the palace, called Prince Baldwin, bravely leapt in to save the king and killed the lion with his bare, medieval hands. As he wiped the lion blood on his jerkin and parti-coloured hosen, he was delighted to hear the King promise him literally any reward he chose to name. He named Princess Rosalia.

Since Rosalia was one of his royal chattels, and ripe for marriage at a mature thirteen years of age, King Roger foresaw no problem. Yet Rosalia immediately declared she had decided to become a nun instead, and ran off to the nearest convent. This was most embarrassing for King Roger, and for Rosalia's parents, and indeed a disappointment for Baldwin. All of them took to visiting Rosalia constantly, urging her to remove her nun's habit and marry the lion slayer.

Instead, she got hold of a pick axe and ran off into the mountains, where she hid from everyone, slept in a cave, and ate whatever she could catch or pick. Despite her tender age and extremely restrictive upbringing, she must have been a resourceful little girl indeed, for she lived on various mountains as a troglodyte hermit nun for over sixteen years, avoiding all the lions, hacking out rocky shelters for herself and praying constantly. She ended up living in a cave at the top of Monte Pellegrino, or Pilgrim's Mountain, and she carved on the cave wall 'I, Rosalia, daughter of Sinibald, Lord of Roses, and Quisquina, have taken the resolution to live in this cave for the love of my Lord, Jesus Christ.' The reason this cave was such a testing place for her to live was because, from its entrance, she could look out over her home town. Not only this, she could also clearly see the actual Norman Palace where she had grown up, and where her family still lived. She stayed in the cave until she died in her thirties.

By the time Valentino finished the story, the day was warming up and I was smelling overwhelming clouds of Chanel no. 5 with undertones of gorgonzola wafting up from my own feet. I think some of the fumes were even rising up my trouser legs and evaporating out of the waistband. I walked faster and faster, trying to get upwind of my own scent and hoping Valentino would follow me fast enough not to notice it.

Thanks to our new spurt of speed, we overtook a man with bare feet, walking steadfastly with his head bent down in pious concentration. He was muttering constantly under his breath, too quietly for me to hear whether he was fervently chanting prayers in Latin, or swearing about the painfully hot and lumpy cobblestones scattered with cactus thorns and lizard poo.

"I wonder what vow he's made," commented Valentino under his breath. He raised an eyebrow. "A vow to remember his shoes next time?"

Valentino pulled a bottle of water from his backpack and handed it to me.

"Slow down," he said, sounding a little puffed out I thought. "Shall we sit down and take a break?"

What, and get asphyxiated in a noxious cloud of French perfume and rancid Stilton? I started walking even faster.

"No no no!" I said over my shoulder. "There's still a long way to go! I enjoyed the story of Rosalia. Tell me, did you like history at school?"

"I hated it," said Valentino, trotting to catch up with my perfume-fuelled stride. "I learnt all this when I worked as a tour guide. I qualified as a yacht skipper and then worked in a holiday resort, teaching the tourists sailing and taking them on guided tours of historic sites."

I stood in the shade of a sprawling prickly pear tree and waited for him to catch up with me, holding my nose discreetly and darting off just before he reached the odour zone or, as I now thought of it, the Cheese Event Horizon.

"I would have done that job my whole life if the pay had been decent," Valentino went on. "The job I do now is dead boring, but it gives me a secure salary."

As we cantered up the path together, it gradually became narrower and rockier. The mist across the bay of Palermo was clearing and revealing a vast and beautiful panorama. The path was getting steeper, and in some places I had to put my hands on the ground to steady myself as I climbed up.

The path suddenly turned into a short flight of steps made of loosely piled up stones, and Valentino caught up with me. He showed no sign of flinching as he crossed through the Cheese Event Horizon, indeed, his nose hardly twitched.

He jumped onto the steps and held out his hand to help me up. Afterwards I did not want to let go of it. I think he wanted to keep hold of mine too, but we both still felt a little awkward about it so, after a slightly longer pause than was necessary, we let our hands fall to our sides and walked on.

"Would you like a rest now?" suggested Valentino. "Please?"

"I'm not tired, but let's have some water," I answered. We sat on a low wall and looked out over the bay of Palermo. The sea sparkled in the sunlight as if it were covered in gemstones, and the vast city sprawled all around it. There were fewer prickly pears up here, and more tall, whippy shrubs, a type of Mediterranean broom with small yellow flowers. I choked a couple of times in the odour from my footwear. Valentino, who seemed immune to the pong, pulled two bottles of water out of his backpack. I drank all of the one he handed to me, while he took two sips from his.

"That went fast," he commented. "Would you like some of this too?"

"Yes please," I said. "Can I have it all?"

"Alright," he said. I downed it in one. Outrunning my own smell was thirsty work.

"Will we be able to buy something else to drink at the top?" I asked.

"Yes. And they have toilets up there too. I think you might need those." He winked at me.

"No, it's all evaporating off the top of my head," I told him.

We were passed by the man piously muttering Latin prayers, or possibly moaning about the rocks on the ground, which must be hot enough to fry an egg and were probably blistering the soles of his feet.

"They used to call this the Conca d'Oro," Valentino told me, looking out over the distant countryside, "the Bay of Gold."

"Why?"

"It was full of orange and lemon trees. They sold them to the ships that stopped by, to prevent scurvy when they sailed on to Asia. Imagine all those fruits ripening in the sunshine. It must have been so beautiful."

I looked out over the beautiful bay in thoughtful silence.

"What do you want to ask the *Santuzza* for?" asked Valentino, "if that's not too nosy."

"It's a secret," I answered. I decided to think about it, and decide what to ask Rosalia for while I continued on to the summit. "What are you going to ask her for?" I asked.

"I'm going to thank her for guiding me away from my ex-girlfriend," he answered.

"When did you break up?" I asked.

"Three weeks ago."

Oh. I suddenly felt deeply, horribly jealous as he told me about his ex, and how badly she had treated him. I think I felt jealous because some of the things he said made me fear that he still had feelings for her. There I was, desperately wishing he would kiss me, whilst listening to him talk about this other woman.

We set off again, and I tried to put thoughts of his much-too-recently ex-girlfriend out of my head. We walked up the last few yards of the path, turned the corner, and there in front of us was a stunningly ornate church facade, at the top of a very long and steep flight of stairs.

Walking through the doorway of a magnificent Baroque church, and finding yourself in a gloomy cave with water dripping on your head, has to be one of life's more unusual experiences. In the damp, craggy entrance area was a life-size statue of Rosalia in her brown nun's habit and crown of roses, holding her pickaxe aloft. The statue was festooned in votive offerings, left by people thanking her for wishes she had granted. There were miniature kidneys and lungs, arms and legs, and even a coiled up mass of intestines, all crafted out of silver and hanging from pink and blue ribbons. She had thick sheaves of hand-written thank-you letters wedged in her hands. She was draped with jewellery, wearing about six pairs of diamond earrings and necklaces galore.

"The priests have to take all these offerings off her almost every day," Valentino explained.

We watched a man place a motorbike crash helmet at her feet.

He told us he had survived a near-fatal accident by praying to her desperately while he was lying in the road waiting for an ambulance. The man with bare feet arrived and hooked something small over her fingers whilst I hovered nosily until I could get a look at it. It turned out to be a little pair of silver feet.

Had she cured his bunions? Ingrowing toenails? Chronic foot cheese problem? Should I leave my sister's trainers up there as an offering of my own?

Before I could make my mind up, Valentino led me towards a display case of precious antiques left as offerings over the centuries. They contained Sicilian Baroque pearl and ruby necklaces and earrings, drinking vessels in silver, and a ship about three feet long made of solid gold and encrusted with precious gems, which had been left after a near fatal storm about four centuries ago.

Beyond the entrance area, the main body of the church really was a very bat-cave-like place. Water dripped constantly off the ceiling and was channelled by hundreds of shiny brass guttering tubes, suspended from the ceiling at all angles in a crazy zig-zag melee that looked like a modern art installation. Valentino and I sat side by side on a pew, and periodically wiped ourselves when an occasional stray drop splashed us.

"I love the dim candle lighting and the cool smell of dampness," I commented.

"Oh, does it smell of damp in here?" Valentino asked. "I don't have much of a sense of smell. I'm just glad to be sitting down at last after that mad dash up the mountain. They didn't even make us train that hard when I was doing military service."

I sat in silence for a while. I did not know what to say.

"How did Rosalia become the patron Saint of Palermo?" I asked eventually.

"She ended the plague of 1624 in Palermo," he answered. "She saved most people in the city. Look at all the gifts they left to thank her."

He pointed to the glass case to our left, in which lay the statue of Rosalia that took pride of place in her mountain-top sanctuary. Her flesh was of white marble and her nun's habit and crown of roses was solid gold. Rosalia reclined almost seductively, Baroque and chubby-looking, holding her gold skull in her hand and a gold pick-axe for hacking her way through rocks. The beautiful statue was surrounded by gold jewellery, huge rubies and diamonds, showy necklaces, rings and earrings and heaps of gold coins, all enclosed in the glass case with her. It was essentially a time capsule for, like the statue, all the offerings dated from the seventeenth century too.

Apparently the plague had been brought to Palermo by a trading ship from Tunis. The people in the port tried to stop it docking because there were rumours that Tunis had the plague, but Viceroy Emanuele Filiberto of Palermo – who was of freakishly short stature - let the ship unload because it was full of gifts from the King of Tunis. The ship's captain gave the acquisitive midget jewels, camels, lions, exotic foods and tiger and zebra hides.

The Viceroy had very little time to parade around in his exotic pelts, as he was one of the first to die of the plague. The sickness soon spread through the whole city. Palermo was sealed off, and nobody could enter or leave. The authorities blocked off the ports and the streets, to make sure nobody could leave the city, not even the corpses. Every minute must have been terrifying. It lasted the whole month of May and to the middle of June, with people dying in their thousands and dead bodies covered in buboes rotting around them in the sweltering heat.

The citizens of Palermo prayed day and night to their four patron saints: Santa Cristina, Santa Ninfa, Santa Olivia and Santa Agata. They organised religious processions. The churches were packed. Mass went on around the clock in every church. They begged God and Jesus and the Virgin Mary for help. But the plague killed more and more people.

A soap-maker named Vincenzo Bonelli went hunting on Monte Pellegrino and had a vision: Saint Rosalia guided him to the cave which had been her former residence, where he found her bones. If they were taken to Palermo and given a Christian burial, Rosalia told him, the plague would stop. He took the bones to the Archbishop of Palermo, who ignored him. The plague continued. The soap maker returned again and again. He refused to take no for an answer, and eventually a procession through the city and a funeral were organised.

The plague immediately stopped spreading. Rosalia was made the new patron saint of Palermo and the four old saints were fired. Their statues still stand around the four corners of the Quattro Canti crossroads in Palermo, looking majestic but redundant.

I felt a sudden urge, almost a need, to pray. I knelt at the altar and said a prayer to Rosalia, asking her for three things.

"Please help me find a man who loves me, Rosalia. Please give me a husband. Please give me at least one baby. I want all the things that you did not have, Rosalia, I want to be the opposite of you. Please can you give me the things you never had?"

The night after our trip up Monte Pellegrino, Valentino took me out to dinner in a small fishing village called St. Elia. We sat outside sipping champagne, overlooking the sea with the fishing boats bobbing in the harbour, and after the meal we went for a walk by the beach. I was wearing my six-inch stiletto-heeled sandals and he was most impressed by my ability to walk across cobblestones, sand and small cacti in them, without needing to slow down. We followed a twisting path up to a rocky promontory with a little statue of the Madonna on top, looking out over the most beautiful stretch of coastline I had ever seen. The rock fell away steeply and the sea curved all around us far below. The only light came from the moon and the stars.

Valentino slipped his arm around me and then turned to face me, and hugged me tight. He held onto me for about three minutes before running his hand through my hair and kissing me.

"I'm so glad I found you at last," he told me. "I can't believe how lucky I am."

Valentino visited me in London three weeks later. While he was there, he told me that he loved me. That was a relief, since I was already in love with him. Rosalia was turning out to be a fast little miracle worker, as she had already fulfilled wish number one.

I visited Valentino in Sicily again two weeks after that. Then he visited me again. A certain budget airline made handsome profits out of us. Each time I went to Palermo I stayed with Valentino at The Godmother's house for, like all self-respecting unmarried Italians in their thirties, he lived with his mum so that she could wash and iron his clothes for him and cook his dinner.

We flew to and fro between London and Palermo every fortnight for three months before deciding that we wanted to spend the rest of our lives together. It was essentially a mutual realisation but, of course, Valentino was certainly not going to pass up the opportunity to make a magnificently romantic proposal. One does not fall in love with Italians for nothing.

He took me out to dinner in a restaurant inside a conservatory, which overlooked the beautiful bay in St. Elia where he had taken me for our first kiss. After the meal he led me to the same lovely spot and, under the stars whose reflections danced in the deep blue water of the sea, he got down on one knee and asked me to marry him. He slipped an emerald and diamond ring on my finger and kissed me.

"I want to make you feel like a woman, and I want to make you feel important," he told me. "For the rest of your life."

4

CASA NOSTRA: OUR LITTLE CROOKED HOUSE

Valentino and I decided to sit down for a long talk to choose whether we would live in England or in Sicily, considering the issue from all angles and weighing up the pros and cons carefully. Ten seconds later we definitively decided that it would be Sicily.

Valentino began to spend his free time traipsing all over the Palermo area looking for a house which fitted both of our requirements. I wanted a villa which lived up to my image of a Mediterranean dream home, with a rustic style farmhouse kitchen and a garden of citrus trees located in a romantically quaint, old-fashioned village by the sea, unspoiled by tourism and full of picturesque traditional local activities. Valentino wanted to be near a source of fresh seafood. In the end he found a small fishing village within commuting distance of Palermo, where some new villas were being constructed. The external walls of the one unsold house were already built, but we could specify whatever we wanted inside. Valentino took me to see the area and, for the second time, I fell in love at first sight.

We went for a walk along the beach to make our decision.

"Are you sure about this?" asked Valentino. "I just wish I had more money to put into it. You've got to sell your house in London to pay for this. You have to be certain."

"I think I am," I answered.

"To get an offer accepted on a house in Italy you have to pay at least thirty thousand Euros immediately," he said, picking up a pebble and skimming it across the waves. "As you're paying, I think you should fly home and come back next week if you're still sure this is the villa you want."

"Is it the one *you* want?" I asked.

"Let's buy a sample of prawns and a squid off those fishermen up there, and then I'll tell you," he answered.

I love the look on his face when he makes these jokes, the half-smile he does when he is not just teasing me, but making fun of himself as well. His eyes are very dark brown but, somehow, light shines out of them. I kissed him, and he put his arms round my waist and swung me in a full circle, squeezing me tight before taking my hand and leading me towards the blue and orange fishing boats. A group of fishermen was playing cards on the hull of one of the boats, using Sicilian playing cards with caveman clubs instead of the usual clubs, and coins and cups and swords instead of normal playing card symbols. The players had placed some high stakes and the whole crowd of onlookers let out a roar each time a card was turned. As we drew near, one player clearly had a winning hand. He raised his arm up over his shoulder and triumphantly threw the cards down as if he were smashing an axe into a block of wood.

We bought some fish and left it in the fridge at The Godmother's house for Valentino to sample later, then set out for the airport. By this time the Sirocco wind was blowing up violently. It was so hot I felt as if I were gasping for air as I tried to breathe it in. It rocked the car from side to side as we hurtled along the motorway between rows of prickly pear cactus plants, giant agaves fifteen feet tall, and mile upon mile of pink-flowered oleander bushes and dwarf lemon trees. Clouds of red dust swirled around in the air and some of the older trees lost branches, which rocketed through the air like missiles. Valentino left me at the airport drooping with sadness, and I worried about him as he drove off.

By the time the aeroplane had been delayed for four hours, and we prospective passengers were all on first name terms and had exchanged e-mail addresses, recipes and, in one case, bodily fluids, we started to realise this dust storm was not simmering down. Looking out of the airport windows showed little except an impenetrable red mist and the occasional outline of airborne citrus fruits and small saplings hurtling past. Eventually the airline announced that no flights would be leaving that day, so I called Valentino to return to the airport and take me back to Palermo.

"It's fate," I said.

"I thought the same thing," Valentino answered. "Destiny is telling us something."

We went straight back to the constructor, called Engineer Fortunato Mastronzo, and completed all the formalities. The constructor's name, Fotunato Mastronzo, literally means 'lucky, but a turd'. We should have realised what we were in for.

Valentino is an official in the High Court at Palermo. Whenever a judge issues a verdict, the winning lawyer brings the decree to his office, takes a number, waits all morning and is then called to a window where he gets the documents copied in triplicate, rubber stamped, covered in sealing wax and signatures, and has special expensive stickers pasted everywhere to show he has paid fees for this process. Then the office notifies the bailiffs to sequester property, or the prison service to lock the condemned man up in prison, or to release him, or whatever. Valentino is thoughtful and analytical and this job is mind numbing but he appreciates it, because it is safe. It also means that as soon as anyone is found guilty of anything in the whole Palermo area, he gets to know about it.

Little did we realise, when we bought our house, just how many times this source of confidential information would reveal shocking information about our own home. The series of revelations which simply fell onto Valentino's lap turned his hair white in two years. Maybe being a public official is not always stress-free, after all.

Having just unwittingly made our pact with the devil, Valentino and I decided to go out for a spleen sandwich dinner, then have a celebratory drink with a group of friends, and then go dancing.

When we reached the small bar where Valentino had told our friends to meet us, there were about seventeen or eighteen people already there. Valentino went to the bar to order champagne and, a few minutes later, one single bottle turned up, with glasses for everyone.

"They are bringing more bottles, aren't they?" I asked after we had chatted for a while.

"No," said Valentino. "Why?"

"Well..." I trailed off.

Valentino opened the bottle and poured about three bubbles into each glass.

"Stop! Stop!" several people protested, as if he were trying to make them become alcoholics.

There was even some champagne left over. Seeing a single champagne bottle fill so many glasses was a little like watching Jesus with those loaves and fishes. I tried to calculate how many bottles of champagne it would have taken to satisfy a group of English people in toast-making festivities, but lost count. Everyone engaged in a jovial and raucous series of toasts but most of our chums left a bit of the champagne in their glasses.

"You don't want me to get drunk, do you?" several of them laughed.

It was impossible to convince anyone to polish off the rest of the bottle.

"I feel tipsy already," said several others.

So the bottle sat there, begging me to empty it. It was good champagne.

As we left the bar, Valentino and several of his cousins followed me closely, as if ready to catch me should I collapse to the floor in a drunken stupor. I made it all the way to the nightclub, to everyone's amazement. I was actually pretty amazed to make it there myself, not because of the three drops of champagne but because the spleen sandwich was weighing down on my pelvic floor so heavily it threatened to smash a hole in the pavement. Valentino and I danced like maniacs to burn off the two million-odd calories we had consumed for dinner and eventually we fell into bed, happy with the deal we had made and excited about our new home.

The next time I flew down to Palermo, a few weeks later, we arranged an appointment with Engineer Mastronzo at the construction site to discuss how the house was coming along and to agree on a few details. We waited for two hours while the builders all sipped beer and wondered where he could have got to. Eventually he turned up with a cigarette hanging from his lip and a very pale pink shirt with extensive wet patches under the arms. He smelt of sweat and too much aftershave and he left us standing around for another quarter of an hour while he talked on his mobile phone, the cigarette glued to his lower lip wagging up and down dangerously until a particularly extravagant hand gesture sent it flying and he sprang backwards, brushing the scorching ash off his paunch.

Like many Italians, he carried two mobile phones. Italians used to do this so that they could save money by using the SIM card from one company to call friends who used the same company, thus enjoying a lower call tariff, and equipping the other phone with a SIM card from the main rival service provider to call their friends registered with that company. Nowadays the phones in Italy are all made to hold two different SIM cards. Engineer Mastronzo's two phones kept ringing simultaneously and several times he created a kind of party line by answering both at once. He was worse than the brokers I used to work with in London.

We walked around our future home. We had chosen pale cream marble for the staircase and matching tiles for all the floors, with black wrought-iron banisters. I loved the way my heels tapped on the hard floor and echoed back at me. It made the house sound spacious and grand. The staircase curved up the centre of the villa, dividing the kitchen from the living room. Upstairs the perfectly cubic master bedroom with its lovely high ceiling had a square window set bang in the centre of the outside wall, and overlooked an orchard of lemon trees bowing down with fruit, and a snow-capped blue mountain range in the distance. The perfect proportions of this room were so serene and harmonious that it was this view which sold me on the house. The kitchen looked out on the same view through a wall of French windows but, being lower down, offered a closer look at the other trees among the lemons; the pomegranates, the figs and the fruit-bearing prickly pear cactus trees. On the top floor we had an open-air roof terrace which looked out on the same rolling mountains and a vast, open, royal blue sky. To the right we could see part of the village and to the left we could see the turquoise sea. Valentino put his arm round me as we looked out across the countryside together and squeezed me tight.

"Are you still happy you chose this?" he asked.

"It's wonderful," I answered. "It's a dream come true."

As we walked back downstairs we looked at the two smaller bedrooms. When I looked at the marble windowsill in one of them I realised it was sloping inwards, not outwards. It was angled to make all the rainwater flow straight into the room. When I pointed this out to the Engineer, he vigorously denied it, so I picked up an off-cut of copper piping, left lying around by the plumber, and placed it on the windowsill. We watched it roll rapidly towards us and land on the Engineer's foot. He flinched when it landed and I was not completely sincere in my apology.

"It's too late to rectify now," he said stubbornly. "It would mean pulling half the house down."

"Why?" I demanded.

"Because the walls of the next two floors are resting on it," he said dismissively, answering another phone call.

When he had finished, I persisted.

"There's a lintel and you could take out this piece of wall," I said, indicating with my hand.

"No, Signora, we cannot," was his smug answer.

Signora means Mrs. or Madam. Some Italian men, fortunately the minority, insert it into the conversation and pronounce it in a way which means 'You're just a woman and I'm a man so stop telling me what's right and wrong'.

"Sort him out," I whispered in Valentino's ear, and left them talking in Sicilian while I wandered off to the kitchen to fantasise about Mediterranean-look overhead cupboards, while the high-pitched buzzing sound of cicadas came in through the empty window frames. Valentino was far more patient and tactful than me and using Sicilian was a way of taking a relationship to a more chummy level, even if it was phoney chumminess. I think using their own language reminds them that they are the rebels of Italy, the ones who know how to flout the rules better than anyone else and who have always had to stick together against century after century of foreign invaders. Yet knowing the right moment to switch from speaking Italian to speaking Sicilian can take judicious subtlety. I often heard people, who fired off in Sicilian as soon as they met someone, denigrated as comical characters, or else such uneducated plebeians that they had to use Sicilian because they had no idea how to talk Italian properly. Having said that, nearly everyone in my village talked to me in Sicilian until I asked them not to.

Eventually Valentino and the Engineer clomped down the stairs, both looking relieved to have concluded the tense negotiations.

"I've agreed we'll sort out the window sill ourselves," Valentino said, "and as compensation the Engineer is going to give us a discount on the burglar alarm."

I could tell by the way he said it that I must make no comment until we were alone together.

"What happened," I asked, when we were eventually in the car.

"I don't want his builders trying to rectify anything related to horizontal surfaces," he said. "They'll only make things worse. I went round the house with that piece of piping you used and everything slopes downwards away from the drainage holes. I asked one of the builders to lend me his spirit level and, just to test him, I asked him to show me how it works. He explained that the bubble 'sinks down to the bottom' so you have to get that angled towards the place you want the water to drain to."

"Did you teach him how spirit levels work?" I asked.

"He smelt of beer and he didn't seem able to speak a word of Italian. In fact even his Sicilian was fairly incomprehensible. So I just left it."

Besides never apologising for his lack of punctuality, Mr Faeces the Engineer was completely unruffled by our complaints about the construction. It was impossible to find a right angle, a horizontal surface or, for that matter, a vertical one anywhere in the entire building. I suppose all this frustration should have been thoroughly predictable, since England's national monument is the biggest clock in the world, whereas Italy's most famous building is a tower which leans off at thirteen degrees to the perpendicular. During some of the long sleepless nights, I would draw comfort from the fact that, despite its being so squiffy, the Italian builders have nevertheless made the Leaning Tower of Pisa remain almost upright for the last eight hundred years.

Our problems multiplied as time went on. The man we hired to tile the bathrooms could not find any way to disguise the fact that the shower cubicle is seven tiles wide at the bottom and eight tiles wide at the top. The large rectangular mirror we ordered, to be set into a space in the tiles above the sink, had to be trimmed to a rhombus to make it fit. The glass shelves for toiletries were aligned with the edges of the tiles but then, when we watched my perfume bottles accelerate one after another onto the floor, we realised the shelf was set at a one-in-ten gradient. The men who fitted my beautiful rustic Mediterranean-style overhead kitchen cupboards, which I had devoted so much time to daydreaming about, asked me if I wanted them to make contact with the wall at the top, or at the bottom; both was not an option, he carefully explained. When the wardrobes were being assembled in the bedroom, the carpenter commented how fortunate it was that we had not chosen fitted ones, since they touched the wall up at the cornice whereas, down by the skirting board, he could insert his leg as far as the knee.

Eventually the big day came when it was time to move into the house. This occurred before we had finished paying for it, obtained the title deeds or, indeed, seen any documentation regarding building regulations approval or even planning permission. For someone who comes from England, in fact for someone who applies logic to any aspect of their life, this is not possible to imagine. I was rapidly realising, though, that in Sicily unimaginable things happen on a daily basis. Meanwhile the sale of my house in England had marched ahead with rapid efficiency and, on completion day, my possessions had rolled away in a very large lorry.

I overtook them by plane and spent a few nights with Valentino in our very empty, echoing house waiting for them to arrive several days later. In that strange phase we all go through in a new house, when we cannot remember which switch operates which light, and we wander about the house deciding which socket we fancy best for charging our phones, Valentino and I noticed more and more blemishes in our new house. The plaster in the downstairs bathroom had warts. The cast iron bannisters continued too far down, so that you could not actually access the little storage section below them – Harry Potter's bedroom, so to speak – unless you held your breath, sucked your tummy in as far as you could and squeezed painfully between the wall and a cast iron strut which was trying to draw and quarter you. Perhaps most infuriating of all, the supposedly solid cherry wood doors throughout the house were actually just made of Weetabix with a plastic coated photograph of wood glued on top.

As soon as the entire contents of my former house arrived from England, and the Sicilian house was full of furniture in pieces, cardboard boxes and dust, I stopped worrying about all its irregular angles and distinguishing features. I had other things to worry about.

As I perused through my two-hundred and twenty boxes of possessions left by the removals men, I had ample time to ponder how I had accumulated so much stuff and, more bewilderingly, how I had ever thought I needed it. The problem was compounded by the fact that people in Sicily kept giving us more things, not realising that we already had too much.

Valentino's grandmother gave me a complete dinner service containing a staggering thirty-five place settings. It was not just a thirty-five person dinner service, but a nine-course thirty-five person dinner service.

"I'm sorry a couple of items have got broken over the years," Nonna apologised.

A couple of pieces missing? Did she actually think I might notice?

I piled all the towers of variously sized plates in my antique dresser, then added soup tureens large enough to use as bath tubs, bowls you could live in and oval platters big enough to serve Silvio Berlusconi roasted on a spit. The dresser bowed under the weight, and the shelf inside turned into a kind of wooden hammock. All I needed next was another four dinner tables and I would be able to cater for the whole family in one sitting, although, since I already had three dinner services of my own (yes, I know that is excessive) I concluded the best solution may be to hold a Greek-style wedding to clear out some space, smashing the entire dinner service on my way to the church in order to ensure good luck - the good luck not to be asked ever, EVER to cater for thirty-five people all at once.

Of course, The Godmother thinks nothing of cooking up meals for thirty-five people at a time. Apparently nobody in Sicily feels remotely daunted by the idea. Indeed, they seem to positively relish the prospect, and would not dream of shying away from preparing the most complex and elaborate dishes imaginable. Personally, as soon as more than five people expect me to feed them, I panic and yearn for Marks & Spencers, with its ready meals that look as if you laboriously prepared them all by yourself, so long as you can hide the packets where they'll never be found.

The housewarming presents from The Godmother multiplied. Her generosity almost embarrassed me. I had been used to earning my own money, living in my own house and paying for my own stuff for years. She gave me several complete sets of bedding, embroidered hand towels and sets of bath towels, a summer bedspread and a winter bedspread. She handed me boxes and boxes of unused socks and underpants for Valentino, all individually wrapped in cellophane and beautifully packed in tens in boxes with gold logos on the lids. There were stacks of white T-shirts (his winter underwear) and white cotton vests (his summer underwear, indispensable for all Sicilian men of course) in their original packaging, all inside wholesale boxes of six at a time. There was enough clothing to last him a lifetime and possibly sell some surplus by opening a department store as well.

Eventually it dawned on me that The Godmother was actually sending her son off with a wedding trousseau. Reflecting on this I realised that, without planning it, I had turned up with the biggest dowry Sicily had probably ever seen. I had brought a house and its furniture with me. And money. The Godmother was making sure she kept up her side of the bargain. The strangest thing was that she was handing all Valentino's clothes to me. Presumably I was supposed to dispense them to him in appropriate quantities and dispose of the old ones, over the years, as I saw fit.

One day some men turned up with a fridge. This was not only a remarkably generous gift but also a much-needed one. Fridges, it turned out, have motors proportional to the ambient temperature. For a fridge to keep your food nice and cold in the sweltering heat of a Sicilian summer it needs the kind of motor that could power a Boeing 747, apparently, and my poor feeble English fridge was groaning, moaning and having a breakdown.

Another day my father-in-law to be, Don Ciccio, sent us off to a furniture shop and arranged a five-year loan to buy us the most magnificent complete set of bedroom furniture I had ever seen in my life, all made of walnut wood.

The most unexpected of gifts, however, was the Cleaning Products Cupboard, replete with a lifetime's supply of everything you could possibly imagine using to clean things, along with plenty of other things I had never seen before in my life. It was so large we could not fit it inside the kitchen, so it had to live on the balcony.

Another day The Godmother turned up with some colossal saucepans. The indispensable course of any Italian meal is the pasta, naturally. The Godmother herself has a saucepan large enough to boil a dead body in hydrochloric acid and then bury the gold fillings. It is so large that, when she is carrying it, it looks as if the pot has grown two feet and is waddling along all by itself. Of course she has never really boiled a corpse in it! That would taint the taste of the pasta.

I realised eventually that I was probably going to live with unopened boxes full of stuff from the removals men, stuff I never needed, for the rest of my life. I made a mental note to look for a metal worker and get that last section of bannisters removed, so I could cram them all in Harry Potter's bedroom and never think about them again.

5

WE WARM THE HOUSE

Since we were now living in a house which was only one third ours, I authorised Valentino to make the second payment from our account to Fortunato Mastronzo's account. Valentino does not have what I would call "business acumen". He was unaware of the very simple business concept that, while money is in my account, *I* am getting the interest, and once it is in your account, *you* get the interest, so I should always pay just before the deadline, not as soon as the bill comes. He does not know how to dangle money under people's noses as an incentive. He does not understand that people are often less motivated to deliver what you are asking for, or rectify mistakes, *after* you have already paid them. He kept rushing to pay people in advance because he thought that would show them he was a nice person, so they would be nice in return.

Mr. Lucky Faeces was not a nice person. We had to go to his office and grovel for the receipt for the particularly large sum of money we had paid him. His office had a yellow ceiling and smelt so badly of smoke that I opened the window without even asking permission; I had to take this precaution because I anticipated shouting, and realised that without a safe oxygen supply I might be risking an asthma attack. The usual cigarette dangled from Engineer Mastronzo's lip, and he handed the receipt over to me like a surgeon giving the scrub nurse a fetid, malignant tumour dripping with blood that he had just removed from a patient's large bowel.

The receipt did not satisfy me at all. It did not specify what the money had been paid for, or what it entitled us to, legally. It did not have the engineer's signature, or indeed any signature, on it. All it contained was a date and a few bits of incomprehensible garbage. Maybe Mr. Lucky Faeces knew a lot of people willing to do business like this; but I was not.

There was also still the fact that the expensive tiles we had bought for the upstairs bathroom were nowhere to be seen, the bidet and other fittings we had paid for were not inside the house, and various other fundamental house parts were not yet completed. When I started asking about when this work would be done, Mr. Faeces ignored me and spoke to Valentino instead, in Sicilian.

"Oh, these Anglo-Saxons," was the only part I understood. No doubt he was making fun of my 'fussy attention to details' and lack of understanding about how these things are sorted out between men. Staring at his fake-jovial face without the distraction of following what he was saying gave me the chance to weigh him up coldly. It was clear he had worked out Valentino was the financially naive one. He had figured out a way of excluding me from negotiations whilst pretending to be chummy. He may be used to bamboozling and bullying people, but I had his number. I left the meeting feeling angry and uneasy but, at least in theory, we now owned two-thirds of the house.

I was walking alongside the beach one day when I saw the fishermen bustling around a fresh swordfish which they were selling by the slice. Its doleful eye, the size of a cricket ball, was still so clear and fresh it looked as if it were imploring passers-by for help. Catching a swordfish is a rare and highly lucrative event, so there was a bit of a party atmosphere.

"Ciao, Veronica!" one of the fishermen shouted out. "Buy a couple of slices."

"I'll have twenty, please," I shouted back.

While he sliced the swordfish and added some prawns and a large octopus, I called my Sicilian mother-in-law to inform her I would be having a barbecue at my house. That was the only organising I needed to do, as far as arranging a thirty-person barbecue party was concerned.

As soon as I called The Godmother, she logged on to the Auntienet and by midday my house was so full of relatives with wooden spoons I could hardly move. The Auntienet is like the Internet except it doesn't need wires or computers and is mainly used by aunties, mothers, grandmothers and godmothers who need to know whether their kid needs a jolly good spanking *before* he actually gets home. Sicilian kids dare not swear in public or pat dirty stray dogs, as *The Godmothers Are Watching*.

Sicilians never expect their hostess to cook. They expect the whole family, men and women, to squeeze into the kitchen and cook together. So while a few uncles were lighting the barbecues outside, Valentino and about twenty relatives of his were jammed into my kitchen like the black hole of Calcutta, squeezing lemons for marinade, stuffing artichokes, and doing unspeakable things with offal.

As more and more people, and more and more items I had never previously regarded as food, were crammed into my kitchen, I found myself physically ejected into the garden. I simply popped out of the door involuntarily, like toothpaste from a tube, and ended up watching the preparations in my kitchen through an open window. My father-in-law, whom everyone calls Don Ciccio, is the only Sicilian I know who does not participate in these guerrilla cooking activities. He is a small, shy Sicilian speaker who tends to struggle with Italian, so we just stood together in companionable silence, watching the frenzy inside as the smell of pine cone-scented barbecue smoke wafted around us.

The entire kitchen was being expertly co-ordinated and guided by The Godmother in her frilly apron, I gradually realised. What looked like chaos was actually more like a symphony orchestra playing *The Flight of The Bumblebee*, perfectly, inside an elevator, and she was the conductor.

Valentino, was wrestling with a fifteen-inch-long octopus which was still alive and kept suckering onto his arms. The one I had bought, which I had thought was quite impressive, was probably one of its babies. He suddenly raised the squirming octopus to his mouth, biting at the base of one of its tentacles until it flopped limply.

"Did you just kill it with your teeth?" I shouted through the window.

Valentino's big, dark eyes glanced up at me with the guiltiest expression I have ever seen on anyone, seven inches of greyish tentacle dangling from his mouth. He sucked it in slowly, and swallowed it with a gulp of satisfaction.

"No I didn't kill it, it was only paralysed," he said.

"That's gross! I'm not kissing you for a week!" I shouted in through the window.

A couple of minutes later he passed me a mug of tea out of the window.

"Ere, ava cuppa-teano," he offered.

I love it when he tries to talk English. His accent is so strong it always makes me laugh, but it sounds sexy at the same time.

Amid the seething mass of hands, I picked out Valentino's Uncle Pasquale with his hands inside a squid of monstrous dimensions. It was almost a kraken. Pasquale's name derives from the Italian word for 'Easter'. When The Godmother had finished committing genocide against vegetables and Uncle Easter had extracted the ink sac from the squid, everyone was ready to proceed outside towards the row of three smouldering barbecues. They roasted peppers whole and peeled the skin off when it started to bubble, they drizzled stuffed artichokes with olive oil and lemon juice while they roasted on the grill, and they barbecued marinated lamb chops, chicken and beef steaks which they progressively heaped up on the table until it started to creak.

Meanwhile the aunties indoors whipped out from nowhere the two largest saucepans I have ever seen. They would have been amply big enough to casserole Tarzan in one and Jane in the other. They used the Tarzan one to boil about thirty kilograms of spaghetti and the Jane-sized one to prepare swordfish in tomato and white wine sauce. As the pasta was bubbling away nicely, there was a call from The Godmother's brother, Uncle Natale. Natale means Christmas. Most of us call him Uncle Christmas but his two sons often call him Father Christmas. Honestly, they do.

The Godmother wiped her bread-crummy hands on her apron to answer her cell phone. Most people in Sicily give their old phone to their mother each time they buy a new one, so you see a lot of elderly ladies in Sicily engaging in vintage telephony with enormous handsets.

"*Pronto!*" The Godmother screamed into the phone, so loudly that Natale probably did not actually need his phone turned on to be able to hear her. "I see, I see," she yelled, nodding her head vigorously, and then she held the phone at arm's length and peered at it over the top of her glasses to locate the "off" button.

"*E arrivata La Nonna!*" she announced. "Grandmother has arrived!"

Nonna is over two hundred years old and looks like Jabba the Hut. She flares outwards continuously from the head down, her face widening into a collection of broad chins which merge seamlessly with her bust and even wider waistline, which in turn continues outwards into immense hips and finally a pair of legs which each need a chair of their own. 'Nonna' simply means 'grandmother' and everyone calls her that, including all the neighbours and the butcher and the baker (two dear, dear friends of hers). Apparently she did have a real name once, but nobody knows it now.

The news of Nonna's arrival mobilized her grandsons into a crack military-style squad. To reach our front door she would have to walk about a hundred yards, something she apparently had not done since last time England won the World Cup. Valentino and his brother Manfredi began testing the strength of various chairs by jumping up and down on them as hard as they could, while The Godmother listened for cracking wood or other signs of structural weakness. When the two strongest chairs had been chosen, they picked up one each and sprinted to the car with their special moving equipment, accompanied by myself and several uncles, along to enjoy the spectacle. Manfredi skilfully used Nonna's walking frame and one of his legs to lever her out of the car, with Uncle Christmas exerting all his strength to push from the inside.

"Ai yaaaa! Ow! Ow! Ow! You're trying to kill me!" shrieked Nonna until she was finally out. Then she demanded the two chairs, which were carefully positioned side by side, one for each buttock. We thought they were going to give when she collapsed down onto them, but luckily they resisted until she regained her breath and authorised Valentino and Manfredi to lift her up to her feet.

"Ai ya! Ow ow ow!" gasped Nonna.

"Uuurgh," groaned Valentino, red in the face.

"I think I've got a hernia," squeaked Manfredi.

Uncle Christmas positioned the walking frame in front of her and she took five paces before yelling for the chairs. Valentino and his brother put on an alarming performance of heavy breathing. They were both dripping with sweat. Nonna panted louder than either of them, but she does that even when she's in bed so I was not so worried about her. After a long pause they lifted her up again, and she managed another five paces before collapsing onto the chairs as before. The whole hundred yards was negotiated in this way.

By the time she reached the house, the pasta was ready and stood on a very long table in the garden, which was actually three of our tables in a line plus one borrowed from the neighbours. Nonna was installed on her two chairs at the head of the table, and gave the order for the feast to commence. Nonna herself had the largest plate of spaghetti, almost taller than it was wide. To one side of her sat her three children, her holy trinity; Natale, Pasquale and Crocifissa, the Godmother.

"My sister's the youngest," Pasquale told me. "They had run out of festivals when Nonna got to her, so she moved on to artefacts."

"I'm very ill, you know. I've got no appetite at all," cut in Nonna as she twirled the last strands of spaghetti into her mouth. "I'm just eating out of politeness."

The fresh swordfish in its tomato and white wine sauce was so juicy and delicious I was tempted to take second helpings, but Valentino whisked my plate away and brought me a clean one to embark on the meat courses. At the English barbecues I have attended, I was served a blackened burnt offering marinated in lighter fuel which, when cut open, turned out to be raw chicken inside. At this Sicilian barbecue I was served grilled delicacies where the marinade was made from fresh herbs gathered from the garden early in the morning, the smoke from the fire was sweetened with pine cones and the chicken was drizzled with olive oil as it cooked, to keep it tender. My mouth watered as I let go of all restraint, and ate like a pig.

"I've had enough food for a family of five already," I announced as I eased my belt out three holes.

"I've hardly eaten a thing," said Nonna from behind a tower of chicken bones heaped on her plate. "I'm practically fasting today."

Then we ate the sweet, roasted artichokes with garlic butter filling. Artichokes are tough on the outside but, when you get to the centre, where the flower forms, they are soft and juicy and they leave such a sweet after-taste in the mouth that you have to leave a long pause between each one to fully savour the flavour.

Except if you are Nonna. After she had made short work of the artichokes we started on the grilled peppers dressed with olive oil and balsamic vinegar. Finally we attacked the seafood.

"I'm getting so thin these days I'm wasting away. I can hardly force this down," remarked Nonna as she tucked into her third cuttlefish.

After the barbecued cuttlefish and squid and lobster, the boiled octopus was ready. Octopus is a strange food. When raw, it is grey and translucent and, once finally dead, it flops down so flat that it looks like a massive dollop of mucus. Yet even when well and truly deceased, if you poke it, it still becomes bright red, the way live octopuses do when angered by predators and preparing to squirt their black ink. When you boil it, it perks up and looks far more alive than it did when it actually was alive: It turns pink, it is no longer see-through, and the tentacles coil up and bounce around when you try to cut it.

Valentino brought a large oval platter to the table; his nemesis sat at one end, its seven remaining mighty tentacles bobbing around menacingly, while my own humble purchase sat at the other, nestling amid a tangle of tentacles that reminded me of plastic soap-dishes from the seventies.

"Do you cook your octopus the same way as this in England?" enquired Auntie Giovanna politely.

"Erm, no," I answered.

"You will try some, won't you?" said Valentino, leaning close to me and putting his arm around me.

"Go on, then," I said.

He put some tentacles on my plate. This was the first time I had tried octopus. It was so rubbery it made my gums swell up from chewing it.

"Wow, this is the chewiest octopus I think I've ever eaten!" said Valentino. "It's wonderful!"

Everyone else agreed vociferously. I asked Valentino to explain why rubbery was good.

"The golden rule on sea life is, the fresher, the rubberier," he answered.

"You know, I've heard some mainland Italians, *Continentals*," cut in Uncle Pasquale with disdain, "complimenting octopus dishes in restaurants for the 'tenderness' of the flesh!"

Everyone around me laughed heartily - nay, scoffed - at such ignorance. The Godmother leaned over and touched my arm.

"That means the octopus has been frozen," she whispered conspiratorially.

"Or worse," added Manfredi, "left slopping about at the back of some restaurant fridge for goodness knows how long, until it's nearly going off."

We sat down to start eating at two o'clock in the afternoon and, by seven in the evening, items were still coming off the barbecue and, incredibly, still being eaten. At this point, the various diabetic members of the family sneaked off to inject themselves with insulin before pudding. It seems nearly everyone over fifty in Sicily has type two diabetes; I cannot imagine why. Nonna was medicated at the table as it would have been too time-consuming to move her. Valentino expertly filled a syringe and injected it into her upper arm (at least, I think that is where it went in) with a flick of the wrist like a professional darts player. He has been doing this since he was ten years old, as so many Sicilian children do for their grandparents. The elderly often refuse to learn how to inject themselves because it is a way of ensuring their relatives have to visit them several times a day.

After the old-timers had finished shooting up, Valentino and his brother Manfredi disappeared in the car for a quarter of an hour and returned bearing five large trays, laden with what looked like elaborately iced cupcakes topped with a variety of fruits, chocolate drops and sweets. When I touched them I realised they were all made of ice cream. Everyone had two each, except Nonna, who had the rest of the tray.

"I'm only eating them because I've had my injection," she explained. "You have to regulate your blood sugar."

"Remember, we have to get you back to the car later," said

Valentino and Manfredi, looking scared.

The house well and truly came to life that day. Since then I have never felt like complaining that I need a larger kitchen. I may have a larger kitchen, actually, caused by the outward pressure exerted against the walls by all those relatives.

6

A VISIT FROM THE GODMOTHER

Sicilian housewives are scrubbers. Honestly. They spend more time scrubbing things than in any other activity, save possibly ironing.

One day, The Godmother came round to my house when I had just swept and mopped all the floors. Shafts of early morning sunlight were streaming in through the French windows in the kitchen, reflecting off the shiny floor tiles, sparkling off all the glassware, and glowing against the cherry wood cupboards. The house was immaculate, the weather was glorious, and my armpits were sweaty.

The Godmother was wearing her black skirt and black blouse, which is what she puts on when she really means business.

She gave me a pitying, or perhaps critical, look and said,

"Oh, you poor thing! You must be so worn out with all this unpacking and organising that you haven't had time to clean the floor."

"Erm, yes," I said.

"Don't worry," she answered, her nose already in the Cleaning Products Cupboard she had given me as a house warming present. "I know you get confused when you have to do real work."

What?

"I'll take care of it," she told me.

"Are you telling me I don't know how to clean my own house?" I asked, smiling. She was to be my mother-in-law and I wanted to be on good terms with her.

"Poor Valentino, I don't want to leave him to do everything by himself," she said.

She almost disappeared inside the depths of the cupboard of mysteries, extracted a thing which looked like a broom with no bristles, and then wrapped it in a cloth which she dipped in something that smelled pungent enough to make my nose run. She proceeded to rub it all over the floor with so much verve I thought she might actually erode the glaze off the tiles. Her white bouffant hair occasionally wobbled.

"That's just given it a quick removal of the main dirt," she said, as she got on her knees and proceeded to pull the plinth away from the fitted cupboards under and around the kitchen sink. She put the steel strips out on the balcony, and then proceeded to remove the entire underside of the island unit as well. Not satisfied with this, she prised all the knobs off the hob, did something that looked downright painful to remove the oven door and then turned the extractor fan over the cooker into no less than eighteen separate, yet almost identical-looking, pieces of plastic grille.

Whilst I was profoundly shocked to see her calmly pull my brand new kitchen to pieces, I was also flabbergasted that she was actually able to. For my whole life, up to that point, I had believed you needed men with exposed bum cleavages to do that type of thing.

When I was single and worked in a bank in London, I had thought that being able to sew would stand me in good stead when I became a housewife. I thought it meant I had potential. Then I met The Godmother, who is the very walking definition of uxoriousness in flesh and blood, and I realised becoming a housewife may be the hardest thing I had ever attempted in my life.

For example, I had always thought – foolishly, as it now turns out – that there were certain objects in this world which it is simply never necessary to clean. Ever. The road, for example, was something I had never once looked at in my life and thought, 'Well now, I think I'll give that a jolly good scrub.' Yet, apparently, to be a decent housewife, a decent Sicilian one at any rate, it is essential to wash the pavement outside one's house quite regularly, on one's hands and knees, using a scrubbing brush that could flay an elephant and the kind of cleaning products that you probably need a special license to purchase in other countries. Similarly, I had never once been tempted to lather up a set of iron railings and then rinse them down, dry them and buff them up with a soft cloth. I just figured that the rain took care of removing clumps of dirt, slattern that I was.

I stood watching The Godmother toiling away – entirely sweat-free, I noted – and felt clueless and redundant. I wanted to join in, to show willing, yet I had no idea what needed to be done. I had thought the house was clean already. I just stood and watched her, perspiring by proxy.

The Godmother calmly filled the sink with several potent

products, which foamed and gave off a greenish hallucinogenic vapour, and put all the small components of my ex-kitchen in it. While I sat down to regain some breath, she filled a bucket with whatever the Mafia use to dissolve dead bodies away to nothing except a few gold fillings, and started rubbing it into the pieces of stainless steel plinth she had yanked off the cupboards. I had chosen a matt finish but she kept working away at each piece of metal until she had made it look like a mirror.

I felt exhausted simply from watching all this manual labour, but I also began to realise I was suffering an acute respiratory crisis. I was wheezing loudly and my vision was clouding over as if there were some type of jelly stuck to the front of my eyeballs. Apparently my eyes were turning maroon and I sounded like a Fiat that had accidentally been filled with diesel. I was having a severe allergic reaction to The Godmother's cleaning products.

I dashed into the bathroom and begged her to identify the pack of antihistamine I knew I had stashed away somewhere. She rummaged about and asked how many tablets I wanted. I told her to give me all of them. As I was shovelling them into my mouth, I realised she was buffing up the mirror with a dry cloth between popping the pills out of the foil blisters. She is the kind of woman who, if one of her children got his head stuck in a saucepan, would give it a jolly good polish before taking him to the hospital. If someone broke into her house by throwing a brick through the window she would wash the brick before calling the police. If she ever drank tea she would iron the teabags before using them.

I made my way out of the house, out of the chemical inferno which had once been my kitchen, sneaked into the lemon orchard behind the house, and sat on a patch of scratchy grass under a tree. The view of this lemon orchard from the kitchen was what had first made me decide to buy my house, with all the lemons glowing like gold in the Mediterranean sunshine. It was still swelteringly hot, but at least there was some shade which protected my watering eyes from the full power of the sunlight.

I would like to say, especially if any minors are reading this, that overdosing on oral antihistamines and snorting kitchen descaler is a stupid and dangerous thing to do. I felt as if I were drifting out of my body and wafting around among the leaves of the lemon trees in the form of a curly green waft of vaporised ammonia, carbolic acid and hydrogen peroxide. I think I hallucinated the bit where the lemons were talking to me about how they liked me wiping them clean with my eyeballs. I think the bit where I slumped against the trunk of a tree and slowly keeled over through lack of oxygen may have been real. The bit where The Godmother shouted "Veronica, Veronica, wake up!" was definitely right here on planet earth, and it worked.

Before leaving, the Godmother presented me with a direct challenge. Her son needed a woman who knew how to look after him properly, and if I could not rise to the challenge, I would do better to pack off back to England and let the vacancy be filled by a better woman.

I was too busy wheezing like Darth Vader, and reeling in shock, to come up with any response at all. I just waved her off from the balcony as she farted away in her rusty Fiat Punto.

When I recovered from this experience I did a lot of soul-searching. The Godmother was not impressed by me. I was betrothed to a Sicilian man who, up till now, had spent his life wearing steam-ironed underpants, coming home to a front door that was boil-washed daily, and eating fresh spaghetti which his Mamma had personally ground, mashed and extruded in her own kitchen.

I, on the other hand, had been encouraged to prove my worth in this world by excelling academically, and then in my career. I had wanted to be a housewife, but only in the way Marie Antoinette wanted to be a shepherdess; I hadn't *actually* wanted to be good at it. I am the kind of woman who will happily step over a squashed slice of cake on my way to the kettle; when I want a cup of tea, I never lose focus. For me, the most laborious part of preparing a slap-up meal is rinsing the can-opener afterwards. My mother never taught me how to cook. She was too busy teaching me how to think. I remember watching her making sculptures, sawing branches off trees in the garden and making furniture all over the house, but I struggle to remember ever watching my mother washing a floor or cooking a meal. Cast in a similar mould, I had travelled the world and led business deals on three continents, and earned and saved enough money to buy a villa in Sicily with cash. I thought I had done enough.

Now I was to be married to a wonderful man, to the love of my life. What if Crocifissa, The Godmother, was right? What if I was not what he wanted? What if, ultimately, I could not make him happy?

I realised we were in a woman-to-woman, scouring-pads-at-dawn type duel. The Godmother had thrown down the gauntlet, so to speak, or rather the rubber glove, and I had no choice but to accept her challenge.

7

GETTING TO KNOW THE VILLAGE

Once I had my house superficially tidied up and organised, and had reduced the number of cardboard boxes full of junk down from triple to double digits, I explored the village thoroughly. I went for a walk every day, and made a new friend almost every time. I always followed the main road along the sea front and greeted all the fishermen.

"Fresco!" shouted a little puny one, every day. That means 'fresh'. The rest of them usually just said "Ciao" instead.

After that I would duck into one of the tiny side streets at random, just to see what I would find. I once passed down a small street so narrow that I could reach out and stroke my hands along the façades of the houses on both sides as I walked. Many of the houses had cords wound around their window fittings leading off to the nearest lamp post, upon which assorted laundry was pegged out, so working my way down this street involved clambering between jeans, shirts and occasionally some massive pairs of knickers fluttering in the sea breeze.

Outside one house there was a man on a wooden kitchen chair, with tubes up his nose, breathing from an oxygen tank. I paused to say hello, and had a brief chat. He was breathless and spoke in a mix of Italian and Sicilian, but I managed to understand him. He could hardly believe that I had left London in order to come and live in this ramshackle village. The idea made him laugh so much that his wife popped her head out of the window to check whether she should call an ambulance.

There was a shadowy presence in the house next door which eavesdropped as we spoke. I was aware of it because the net curtain twitched. Sometimes the vague outline of an emaciated form was vaguely visible, hovering. Eventually the curtain-twitcher became just a tiny bit too curious and unintentionally poked her head out of the window just far enough for me to catch a glimpse of her bony hand and pinched, angular face.

"Buongiorno!" I called out to her, as loudly as I could. "How are you?"

She was so embarrassed that she had to answer.

"Fine, thank you," she blurted out, then retreated.

A little further up this tiny alley was a cul-de-sac where I saw a fisherman mending his nets. The fishermen's nets are constantly in need of repair, so they are always at work not out at sea. They keep reels of different thicknesses of nylon thread, which they loop and tie up to fill in all the holes ripped by rocks on the sea bed.

"Just doing a bit of embroidery!" he called out as I watched him hunched over his work, brandishing his long curved needle made of bone.

The next day, when passing, I had another chat with Oxygen Man and then stood outside Curtain-Twitcher's window and called out loudly,

"Buongiorno!"

"Buongiorno," she mumbled back, from right behind the curtain. She frowned upwards, as a basket tied to the end of a rope descended from on high. A woman in the top floor flat was lowering the basket as a tiny lambretta roared up behind me making more noise than a jet engine. A pimply boy jumped out, and shouted up to her in Sicilian: the woman shouted something equally incomprehensible in reply, upon which the boy took some coins out of the basket, and put in a loaf of bread from the back of his well-stocked van. He sped off with a deafening roar as the old lady hoisted her bread up three storeys, ready for her lunch.

At my end of the village there was an ice-cream parlour. which had black granite counters that reflected like mirrors, glass and chrome display fridges of mouth-watering temptation, stunning displays of cones and cups in all sizes, and home-made ice creams in flavours like mulberry, peach, mandarin orange, black cherry, pistachio, hazelnut and chocolate gianduja. As if this were not enough they also had a glass-fronted freezer displaying two and three tier cakes, made entirely of solid ice cream and elaborately iced like wedding cakes, with flowers made of white and dark chocolate on top.

I had to walk past this place every day to get into the village and, naturally, I had to try out each flavour of ice cream, just so I would know which ones were the best. The man who worked there was called Giuseppe, and I was usually his only customer in the mornings. I got to know him well and looked forward to our morning chats. He confided in me that the owner treated him badly, and he often sneakily gave me freebies when he could get away with it. He also introduced me to other customers whenever they came in, so through Giuseppe Ice-cream my circle of friends gradually grew.

One day he introduced me to Giuseppe Wheelbarrow.

"He's rough round the edges but has a heart of gold," he told me.

Giuseppe Wheelbarrow was indeed a diamond in the rough. His livelihood was his wheelbarrow, the only asset he owned, and he survived by moving things around the village in it for anyone who asked. He gathered scrap metal or anything metallic that he could sell for recycling. He was one of nature's gentlemen, for he always insisted on paying for a coffee for me and would not consider letting me treat him, ever. He would plunge his rough, calloused hands into various pockets, pulling ten cents out of one, then a twenty cent coin out of another, until he eventually gathered up enough money to pay for two coffees; sometimes he fell a little short, and he would tip a wink to Giuseppe Ice-cream, promising to pay the rest when he could.

"So, yes," he told me one day, as we sat at a table outside the ice-cream parlour looking out over the deep blue waves. Some of the fishermen's orange, white and blue-striped boats lay on the beach, but several were out fishing. "I'm one of twelve brothers. They took most of us away when I was seven and put us in three different orphanages, and just left my mother with the two youngest. I came back to live with Mum when I was eighteen."

"That must have been frightening for you," I remarked. "Why did they take you away?"

"My mother couldn't cope at all and we were running wild like animals. She kept having babies incessantly. She was always breast feeding one, while pregnant with the next one. Sometimes there were two babies, both being breast fed as if they were twins."

"What was it like in the orphanage?" I asked.

"I cried a lot at first, because I missed my Mum and I was scared. But really it was nice. We all had clothes, and they gave us food every day. They took us on outings too. I saw lots of beautiful places and learnt a lot there. Most of the other children were nice. I had two brothers with me, and there were five in another orphanage and two sisters in a different one. They were very far away too, so we didn't see each other often at all. I lived right over in Mondello, the other side of Palermo."

I was a little too stunned to respond. It was really nice because *they gave him clothes*? And *food every day*? Whilst my brain was struggling to make appropriate neural connections, both Giuseppe Ice-cream and Giuseppe Wheelbarrow called out

"Ciao, Giuseppe!" to the village idiot, who was cycling past.

The village idiot always rode his bicycle around, in no particular direction, and people flew out of his way, dropping babies or bags of vegetables or whatever they were holding with reckless abandon in their haste to clear a path for him. This was because he had customised his bicycle in such a way that he could not see where he was going. He had painted it fuchsia pink and twined ribbons gaily around the entire frame, he had embellished the wheels with fluttering ribbons and strands of wool, and, most importantly, he had somehow attached a music stand to the handlebars, rising up well above his line of vision and displaying photographs of all his favourite football players, taped on firmly. He would occasionally hit unmovable objects such as parked cars, and simply get back on his bicycle apparently unperturbed and continue on his way.

On this particular occasion he scored a direct hit against a lamppost and he and his bicycle flew off in opposite directions. As he picked up his bike he apologised to the lamppost, then realigned his music stand and continued on his way.

"There are lots of Giuseppes in this village, aren't there?" I said, for want of a better comment, as I watched him cycle away.

"Oh, if you ever forget someone's name, try calling them Giuseppe and you'll probably be right!" said Giuseppe ice-cream.

I had only been home for about fifteen minutes when Mister Faeces the Construction Engineer turned up, with a hammer in his hand. I was preparing a pot of tea using nine Italian teabags, which is the equivalent of one English teabag. As usual he acted as if the house still belonged to him, and simply sauntered into the garden, puffing his cigarette obnoxiously as he called out to ask if I were at home. Since all the doors and windows were gaping wide open, it would have been pretty hard to hide behind the sofa and pretend that I was out. It would also have been difficult to point out that he was barging unwelcome into my house because, on paper, it actually did still belong to him.

I wondered whether it would be a better tactic to start playing hard-ball and inform him that I would initiate action with a lawyer if he did not complete the construction and deliver the fixtures and fittings I had already paid for right away, or whether to continue Valentino's preferred strategy, which was to carry on acting as if we were friends, as if we liked him, and as if we had no doubt he would set everything straight as soon as possible. Since he was waving the hammer about like a baton twirler, swinging it about to and fro as if weighing up the damage he could do with it, I decided to fall in line with Hubby.

He sat down at my kitchen table and puffed away, apparently oblivious to the hammed up theatrical coughing, spluttering and choking noises I was making. He laid the hammer on the table and caressed it with his hand, the way evil masterminds in movies fondle their cats.

"I cannot tolerate any more of that smoke" I told him eventually, "you'll have to put it out. And I want to talk about the bidet and other fittings that still haven't been delivered."

"Yes, it's going to take more money," he told me. "Some additional expenses have come up."

"I've already paid for the tiles and a bidet," I insisted, "so let's say you deliver them first, and *then* we'll see about paying for more things."

"You obviously haven't understood, Signora," he said, his grip tightening around the hammer. "The house could fall down on top of you if we don't get some more money to fix a few problems. It could cost as much as twenty thousand euros. It's happened before, you know, that people didn't pay what was necessary. You had better pay or you'll come to regret it."

Was he trying to extort money from me? I sat at the table and took a deep breath, my mind racing as I wondered what to say next. The open teapot was sitting in the centre of the table, already containing nine teabags and surrounded forlornly by their little strings and paper tags, which I had been pulling off. I always remove the strings. These 'Sicilian sachets' may not have real tea inside but at least I can try to maintain standards by making them look as much as possible like real teabags on the outside. Tampons have strings on, not teabags.

With a deft flick of the wrist, Mister Faeces tossed his cigarette butt into the teapot, without even pausing first to stub it out. For a lingeringly portentous minute nothing happened, and then, with a huge whoosh, a tongue of flame burst out of the top of the open teapot and very gratifyingly made him leap up from the table and bang the back of his head on the dresser doorknob. They may not brew good tea but, goodness gracious, Italian teabags make outstanding kindling. Before our horrified eyes the flame grew higher and I was just drawing near with a plastic washing up bowl full of water when the teapot cracked into two pieces with a fairly loud snapping noise. I had to douse the whole table, in case the tablecloth caught the flame, and I am proud to say that I managed to put out the whole fire successfully whilst also drenching Mister Faeces' trousers.

I am also very proud to say that, while he staggered back, pulling at the sodden fabric around his gonads, I had the presence of mind to grab his hammer off the table and throw it out of the window. If he wanted it back now, he would have to go outside to get it and I could lock the door after him. I was still wondering if he was genuinely trying to extort money from me, or if he was simply toying with me because he enjoyed frightening people. I suddenly lost my temper. The softly-softly approach had never been my style, anyway.

"I don't have an extra twenty thousand pounds for you, and I have no way of getting twenty thousand pounds to give you, so I am going to pretend you never asked for it," I told him. "And I think you should do the same. Just forget about the sink and the bidet and the actual quantity of tiles I have already paid for, if you are short of money, but don't ask me for more cash, because I cannot help you. You'll have to ask someone else."

He did not look me in the eye as I spoke. I think he found being spoken to like this by a woman so unexpected and bizarre that he simply did not know what to do. He stood up, making a bid to leave, so I delivered the rest of my address to the wet patch on his trousers. I hoped he would find it as disconcerting as I do when men talk to my tits.

"Don't ever come and visit me here again when I am at home alone," I told his dripping testicles. "It simply isn't done. Have I made myself clear?"

He laughed at me, slowly, and walked out without looking back. I slammed the door noisily behind him and hoped he could hear the key turning in the lock.

To get over this episode, I had to make the world's largest cup of tea, by putting all the remaining teabags I had into a saucepan and emptying half the sugar bowl in on top of them. When I told Valentino about it later, he looked deeply worried and said nothing at all.

From this day on, Valentino took to telephoning me from work every half an hour. Friends of his would often drop in on me unexpectedly to check that I was alright. I realised he was very worried and did not like leaving me alone for one minute. I started to relax as day after day passed without any sign of Mr. Faeces darkening my doorstep.

Once I had explored it thoroughly, I established that our village contained a baker's, an ice-cream shop, a barber, a ladies' hairdresser, a hardware shop, a purveyor of rotten meat, five cafés and a post office full of fighting old age pensioners. There was no queueing system and no take-a-number system. In fact, the only system was survival of the fittest, and may the old timer with the sharpest fingernails get to the service hatch first.

My first foray into the village's only supermarket was something of an eye-opener, too. I went looking for tea, though I should have known better. Eventually I found myself in an aisle with a pasta section, in which all the bags of pasta were simply enormous sacks. There was no packet smaller than a pillowcase, and they were all on the upper shelves. Stacked below them, rather off-puttingly, were cans of dog food. I scanned the packs looking for some of the famous Italian pasta brands I might recognise, yet there was nothing familiar. Then I read the label carefully and learned that this was pasta for dogs. Oh yes, of course! Pasta for dogs. In Italy, you can buy your canine friend fusilli, tortellini or almost any other shape of pasta he may have acquired a taste for, and then add a sauce of chummed up Pedigree Chum, or whatever.

The concept of dedicated dog pasta should not have taken me by surprise, since I had already seem Valentino lovingly warming up leftover pasta to give to his dog, Leo. He kept a supposedly fierce guard dog at his grandmother's house, supposedly to protect her. I am making generous use of the word "supposedly" because the dog was in fact the greatest canine scaredy-cat I have ever seen, and would hide under the bed at the first sign of a postman. Personally I attribute this to being abnormally pampered in every way, starting with food.

Dogs are supposed to munch up leftovers without complaint, whatever they may be. That is why we sigh and say "Ah, it's a dog's life." That is the canine condition. It is the very nature of dogginess. But not Leo. Valentino would stand at the stove lovingly warming up leftover pasta for Leo, tasting it and adding a pinch more salt or a touch of fresh basil if he felt its flavour needed improving, and checking that it was the ideal temperature by dabbing some onto his inner wrist, like testing milk for a baby, before finally serving it up for Leo in the garden. He often serves it with a side dish of salad, or some parsley garnish. I watch carefully because I am convinced that sometimes, when he wanders into the garden with a glass of red wine in his hand, it is actually an aperitif for Leo. If he feels that Leo may be suffering from poor digestion or trapped wind he massages his tummy. After dinner he often gives him an after eight mint.

"Why don't you just give him the leftover food as it is?" I dared to ask one day.

"What?!" responded Valentino, scandalised. "Would you eat cold pasta?"

I realised it would be pointless trying to argue that I am not a dog. I also felt embarrassed to admit that, actually, I do fairly often eat cold pasta out of the fridge, when I cannot be bothered to warm it up. I decided to say nothing, and just wuzzled Leo's ears instead.

Moving hastily away from the dog food section, I located the miserable offerings on sale by way of compensation for the lack of actual tea in Italy. I loaded about twelve packets into my trolley, calculating that, since you have to use six teabags per cup to get any flavour whatsoever, this would last me about four days; and resolved to try to acquire a taste for coffee as soon as possible.

The real, human pasta section was remarkable not least because it occupied both sides of two full aisles, in a supermarket with no more than ten aisles altogether. I spent ages looking at the names of each pasta shape and thinking about what they actually mean. Every pasta shape has a name which is highly descriptive and apt. *Farfalle* are butterflies, *spaghetti* are short bits of string, *vermicelli* are little worms, *linguine* are little tongues, *conchiglie* are shells, *gomiti* are elbows, *orechiette* are little ears, *lumache* are snails, and *ravioli* are little frilly cushions stuffed with vomit. I confess I am not absolutely certain about the translation of that last one, but I think it means something like that.

Like all normal Italians, Valentino is utterly convinced that failing to eat any pasta during one continuous 24-hour period means certain death. To avoid such danger, I loaded one bag of almost every pasta shape I could find into my trolley, plus four packs of spaghetti for good measure.

I went rather wild at the cheese and delicatessen counter, buying a vast selection of smoked Sicilian cheeses, smoked hams and mortadella. They were displayed so temptingly and they sounded so appealing. Frankly, a lot of Italian food is the same as English food but, somehow, the Italians just do it better. Mortadella is a good example because it is actually spam. The only difference is that spam tastes like what it is, namely, a pig's snout, lips and earlobes mixed up with a little bit of its backside, whereas mortadella tastes like a fabulous delicacy because it also has garlic, pistachio nuts and an Italian name. The Italian Christmas Panettone is actually only a giant-sized loaf of raisin bread. Even pizza, if you think about it, is just a glorified version of cheese on toast. It is all a question of presentation and branding.

Another great Italian marketing triumph is minestrone soup

which, as we all know, is ketchup with some leftover vegetables and pasta tipped in. The all-time greatest Italian makeover story has to be, of course, Parmesan cheese. This is no more than ordinary cheese that got left in the larder three generations ago and was rediscovered in a partially mummified condition, grated to look like dandruff, and then sold in automatically reloading sprinkler devices so that Italian waiters could use it for getting revenge on women who rejected the suggestive advances they made with their massive phallic black pepper dispensers.

My trip to the supermarket was only complete when I had made my careful selection of a plastic laminated washing-machine cosy. Many Sicilians keep their washing machines on the balcony, insisting it is astoundingly convenient as you simply remove the clean clothes and hang them up right there, on the spot. To maintain standards of modesty and cleanliness, they protect their washing machines with zip-down covers, rather like a plastic table cloth in three dimensions.

Happy with my selection of items, apart from the tea of course, I tottered off to the till with my trolley which, its gammy wheels weighed down with pasta, was determined to roll off sideways into the sunset. The strangest thing about the village supermarket is the woman who works on the till. She is always there, and there is only one till. I have never seen anyone else capable of looking so close to death, for such a prolonged period of time, without actually dying. Her name is Angela, but I think of her as Vampire Angela. Her face is a translucent blueish white, her eyes are hollow and sad and the exhaustion on her face is so profound that even her whitish-grey hair looks as if it is too tired to keep holding onto her scalp for much longer. The cadaverous look is enhanced when she smiles and reveals teeth that look dry and loose in their sockets. Yet she keeps on going, day after week after month, just the same, and she always says she is fine every time I see her. In this village we see everyone all over the place. It is too small not to. Yet I have never seen Vampire Angela anywhere except in the supermarket, sitting at the till, looking whiter and greyer every time I lay eyes on her.

After I had been living in the village for a couple of months, I went strolling along the sea front as usual and noticed the regular fisherman looking highly excited. They had an adult swordfish laid out on a bench, and were selling it by the slice. I had only seen a swordfish for sale in the village one other time, when I had bought twenty slices for my housewarming and, as on that occasion, the fishermen were in high spirits. Its eye was staring out at passers-by, imploring them for help. The sword growing uselessly from its nose only added to the pathos, as the poor creature had never even had the chance to try bayoneting its final predators.

"*Fresco!*" shouted the little puny fisherman, selling various types of fish and some prawns. "*Fresco!*" he shouted again, but nobody was looking at his fish.

I pushed into the festive atmosphere until, among the crowds of men in long green waders, I found the fishermen from whom we always buy our fish, Giacomo and Filippo. They had been introduced to Valentino by the village barber, who is their cousin, and he immediately made them his New Best Friends. He has their numbers on speed dial and they are briefed to telephone him from their little rowing boats as soon as they have hauled in anything tasty, so that he can meet them on the beach and be the first to buy a ton of it.

"Who would have thought it?" said Giacomo. "Nobody's caught a swordfish round here for five years, then suddenly we get two of them in two months."

"Does that mean the sea temperature is changing, or something?" I asked. "I mean, maybe the water could be getting warmer and attracting fish that don't usually come so far inland. Or could there be unusual currents?"

Giacomo looked at me strangely.

"No. It means that God is answering our prayers," he told me confidently.

I asked if they knew the lads who had caught the swordfish, and Filippo said one of them was his nephew.

"So it's very fresh then?" I asked.

"They caught it about three o'clock this morning," answered Filippo.

Some of the fishermen buy frozen fish at the wholesale market and defrost it in buckets of seawater to sell to people from the city who do not know them. When a fisherman sells fish on the seafront the day after a storm, it is obviously defrosted. Little Signor Fresco does this. The ones who always do this have soft hands and are often weedy little men.

The real fishermen go out in tiny wooden rowing boats, big enough to hold about six people, or a net full of fish. Depending on which type of fish they are after and where they are going, they either row them, or they stagger from home with a Yamaha outboard motor on their shoulder and plonk it on the back. These men only ever sell live, fresh fish. They are burly giants who have calluses and cuts from heavy, wet nets dragging on their hands. It takes a certain physique to haul up a net full of fish struggling for their lives to get away. It also takes a certain toll on the body. The fishermen all have severe, recurring back problems and spend much of their income on physiotherapy and injections of powerful anti-inflammatories. So, if you ever decide to buy fish in a fishing village, do not purchase it from a puny little elf with sprightly movements: look for someone who resembles Arnold Schwarzenegger and, ideally, who winces in agony every time he bends over.

"The lads seem happy," I commented to Giacomo.

"By the time they've sliced that fellow up and sold him, they'll have about a thousand euros," he explained.

"*Frescooooooo!*" shouted Signor Fresco. A couple of smartly-dressed people, probably out for the day from Palermo, started looking at his fish.

"How did they catch it?" I asked Giacomo.

"In one of the bigger boats they use along the coast. They work up there because there are already too many fishermen working here. They both nearly fell overboard. They got dragged around here and there for three quarters of an hour before he finally died. They were lucky. Swordfish die quickly. A tuna could have dragged them around for hours on end."

Giacomo walked back to his net, which was laid out on the sea front for inspection and mending. It was about fifty yards long and occupied the entire promenade, leaving a small space along one side for people to walk. As the seasons changed, the type of nets I saw him working on changed. Depending on the type of fish they were intended to catch, the nets would have larger or smaller holes, and would be longer or smaller. Some of them had pebbles in little net bags fixed all around the edges to weigh them down. Some of them were small but others were more than a hundred yards long. They always seemed to have holes ripped in them that needed mending.

"Just doing some crochet," he usually said when I spotted him mending nets.

I like chatting to Giacomo, partly because he is always smiley but also because he speaks proper Italian to me. The fishermen all speak Sicilian among themselves and, like my father-in-law, some of them seem to struggle with Italian. A lot of the time, they think they are talking Italian but actually they are talking Sicilian.

Strangely, many Sicilians, when you ask them if they speak Sicilian, look at you as if they are the Queen on a royal walkabout and you just said,

"Go on, Your Majesty, pull my finger."

Quite why they find it so insulting is something I have still not fully fathomed. All I can tell you is that they are always the ones who think they are posh. The thing that makes this most mysterious of all is that, later, you notice that more than half their status updates on Facebook are written in pure Sicilian. Meanwhile, there are the fishermen and others who find talking Italian so much effort that, after a few sentences, they just give up speaking altogether and fall into an enigmatic, observant silence.

Sicilian is a fun language. I started picking up odd words from the fishermen and occasionally inserting them into sentences. Many Sicilians who do not know how to talk proper Sicilian - which is a separate language from Italian - do this. Hearing me speak my version of Sicilian always provoked choruses of guffaws from all around me and was a guaranteed way of making new friends in the village. One of my favourite words became *camurria*. Camurria means a terrible drag, or an interminable nuisance. For example, getting stuck in a traffic jam is a camurria; having to take a day off work and wait at home for the man from British Gas to come "some time between nine a.m. and six p.m." is a camurria; an even bigger camurria is having to wait for the Sicilian gas man to come "some time between Monday morning and Thursday afternoon, probably." Another word I love is *fitusu* (pronounced fitoozoo), which means stinky, gone off and disgusting. Rotten fish heads lying about on the sea front are fitusu, so the fishermen always clean them away before they leave. *Piciotti* (pronounced pichotti) is a great word simply because most Italians think it means a Mafia member of the most junior level. What it really means in Sicilian is Lads, or young men. So groups of young men will call each other piciotti, as in "Come on Piciotti, let's go and get some ice-cream and try to pick up some chicks".

Sicilian is a very earthy language. It is equipped with multiple words for different types of farts. The sort that comes out loud and proud is called a *piritu*. (Someone who puts on airs and graces may be called "an inflated piritu".) The type you manage to sneak out secretly, if necessary by breaking it down into several smaller sections, is a *sgurreggiu*. The type which mean you have to rush off urgently and change your underwear is called a *luffione*. I won't list any more, just in case the Queen is reading.

One of the conversations I had many a time arose when I heard a word I did not know.

"Is that a Sicilian or an Italian word?" I would ask, and then a general discussion would ensue, which usually drew in innocent bystanders at the supermarket or people who were passing by in the street. Nobody was sure. The huddle eventually dispersed with a general agreement to look it up when they get home.

Children from full-time Sicilian speaking families do have a reasonable grounding in Italian before they start primary school, but they struggle when they enter an academic environment and have to use Italian exclusively, for writing, for speaking, and for studying. They are learning a lot of new vocabulary, as well as the subject being taught. They must find it a real *camurria*. Throughout their school careers they are told off if they utter a word of Sicilian in class.

The Sicilian language could genuinely be lost one day. It is not an official language in Sicily. You would never see an official website written Sicilian, the way you see them in Welsh; I think even the Sicilians themselves would regard that as hilarious. Nowadays the majority of Sicilians speak Sicilian the way Valentino usually does – Italian with lots of Sicilian words poked in, and a few random Sicilian phrases, which of course is not the real Sicilian language at all. Most of them do not know how to speak pure Sicilian with all the correct grammar and exclusively Sicilian vocabulary. Only the fishermen in my village speak that way and Valentino says that, when they speak among themselves, he does not understand everything.

Sicilians have the terribly irritating habit of starting a joke in Italian, and then delivering the punch line in Sicilian.

"It's just not funny in Italian" they say. And they are right.

They also use Sicilian when they are shamelessly spreading gossip. They lower their voices, lean into each other and mutter in Sicilian, making repeated use of personal pronouns instead of actual names, as they describe shocking and outrageous activities.

Another situation in which Italian will often melt into Sicilian is an argument. When a forthright exchange of opinions descends into a knockdown verbal fight, it inevitably becomes a shouting match in Sicilian. Whilst the language lends itself more readily to wit, it also lends itself willingly to evocative insults and colourful threats. As both parties gradually run out of steam and come to the inevitable making up, which all Italian arguments always do eventually, the participants will revert to using Italian to show that they have regained their self-control. It's almost a pity when that happens.

Perhaps the strangest thing about Sicilian is that it is not just one language. There are so many different dialects, with their own unique vocabulary, that you only have to drive about one hour in any direction and you will find the local dialect is almost incomprehensible, sometimes even to a pretty good Sicilian speaker. Valentino spent part of his military service years in

Catania, and had no idea what anyone was saying the whole time they spoke in Sicilian.

Sometimes when I was out and about, I would bump into the postman and he would pull up on his bicycle and hand me a letter or two. He was amazingly energetic for a man close to retirement age. Once I spotted him walking along the sea front, eating an ice cream with another, older man, whom he introduced as the previous postman. The Ex-postman had lived in America for eight years.

"Howdy" he greeted me, with a strong Italian accent. "'Ow y'all doin'a?"

"Oh, fine, thank you," I said, trying not to laugh. He was immensely proud of his knowledge of English. I could tell it added to his status in the village.

"Y'all 'avin' yourself ha mighty nice day now," he said, tipping his peaked cap as he walked on, and poking his little scoop back into his ice cream. We had had stormy weather the night before, so the fishermen had dragged all their boats off the beach onto the main road, blocking it to the traffic, to make sure they did not get swept away. They lay higgledy-piggledy all over the road, their orange, white and blue painted stripes brightening up the village as if it were ready for a festival. A car was stopped and revving its engine impotently behind the boats, the driver waving his arm out of the window and shouting loudly for advice on how to get to the centre of the village.

"Go to a different village!" the ex-postman advised him.

A couple of weeks later I spotted the ex-postman with another man, even older than himself. This old fellow was wrinklier than a raisin, but he still walked at a lively pace.

"Howdy folks!" I called out. I am not certain why I said this, but it seemed the appropriate thing to say, at the time.

"Howdy!" responded the ex-postman.

He then introduced me to his companion, who was his predecessor, the ex-ex postman. This charming fellow told me he was ninety-seven years old and was the oldest person in the village.

"So your predecessor isn't still around, then?" I asked the ex-ex-postman in Italian.

"No, there wasn't a post office in the village before me," he answered.

Just then Giuseppe the village idiot pedalled past at a leisurely pace on his bicycle.

"Hello Giuseppe" they both called out, and looked relieved when he cycled past ignoring them. He had added a very large radio-CD player to the back mudguard of his bike, with the aerial fully extended upwards, from which was flying a carnation-pink and black Palermo football shirt. He rode diagonally into the road, triggering a screeching of brakes as two cars performed an emergency stop to avoid hitting him, and came to a wobbly halt in front of them. He pretended to turn on the radio, though it did not work, and then rode off delivering what I thought sounded like an excellent imitation of a commentary on a football match. He included the crackling sound of a little bit of radio interference now and then. He had Palermo score a spectacular goal, and they were well positioned to score another one as he rolled off out of earshot.

After watching him disappear down the road, the ex-postman and the ex-ex-postman said they were on their way to the ice-cream parlour, and invited me to join them. My friend Giuseppe Ice-cream was there, keenly awaiting company, as the ice-cream vending business was always slack at this time of day and things could get lonely.

I ordered a coffee *granita* and an ice-cream sandwich. A granita is basically a slush puppie and, if it is a coffee one, that means a cold double espresso has been tipped in with the ice. It was delicious, but I had failed to take into consideration that I was unaccustomed to such quantities of caffeine, and consequently developed a severe, Parkinsons-type hand tremor which made eating my ice-cream sandwich a hazardous challenge to my grossly impaired eye-hand coordination. This Sicilian speciality consists of the largest possible quantity of ice-cream wedged firmly into a hamburger style bread roll. The bread is soft and slightly sweet with a hint of vanilla. The whole thing is ambrosial, provided you are capable of eating it without shaking uncontrollably and thus launching the ice cream component of it down your own cleavage at high velocity, then quickly grabbing it back and ramming the entire thing into your mouth in one go, hoping the ex-postman and the ex-ex-postman have not noticed what you are doing and, as a consequence, developing the worst ice-cream brain-freeze you have ever suffered in your life, so severe that your ears almost fall off and you cannot speak because your tongue is cryogenically frozen onto your soft palate.

Unfortunately Giuseppe Ice-cream did notice, and I think he enjoyed the part where I furtively fondled my own breasts, because after that he offered me free ice-cream not just occasionally, but absolutely every time I went in there. I did not concern myself too much with his motives. I just made sure I went in there every single day for my free ice-cream sandwich, without coffee.

8

WE GET MARRIED FOR THE FIRST TIME, CIVILLY

I usually tell people I love my husband so much that I married him twice. In reality, I married him twice because Italian bureaucracy made me do it. Let me explain.

Although we were living in the house, on paper it still belonged to the Engineer Mastronzo. He had not made any more demands for money above the agreed sale price, so we had concluded the day he came and torched my teapot was just his idea of entertainment. Yet one third of the house really did still belong to him, and he wanted the money for that.

I still wanted him to give me my bidet and bathroom tiles, make the floors and courtyards slope towards the drainage holes, rather than away from them, and stop using my plant pots as ashtrays. A lot of friends told me I was amazingly brave to stick to my guns like this. Most Sicilians told me I was amazingly stupid. Valentino said I was mad to insist, and told me we should just give up and pay. Mr. Faeces was refusing to do the remaining work, Valentino pointed out. He was not interested any more. He just wanted his dough.

I refused to hand over the final payment until we could at least have the deeds to the house signed, notarised and recorded in the land registry the same day. To get the title deeds for the house registered in my name I needed an Italian Residence Certificate and for this, I first needed a *Permesso di Soggiorno* or "Permission to Stay" Certificate. To get this, it turned out, I had to meet certain criteria.

We tried, in those early, naïve days, to point out to anyone who would listen that there is such a thing as the European Union and that, at least as far as Brussels was concerned, I legally had the right to live in Italy just because I wanted to, the way Italians are automatically allowed to live in Britain if they fancy it. In return a uniformed, armed policeman at the Palermo Immigration Office informed me that being a European citizen merely gave me the automatic right to queue hop. Indeed, he withdrew his weapon and forced me to barge straight to the front of a long line of despondent and disappointed Africans, Romanians and assorted Asians who looked as if they had already been waiting in this dismal immigration office, lined with peeling grey paint and posters of people being deported, for months. I was eaten up with guilt when I saw the sadness on their faces as they realised they would have to wait even longer, probably only to receive further disappointment anyway.

"Are you sure England's in the European Union?" the policeman suddenly asked me after elbowing a Moroccan out of the way and physically manhandling me into the service booth in his place.

"Definitely," I said. "We joined before Italy, actually."

"But you don't have the Euro," he objected.

"And a good thing too, don't you think?" I answered.

The Italians see the Euro as the ruination of their economy, and the policeman liked my comment so much he leaned into the booth and told the official to make sure my case was passed without any setbacks or faffing around.

"And don't overdo the stapling either," he added. "She's English, so don't waste her time."

Italian officials love to string things out, so they not only keep people waiting for inordinate amounts of time while they photocopy, rubber stamp and staple reams of paper, but they also send them on wild goose chases to obtain other documents from other public offices, despite knowing that the applicant will only be refused at the end of the whole procedure anyway. This creates more public sector jobs for their friends and relatives. The Lord helps those who help themselves.

The Italian government plays along with this joyfully, as it loves to burden its residents with bureaucracy. It is a cunning political strategy of population repression and it is highly effective, as the Italians would probably have staged a revolution by now if only they could find time between paying their utility bills, renewing their identity and residence cards, updating their national insurance cards and trying to find out who their new driving license was actually delivered to.

The ancient Romans invented this technique to suppress their colonials and prevent rebellion. It worked on all of them, except the Jews. To get permission to do anything at all in Roman Egypt, for example, even to borrow the equivalent of twenty pounds from your own mother, you had to fill out a set of forms in triplicate then have them stamped and sealed; most of them can still be found preserved in the desert sands. Having perfected a system whose inefficiency maintained the *Pax Romanum* for centuries, the Italians have been inflicting the same type of initiative-crippling bureaucracy upon themselves ever since. Its resounding success in population control is the reason why everyone who visits Italy nowadays looks around them and asks how, exactly *HOW on earth* did these people build and rule one of the greatest empires the world has ever seen?

As a result of this cult of bureaucracy, part of the modern Italian cultural heritage is a new art genre encompassing public officials' rubber stamps, dollops of red sealing wax, 'Marche da Bollo' for which you pay lots of money and which are basically government-issue sticky labels in an array of pretty colours, and, for pen pushers at the top of the tree, little tags of red ribbon which are stuck onto the corners of legally binding documents with sealing wax, and even have additional sealing wax medallions hanging off them. Valentino is a member of this elite tier of paper-clip filers entrusted with these sealing wax accoutrements. By the time a piece of paper has passed through his hands, it looks more important than the Magna Carta.

The Immigration Official glared over my shoulder at the Moroccan, who had tried to retake his rightful place at the head of the queue behind me, and was frogmarched away. He told me there were only three ways he could give me a 'Permesso di Soggiorno', or Permission of Stay Certificate. Either I had to be very rich, or I had to have a job in Sicily, or I had to marry a Sicilian.

"Exactly how rich?" I asked.

"Stinking," would be a loose translation of his answer.

"Go on, try me. Give me a number," I challenged him.

Having just sold my house in England and not yet paid for the one in Sicily, it turned out I was that stinking rich. Both Valentino and the Immigration Official said declaring this level of wealth would be a terrible idea, because the government would spend the rest of my life trying to get every penny off me in the form of taxes I had never heard of.

"You'd do far better to just marry him right away," said the Immigration Official, pointing at Valentino. "With all that money you don't need to, but he's very handsome, isn't he? Go on, make a Sicilian happy!"

We chose to embark up on a hasty marriage because it seemed like the easiest option, yet making a Sicilian happy turned out to be terribly complicated. We were working to a deadline and I simply could not believe how many steps and wild goose chases we had to go through to get permission to marry, never seeming any closer to our goal.

We decided to simplify things – and of course I use the word "simplify" in a very relative sense – by tackling the civil bureaucracy and marrying in the village registry office first, so we could legally have the house registered in my name, and then to organise a proper church wedding afterwards, giving ourselves more time to get through the Catholic bureaucracy. The added advantage to this was that The Godmother would have more time to buy herself yet another black dress for the joyous occasion.

Trying to get through the civil administration brought me to make my first real friend in the village. Totò is a sprightly chap of about sixty and one of the few residents of Aspra with all his own teeth. He is related to every other person in the village and they tease him about his famous namesake, for Totò Cuffaro is also the name of the President of Sicily, who governed the island for two years while on trial for being in the Mafia. He was found guilty but decided not to stand down as president, instead declaring he would continue his full term of government and then go to prison afterwards. Whilst this seems impossible to anyone outside Sicily, here it merely provokes a day of grumbling and some groans of irritation, like the here-we-go-again groans of weary irritation on the London Underground when commuters are told their train has been taken out of service because there is a terrorist bomb on it.

Totò Cuffaro works at the village's small Town Hall. The Town Hall in the village is so small that Totò Cuffaro is the only person who works there. I am deliberately excluding the fat lady at the entrance who swats flies away and asks you your name, then sits there not telling Totò, and just waves you through to his office. She is there, yes, but you could not call this work.

Whilst the Town Hall is small, it resides in a grand, late seventeenth century villa with sweeping twin staircases which curve outwards and upwards in semicircles and join at the main entrance on the first floor. This is the classic façade of the Sicilian villa and it is always a terrible dilemma choosing which staircase to walk up, because they are both so badly cracked and crumbling that either of them could give way beneath you and leave you with a broken nose.

"What if I go up this one and break some bones, when I could have used that one and been safe one more time?" I would ponder anxiously at the foot of the staircases.

All the other offices in the building are so badly flooded when it rains that it is like a monsoon indoors, Totò told me, which is why his office is the only room in the building that is used any more.

"Why don't they restore it?" I asked. "This building could be stunning if they fixed the corners back on and filled up the holes in the façade."

"They'll wait until a piece falls on someone and they get sued, then they'll do something. Until then, they won't spend a Euro on it," he told me. "There's one room next door which was restored and painted and looks beautiful, which they use for meetings where they want to pretend to outsiders that things here aren't as disgraceful as they really are. The rest of it can crumble to dust for all they care. Look at the state of this room."

All four walls of Toto's office were lined from floor to ceiling with ominous, bound volumes as gigantic as the Domesday Book. They were heaped up on free-standing metal shelves, and more of them were piled in dangerous towers on three desks. Row upon row of spines six inches thick marked the three types of book, which recorded births, marriages and deaths year by year. The books must have been referred to thousands of times because most of them had spines reinforced with brown parcel tape. The whole room looked as though one false move could bury us both alive in hundreds of tons of paper.

I think Toto started out helping me and treating me so well simply because he wanted to make a good impression on Aspra's only foreigner, but then he realised I made him laugh, and he took to saving his coffee breaks for when I came along so we could have a chat together. He would tell the fat lady we would be out for ten minutes, and then we would saunter over to his favourite café on the sea front, where his old cronies hung out, and spend half an hour over our little cups of espresso, watching the seagulls glide and dive and putting the world to rights. All his friends spoke to him in Sicilian, and it was with them that I started learning to recognise the distorted-sounding words and to pick out meaning from the stream of pouted vowels.

"Sicilian sounds like someone trying to speak Italian with cotton wool in their mouth," my sister once declared, quite accurately.

The initial suggestion from the main council office in Bagheria, the nearest town, was that I would have to go to the British Embassy in Rome or Naples, leave my passport and almost every other official document I own for about two months, and wait for the issue of a 'nulla osta' certificate which would confirm that I was not already married and was free to make a Sicilian happy. I had already been sent from pillar to post enough times to realise that a trip to Rome would turn into multiple trips to Rome and that it would just end in me getting deported, sooner or later, for not having a passport.

Since I already had this *Nulla Osta* certificate issued in England anyway, where it is called a *Certificate of No Impediment*, I objected passionately. I insisted an official translation of the certificate issued in England would have more value. Italian public officials will not let you do anything with no impediment, however. Creating impediments is the reason they get out of bed each morning.

My friend Totò went to endless efforts to help me get my English *Certificate of No Impediment* and other documents accepted, with official translations attached, rather than obey the dangerous proposal from Bagheria. When I actually presented him with my certificate, though, Totò looked at it sceptically. I realised why immediately; it did not have a single rubber stamp or sticky label anywhere, and was utterly bereft of red ribbons. I explained that it bore the personal signature of the chief registrar in England, which was worth far more than a silly rubber stamp which anyone could fake.

"I'm sure that's true, but my colleagues in Bagheria won't think so," he explained. His tone of voice betrayed years of frustration. I think his white moustache actually drooped a little lower as he spoke.

"I could get my fiancé to decorate it at work," I offered. "He's got sealing wax in two different shades of red, you know."

Totò loved that idea, but said we would have to be more cunning. He devised a stratagem involving a mind-bogglingly complex paper trail of translations, endorsements and other additions to a sheaf of documents all backed up by a set of laws he managed to find in a volume which he usually used as a door stop. All the devious twists and turns of bureaucracy which he devised on my behalf were implemented on his aged typewriter, on which he bashed out everything with his index fingers, and the fax machine which was held together by almost one full roll of sticky brown parcel tape and which only worked if I held the plug into the wall at a certain angle for him whilst he operated the buttons.

The final culmination was an excursion together to the main office in Bagheria. He drove me there in his twenty-two year old Alfa Romeo which was largely held together with brown parcel tape, both inside and out. The replacement dashboard was fabricated cunningly out of corrugated cardboard which had once housed a Christmas *panettone,* and the bumpers were cushioned for an extra soft landing, in case of impact, with spongy latex taped round them with the ubiquitous sticky tape.

"Would you mind draping the seat belt across your body?" he asked as I settled into the passenger seat. "I know there's nothing for it to click into, but at least it looks OK if the *vigili urbani* are checking."

The *vigili urbani* are the Italian traffic police.

"I boss them all around, you know, so I'd hate to make a bad impression," he explained. "It would mean the end of my favourite hobby."

Italians are all obsessed with avoiding making a bad impression, which they call a *brutta figura*. This literally translates as 'an ugly figure' and is about the worst form of social suicide an Italian could commit. The only thing worse, in fact, would be to make a *figura di merda*, which means a 'figure of shit'. Accidentally making a figure of shit would, for an Italian, warrant discreetly emigrating to the kind of country that still does not have plumbing, electricity or McDonalds.

When Totò managed to start the engine – third time lucky – he gave me a conspiratorial wink and confided,

"You know, this car hasn't actually passed its MOT for a few years now."

"Really," I said, trying to sound surprised.

To my relief he drove slowly and cautiously. He apologised for this fact.

"My wife thinks I'm a coward on the roads, but I can't risk working up too much vibration in this car. Pieces fall off. It's the tape. The glue melts in the sunshine and it starts to unravel."

When we arrived at the large office in Bagheria we rushed up to the relevant department. I waited patiently in the clammy and overcrowded office, while Totò greeted all his colleagues with kisses and then proceeded to argue with them until voices were raised to screaming pitch and the flailing hands were whirling like helicopter blades. The discussion was largely in Sicilian but, towards the end, as things calmed down, everyone reverted to the more professional Italian and I realised that the deal he had cut with them was that he would mend their photocopier if they would print and rubber stamp the necessary documents for me to get married. Apparently the photocopier engineer had come twice, and merely managed to make the machine not only mash up every piece of paper fed into it, but also to overheat alarmingly and make spooky wailing noises and shrieks like the squealing of ghostly car brakes. The women hated the idea of backing down from their crazed, power hungry bureaucratic ego-trip, yet they clearly knew that Totò was the only person in Sicily with the know-how to make their photocopier work again.

Toto crawled down behind it, unplugged it, bashed the plug against the skirting board a few times, and then plugged it in again.

"It's the electrical current in this building," he said as he stood up. "It fluctuates. And that plug has a fuse that comes loose."

Then he removed the paper jam, calmly made photocopies of all my documents, rubber stamped them himself, and tipped his hat to all the ladies before leaving. They stood around with their mouths gaping open.

"*Grazie*," I said as I followed him out.

I wanted to give Totò a big kiss but instead I settled for a *cafè corretto*, which means espresso with a large shot of spirits in it, which I am sure he vastly preferred.

Valentino and I set the date for our civil wedding two weeks later. It was to be held in the restored room of the Town Hall, the one used for tricking outsiders into believing that Sicily is not so very different from the rest of Europe. My parents flew down with my older sister Susy and my four-year-old nephew, Jim, for a little holiday which would include the civil wedding ceremony.

Almost from birth, my nephew was fascinated by the sea and its exotic creatures. When he was not even two years old, and before he could talk at all, he loved sitting beside me leafing through a large coffee-table book of underwater photographs of animals which live around the Great Barrier Reef. Staying with us by the beach was his idea of heaven. I took him for walks along the sea front every morning.

One day he grabbed an octopus, which was still squirming around, from one of the fishermen's stalls and sprinted off towards the sea with it, to save its life. I chased after him, but I was too late, and only caught up with him as the octopus plopped into the water. I had no idea they could swim so fast! The fisherman thought this gesture so sweet that he refused my offer to pay for it.

Jim took to making me recite the names of every fish, creature, plant and any other life form in the sea, until I started desperately listing stuff like sand, bubbles and sodium. He also took to demanding (and remembering) the name of every fish we saw being sold on the beach each morning, in both Italian and English. When I did not know the English name of a fish, which was most of the time, he would invent one. Therefore we spent a lot of the holiday eating 'Stone fish', 'Stepney fish' and - my favourite – 'Righty-ho fish'. The fisherman memorised these "English" names in case any tourists came along, with cash, wanting to know what the merchandise was.

One day we decided to go to Segesta. This is the site of a miraculously well-preserved temple dating from the Ancient Greek colonisation of Sicily.

Fitting five adults and a child into a Fiat Punto is a test of how much they all love each other. Most of my family are not thin people, and we were crammed into a space which I think might be fairly described as "inadequate". We had to synchronise our inhaling and exhaling as team work, make various stops to exchange positions when body parts became completely numb, and also swear a lot (with our hands over Jim's ears) to release our negative emotions in a healthy way.

As we followed the curving mountain road and drew near to Segesta, glimpses of the temple gradually appeared from a vast sweep of intense yellow flowers which set the valley alight. Words cannot express our relief and delight at being able to explode out of the car. Our limbs gradually re-inflated, like a butterfly when it has just emerged all damp and compressed from its chrysalis and its crumpled wings need to be pumped up. We limped across the dusty car park, as the feeling slowly came back to our battered extremities and tortured joints.

The approach to the temple from the car park is a long walk and a shuttle bus is laid on. We decided to walk, since the idea of cramming ourselves into another vehicle provoked rabid foaming at the mouth in the case of my sister Susy, and almost reduced my mother to tears. As we strolled along the sandy, dusty path, we meandered alongside a low, dry-stone wall. A vast valley and hillside, carpeted with intense yellow flowers as far as the eye could see, spread out before us glowing in the sunshine. The temple stood at the top of a long walk uphill.

"Look," said Jim, "that's a fossil."

"Where?" I asked.

He pointed to a stone near the top of the wall, which displayed some kind of ammonite in low relief.

"So it is!" I exclaimed. "Look everyone."

He was only four years old and he had spotted a fossil which all the adults had missed. I was so proud of my little nephew.

"Mummy, put it in your handbag, please," said Jim. "I want to take it home."

It was a piece of stone weighing at least eight kilogrammes and it was also part of a wall in a protected historic site.

"I'm sorry, but we can't," said my sister.

"I'm not going till you get it," said Jim, crossing his arms stubbornly and sitting firmly on the dusty ground alongside his precious find. A prolonged dialogue of telling off, and refusing to listen, ensued.

"Why is there a sea fossil so far inland?" asked my mother.

"Sicily used to be under the sea," said Valentino. "There are sea fossils all over Sicily."

"Is this an ancient Greek wall?" asked Susy.

"No, it's modern," I reassured her.

"Are you sure?" asked Valentino. "How do you know?"

"I've got a degree in Classics and I've stayed up all night writing essays about Greek walls and columns more times than I care to remember," I said. "Trust me. I know."

"Right then," said Susy. "I'm just taking the damn thing because I don't want to carry Jim under my arm and he refuses to walk. This ruddy fossil is bound to be lighter than he is."

She set about removing the stone, inserting it into her capacious Mummy handbag, and then rebuilding the section of dry stone wall using the rocks she had removed, and another one my father found nearby. He turned out to be rather an expert on dry stone walls. Once we had finished, it looked better than before, although now devoid of a certain prehistoric interest. After the prolonged rebuilding efforts, which were now tending towards excessive perfectionism, I realised the sun might set before we had time to get up the hill and down again.

"Come on!" I commanded, stomping up the hill. "Let's get moving!"

The yellow flowers started swaying in unison and dancing in a warm, gentle breeze. When we reached the temple, it was even more wonderful than I had expected from afar. At first glance, the temple of Segesta seems to be in almost perfect condition, yet a closer look reveals that it was never actually finished. The columns have not been fluted, as they normally would have been in a temple of this period and style. If you look carefully at the base you can see there are still tabs left on the stone blocks, which were used for lifting the blocks into place but were then chiselled off. It also lacks a *cella*, which was the walled-in chamber at the back end where the statue of the god or goddess, to whom the temple was dedicated, was housed and protected from the elements. There is no sign of rubble that could once have been the *cella* and anyway, it would be unlikely to have fallen down when the rest of the temple is in perfect condition, so the only logical conclusion is that it was never built. Finally, the stonework around the top of the temple was clearly never prepared for the roofing structures, so we can be sure the temple was never roofed over.

"How on earth did the ancient Greeks actually design and build something like this?" asked Valentino, "without lasers or computers? And without mechanical excavators and heavy duty machinery? It's so perfect."

"Well, firstly they had to level off the site for the foundations, so they turned the entire plot into a spirit level by filling it with water," I told him. "Then they hit a stake into the ground at each of the four corners of the pool of water, marked the water level and then drained the water."

"I see," said Valentino.

"So the wooden stakes with their labels would be reference points for the height of the temple foundations," I added.

"Yes, I get it," said Valentino.

"Next, they had to get the base and columns perfectly perpendicular. They used plumb lines. The ancient Egyptians used the same methods for their temples. They used string to measure distances, and they used shadows to work out angles and lengths on the ground."

"Owww!" moaned my sister loudly, sitting on the base of the temple. "My shoulder!"

"Don't be so soft," said my father.

"I'm lugging eight kilogrammes of fossil," said Susy. "It weighs a ton!"

"Eight kilogrammes is neither an imperial nor a metric ton," said my father calmly, wandering away unsteadily across some ancient Greek rubble. "I spent a fortune on your education," he added over his shoulder. He sounded somewhat defeated. "Surely they taught you that?"

I swapped handbags with Susy. I immediately regretted it. Eight kilogrammes does weigh a ton, I discovered.

"Are you sure you want this fossil?" I asked Jim.

"Yes!" he said emphatically.

After I put on a great display of moaning and shoulder-rubbing, Valentino eventually took over carrying my sister's handbag. He drew a few strange glances as we came back to the car park, but he wore the bag with aplomb.

"I don't know what their problem is," he commented. "It's a very fashionable bag from this season. This is top quality Italian leather work."

When he put it into the car boot, it landed with a worryingly loud thud. On the way home, he said he thought it might have thrown the car's suspension off-balance. The rest of us were not worried about the car's suspension, as we were struggling to breathe.

"That was a great outing," said Jim, with passion. "I hope we find another fossil tomorrow."

"I don't," said Susy through clenched teeth.

We had intended the wedding to be a small affair with our immediate families. It was, after all, just a civil ceremony to facilitate some paperwork, and the proper wedding would be organised later. In addition to my family, Valentino's parents, his brother Manfredi, and his sister-in-law were invited.

On the day, an extra aunt also appeared. We had not invited aunts as Valentino has about six dozen of them and we thought the ones inevitably excluded could take offence, but this aunt had cancer and it was at her son's wedding that we had met, so in the end The Godmother invited her. We also had a spare, random elderly couple whom Valentino knows. They appeared unexpectedly and it was too embarrassing to get rid of them. Luckily my Father got on very well with the husband and they talked at each other all evening, completely unperturbed by the fact that they did not understand a word each other was saying. In fact, that is probably why they got on so well.

Totò was, naturally, the guest of honour and the proceedings were led by his brother Pepe who, it turned out, was something like the mayor of the village. Pepe had white hair and a playboy-style perma-tan, and everyone thought he had the mannerisms of a gangster. He had the slow, lazy way of talking and the compulsive habit of scanning the room constantly, with an anxious expression on his face, which is typical of *mafiosi*. It is typical of *mafiosi* in Italian films, at any rate. Valentino and Manfredi made a few very hushed comments about how *mafioso* he seemed. We found out afterwards that he has a serious heart condition and a liver disease and simply felt pretty ill. We also found out afterwards that there is usually a fee for registry office marriages, but the brothers insisted we were to pay nothing.

Pepe put on a Miss World style sash in red, white and green with a huge gold crest on his chest for the occasion, and made the ceremony very ceremonious. He and Totò gave me a huge bouquet of strelizia and other tropical-looking flowers and, as a wedding present, a commemorative plate hand painted in traditional Sicilian style by a local artist.

"This isn't a real wedding," announced my nephew Jim fairly loudly in the middle of the proceedings. "At real weddings the lady wears a white dress that's too big to sit down in, and it should be in the church next door. This isn't the church."

We looked round at the large hall, which still had eighteenth century decorations and a sculpted plaster ceiling.

"It's pretty, though, isn't it?" said my mother.

Jim promptly fell asleep.

Valentino bought red roses for all the ladies, which they loved. The Godmother brought several vast trays of elaborate little cakes and several bottles of champagne, which everyone loved.

"Auguri!" everyone wished us, as they toasted us with champagne. *Auguri* is a general purpose word in Italian used to wish someone good things in any situation. They say it instead of good luck, happy birthday, happy anniversary, well done on passing your degree, congratulations on getting your driving license, and so on. It derives from the ancient Roman priests, called augurs, whose job was to sacrifice animals and then read the future by looking at their entrails. Healthy innards meant a good future for Rome, whilst ones marked by disease did not augur well. You see, we use augury too in our language. The Italians just use it more.

After the wedding ceremony, and lots of augury, we all had dinner in a fish restaurant by the sea, in a slightly larger fishing village along the coast from Aspra. Everyone loved the food and Jim had the time of his life, toasting everyone with fizzy fruit juice which we told him was champagne. He kept luring people out for walks by the fishing boats, which fascinated him. They were larger than the boats in Aspra, like little houseboats with a closed-in central section and windows. The fishermen use these boats to go out further to sea, usually staying away three days at a time and thus catching types of fish which the Aspra fisherman cannot catch so close to the shore. Instead of the blue and orange of Aspra, the men from this village paint their boats green and orange although, like the fishermen of Aspra, they do not paint them too often, so they always look peely.

In the evening I flopped into bed with Valentino and thought happily about the fact that Santa Rosalia had just granted my second wish. I said a little prayer thanking her, and mentioned the third wish about having a baby, just to remind her.

When it was time for my family to leave, there was a suitcase-packing crisis. My sister would either have to leave behind almost all her clothes and other possessions, or the eight kilo fossil.

"Why can't you just put it in your handbag like before?" asked Jim.

"They weight everything when you go on the plane," explained

Susy, cuddling him. "I'm sorry, darling. Aunty Veronica will look after it for you, OK?"

Eventually he was persuaded. Thus I became the proud owner of a very large fossilised ammonite pilfered illegally from an ancient Greek monument. I put it on the balcony outside the kitchen, hoping the National Heritage Protection Police would not notice it.

Now we were legally man and wife, Valentino and I could go ahead and pay the last tranche of cash to Engineer Mastronzo, Mr. Lucky Faeces, and sign the title deeds to acquire the house. We transferred the money and went the same day to meet Mr. Lucky Faeces in the offices of a local notary, who immediately gave me the creeps. He wore a sharp suit but had, apparently, shampooed his hair with butter. It was thin on top and instead of having it cut extremely short - the only successful strategy in such circumstances - he had chosen to retain extra length and glue down the surplus. Such misguided attempts at self-rejuvenation are rare in Italy, though of course President Berlusconi led the trend among those with reflective domes by apparently painting his with creosote each morning.

The notary pranced about his spacious, fake antique office constantly, and had an attention span that lasted not more than five seconds. His eyes were a ghoulish see-through watery blue and could not hold my gaze while I spoke, but would wander and dart about as if constantly searching for something more interesting. Since his office was lined with hundreds of brown, leather-bound volumes all of equal height, his efforts were obviously futile.

Mr Lucky Faeces the constructor was obviously on great chummy terms with him.

"Not just a notary but the blue-eyed Adonis of the legal forces in this area!" he joked, flattering the notary and yet apparently actually meaning it, too. Valentino seemed to nod in agreement. I was already aware that Italians think having blue eyes is only one step less marvellous than single-handedly finding a unified theory of physics or achieving permanent world peace; yet apparently they thought this ghastly man was "good looking" merely because his irises were invisible, and that did surprise me. The daftness of heterosexual men never ceases to amaze me.

I felt uneasy and suspicious throughout the whole transaction, not only because the slimy butter-headed notary acted so shiftily all the time but also because Mr. Lucky Faeces kept muttering to him in Sicilian, which was downright rude considering the person buying the house, in other words me, did not understand them.

"Exactly when are you going to come and install the sink in the utility room and the bidet in the downstairs bathroom, which I am now paying for?" I asked Mr Faeces bluntly, when I had had enough of it.

He exchanged glances with Butterhead, and they both laughed as if I were so amusingly quaint.

"Don't worry about that," said Mr. Faeces, waving his cigarette at me.

"I won't worry about it *after* you have done it," I responded.

"It's all in hand," he said.

Butterhead showed us a large, handwritten book, which was leather bound but not the same height as all his others. Apparently this was the *Catastale* and, I deduced, *catastale* means land registry. I had thought that kind of thing would be done by computer, and indeed Butterhead said it would be done afterwards. He said that to his curtains, then paced over to his coffee machine, then back again, without offering us any coffee. He wrote that the house was ours, that the road outside it belonged to the council, and that we had paid about half as much money for it as we actually had paid.

"What?" I asked.

"That means you pay less stamp duty," he explained.

My mouth hung open.

"That's OK," said Valentino, "Everyone does that."

"Good grief," I said, in English, and stared out of the window.

After the creepy, suspicious deal was done, and we were given what I hoped was a legitimate title deed to our house, Mr. Faeces insisted that we all went off to a bar and drank a toast of very strong liqueur together to celebrate the completion of the deal. I am not sure which of us, Valentino or I, was more surprised by the fact that Mr Lucky Faeces paid for it himself.

When we got home, we walked along the central pedestrian path which runs between our house and the neighbour's. It was wavy. It had subsided and the neighbour was outside, standing in the dip, angrily.

"Is it going to collapse like a sink hole?" I asked Valentino.

"I don't think it can do that," he answered, "but this is not good."

We agreed with the neighbour that we would document everything photographically and present Mr. Lucky Faeces with a formal written request to sort it out.

We returned home, into our house which at last really was our house, feeling happy and satisfied but not completely calm. While I started peeling some potatoes, Valentino went outside on the balcony to get some fresh air, and immediately yelped in pain.

"What is it?" I asked, looking out.

He was hopping on one foot and clutching the other while grimacing melodramatically. He pointed at the fossil.

"I stubbed my toe on it," he groaned. "I'm going to chuck it away now your nephew's gone home. It's just a nuisance."

"No you are not!" I exclaimed. "It is a precious prehistoric object of great scientific value, and I am its guardian. I made a promise to Jim that we would look after it. The fossil stays."

Valentino gave me a look. I knew what it meant.

"*Promise* you won't get rid of it," I insisted.

"I promise," he said, reluctantly.

9

THE CHALLENGE OF BECOMING A HOUSEWIFE

Now that I was a wife, I had to figure out how to become a *house*wife. Not just any housewife: a Sicilian housewife.

Before achieving my ambition to become a housewife in Sicily, I travelled the world both for business and pleasure and, being English, tested the tea everywhere I went. In very few places was it up to the elite standards of quality and taste set by those discerning chimps at PG Tips. I can declare unequivocally, though, that the very best tea in the world comes from Malaysia. It is grown in a steamy and spectacular range of jungle-cloaked mountains called the Cameron Highlands, a place so esoterically beautiful and divine in nature that I sat among the tropical flowers, and the air thick with multi-coloured butterflies, and briefly considered never leaving. The tea grown there is called Boh. It is the nectar of the gods.

It was in the Cameron Highlands that I learned about tea production and the different grades of tea. The top two leaves of the plant are the tastiest and most delicate, and only these go into the highest grade of tea. This grade is only sold as loose leaf tea and is never put into teabags. The second grade is made from the next two leaves, and finally the lowest grade of tea is made from the other leaves which are the sort used in most teabags. The good teabags in England, decent pyramid shaped ones for instance, mix a selection of second grade and sometimes some third grade leaves. Cheap, nasty teabags use just the third grade of tea leaves. In this category come nearly all the teabags you encounter when you are in continental Europe, the sort which make you feel wretchedly homesick as you pull on the string to extract them from your cup.

The very last category of teabags are the only sort commercially available in Sicily. They contain no tea at all, just the sweepings of dust, small twigs and maybe a few crushed cockroach carapaces from the tea-factory floor. To this they add crumbled gerbil poos to add bulk and enrich the colour.

One steaming hot morning, I put the usual six of these sachets into a cup and waited about half an hour. While sipping on the resultant urea-coloured gerbil dung infusion, I started to ponder. You might even say I was glooming.

In the British media, leaving a successful career and retiring somewhere too hot in order to become a housewife-peasant is portrayed as being the pinnacle of self-indulgence. It is The English Dream. You sell your home in exchange for a house in the Mediterranean, which you call a villa, because "villa" happens to be the Italian word for house, and that implies that you are living in the lap of luxurious indulgence. At last you have lovely sunshine outside instead of a grey overcast sky and drizzle-streaked windows. You live on your own wine farm or olive grove, lunch on spaghetti and some fresh grapes growing on your own pergola, and flourish on the Mediterranean Diet for the rest of your happy, suntanned days. Knowing I was living in a lemon orchard and sweating my way through five or six fresh pairs of knickers a day was making all my friends back in London green with envy.

Yet this housewife lark was not all it had been hacked up to be. I do not just blame The Godmother with her spaghetti extruder and her bottles of hydrochloric acid. I also blame the British media.

I had been falsely led to believe, by the media, that I would enjoy myself by spending my days sitting about on vibrating white goods dressed in stain-free clothing, like women in advertisements. I would repeatedly swipe my finger through the icing on fancy cupcakes (with no trace of burnt bits) whilst retaining a size ten figure and being able to lick my own digits seductively. I was looking forward to whizzing up a bit of homemade pesto out of my home grown basil, *without* breaking the blender – after all, Nigella Lawson can do it whilst looking hung-over with her boobs popping out of her dressing gown. Perhaps, after whiling the day away shopping for Italian shoes, I would then delight and fob off my unsuspecting husband by serving him a ready meal (from a brand your family can trust, of course) which I would pretend I had slaved over myself for the bulk of the day, carefully hiding the packaging in a neighbour's dustbin. I yearned to smile and chat happily to the women next door while extracting blindingly white, pine-fresh linen from my washing machine, perhaps pausing to enjoy sniffing its bacteria-free cleanliness before hanging it on a washing line and then peeping round it glamorously while reminiscing about my too-good-to-be-true childhood in soft focus. In my ambitious moments,

I had dared to wonder if I might even occasionally have ladies' card-playing and gossip evenings like the housewives of Wisteria Lane.

What I actually had was a mother-in-law who would drop in unexpectedly to spot-check my toilet bowl for lime scale and faint skidmarks.

One afternoon, The Godmother dropped in on one of her regular visits to monitor my domestic performance. Despite our tense relationship, we were living in an uneasy truce at that point, largely based on the fact that she finds ironing so relaxing, she is willing to do mine when she has run out of her own. My own idea of relaxing is to eat chocolates and drink red wine while watching TV, but The Godmother doesn't let me relax while she is busy relaxing. She assigns me tasks.

She had, apparently, decided to teach me how to iron properly for myself. Using her iron.

First she made me gather up the dry laundry. I pottered about sorting it into two heaps; one Mount Everest of things that needed ironing; and a Mount Etna that I could fold and put away. The Godmother popped over to check, and pointed out that I had committed another of my gross domestic blunders. Everything needs ironing!

"What, even towels?" I dared to ask.

The Godmother thought I was just saying this to make her laugh. She rolled up her sleeves.

"I'll show you the best way to iron," she offered enthusiastically. "I have a personal ironing technique which can flatten anything."

She picked up all the clothes and reunited them into a single heap. I wondered whether to tell her that in England we avoid ironing our jeans because the kind of people who walk round with a crease down the front of a pair of Levi's are from South America or Turkey and are simply marking themselves out as illegal immigrants; indeed, that in England we think people who iron their jeans or T-shirts are sick and wrong, and must be stopped. I also wondered what she would think if I told her there was no need to iron her son's pants because he pressed them nice and flat himself with the warmth of his own buttocks as soon as he put them on. If I were a braver person I might also have mentioned that I preferred his pyjamas nice and wrinkly and, really, I was the only person he was supposed to impress when dressed in them. In the end, I was afraid to tell her, so I remained silent.

When I was a business consultant, I calmly met the directors of listed companies which had revenues of millions of pounds a day, and I was not afraid to tell them they were making mistakes in the way they ran their companies and should change a lot of things. If I believed a man was not handling his assets to their best advantage, I set him straight. If I thought someone's gross margin was pathetic, I said so. Now, as an apprentice Sicilian housewife, I was standing opposite The Godmother and she was telling me to iron her son's underpants, and I was too scared to say no. I obeyed.

The Godmother should not really be frightening as a person. She is about a foot shorter than me (albeit two feet wider) and she is old and has arthritis as well. It is just that she has eyes that sometimes look as if she could make streaks of lightning come flashing out of them at will, and reduce any adversary who refuses to wash their face again, and do it properly this time, to a smoking heap of ashes.

Her patented ironing technique involved heating the iron to a temperature that could smelt many types of metal ore, and then releasing a full litre of water vapour into the atmosphere, via the fibres of the offending wrinkly garment, with each push of the 'steam' button. Her iron was no normal iron. It was attached to a large tank which continually refilled it with water via a flexible hose and featured a control panel allowing her to adjust the water temperature and pressure, the iron temperature, the steam squirting rate and many other variables I would only have thought relevant to a space shuttle. Whilst she twiddled the dials and gave me a stream of enthusiastic explanations, I am ashamed to say my mind wandered. It does have an inconvenient tendency to go meandering off on its own, without its owner's permission, from time to time.

The Godmother and I define ourselves in different ways, I realised. For me, my degree, my career, the fact I have travelled to many countries and have friends from all over the world – these are some of the things that make up the woman I want other people to see. People who know all about these things, which I have done, understand the inner me.

The Godmother, on the other hand, defines herself as a lifetime professional housewife. Nonna brought her up that way and gave her no choice in the matter. If a member of her family is wearing something a bit creased, if anyone does not like something she has cooked for them, if there is a speck of dust on her kitchen floor, she feels like a failure as a person. Most of the Sicilian women I had met so far seemed to be like her. They would tell me how much stuff they had ironed, or describe what they had made for dinner last night, by way of conversation. It took me a long time living in Sicily to realise that they were showing off.

Well, the result of my philosophical reverie was that I nearly casseroled my hand, while it was still attached to my arm, by pressing the "eject gusts of vapour at a temperature hotter than the core of the sun" button instead of the "start super-cooling down to ambient temperature over the course of the next four days" button.

Whilst I nursed my hand with a bag of frozen peas, The Godmother attacked a ribbed jumper.

"I'll get all those nasty ridges out of this in no time" she said. She then proceeded to press my jumper so vehemently that by the time she had finished with it, it did indeed no longer have any ridges. It was no longer a ribbed jumper. It was smooth, and four feet wide.

After that she pressed the towels till they were as thin and absorbent as muslin, melted the elastic on all my knickers, and removed the cartoon characters off the front of my pyjamas by making them simply atomise at the temperature of a red dwarf. I was getting scared she might decide to iron me next. Seriously, I was panicking. Luckily, she felt relaxed enough to stop at that point, and permitted me to put everything away.

Another major duel in our ongoing competition had taken place, and I had just been thrashed once again.

I spent a long time, when I first moved to Sicily, thinking the other Sicilian housewives in my street were excluding me from their social activities. Then I became more intelligent, turned into a curtain-twitcher to watch them closely, and realised they did not have any social activities. Literally all they did was laundry, ironing, cooking and cleaning. I also reflected that, even if they did have any social event, I would not have wanted to go, because all they were capable of conversing about was laundry, ironing, cooking and cleaning.

When Valentino and I went out, large social events often ended up splitting into a group of women and a separate group of men. I would start out among the women, unable to participate in their discussions about their favourite cleaning products or their exciting new table cloth. I would sit wondering if there were any woman, anywhere in Sicily, who might tell me about a good book she had just read, clear up some scientific fact I had been wondering about, or describe some foreign country I had never visited. They must exist. Why could I not find them? I invariably ended up among the men sooner or later. They were informed, they had opinions, and they were capable of actual conversation; equally importantly, they listened to what I had to say to them.

The woman a few doors down from me, whom I shall call Mrs.

Sterile, accosted me one morning and almost immediately launched into a detailed account of all the things she had ironed, the order in which she had ironed them, and *how* she had ironed them. She took ages pressing her husband and son's socks because she had boil-washed them and they had become terribly creased; now I knew why her little boy always had flaccid tubes of jersey bunched up around his ankles, and why her husband could not walk five steps without stopping to pull his socks up, again. After a few minutes of these anecdotes about her domestic derring do, we were joined by Mrs. Muppet.

Mrs. Muppet has a mouth that opens far too wide, so that she almost looks as if her head is separating into two halves when she talks. She also has matted bright orange hair, which sticks out all round her head and has the texture of a polyester furry toy that has been massacred in the washing machine. On this particular morning, she had already told me about each of the times her baby had done a poo in the night and, on each occasion, whether it had been she or her husband who had got up to change his nappy, and she was now telling me about all her laundry and what she had ironed that morning. She had already starched all the sheets and table cloths and was pressing the baby's bibs with a lower level of steam when my mind went absent without leave. She must have noticed my eyes glazing over, or maybe crossing, because she made an abrupt retreat.

Later in the day I was too slow-moving to dodge another neighbour, called Carmen. Actually I do like her, because I think she might be slightly unhinged. She sometimes pops over to my house to ask for a couple of eggs or a bit of sugar in her nightie, which, let me tell you, is skimpy. She is taller than most Sicilian men and always wears platform shoes so high and bulky that she looks as if she is standing with her legs akimbo on two separate podiums, or podia perhaps I should say, then clomps about patting other people's husbands on the head. Her hair is waist length and orange and made of nylon.

Carmen said she had seen me through the window, sitting at my sewing machine in the little guest bedroom rather a lot. I had been making curtains for the whole house, but had almost finished and was wondering what to start on next. Carmen asked me if I would mind altering some clothes for her. There is a big market for altering clothes in Sicily, which mostly consists of cutting two or three feet off the bottom of men's trousers and re-hemming them. So that was how I briefly became a seamstress, as Carmen brought me lots of garments and also told all her friends that I could sew.

What a change from business consultancy! In the old days, the kind of things I used to say all the time were, for example,

"Well, if you can't put more than ten million of your own capital on the table you can't expect any venture capitalist even to take a look at your business plan."

Now in Sicily, I more often found myself saying things like,

"Well, for hemming trousers I charge four Euros, but if you want that fly button sewn back on as well, it'll be four-fifty."

Obviously, hemming trousers is more relaxing than negotiating international takeovers or investment programmes, though I must admit I felt slightly nervous about hacking great swathes of fabric off pairs of Dolce & Gabbana trousers and Max Mara dresses. There is a level of responsibility there. What if I suddenly had a bad day and got the legs different lengths?

The fun side, though, was that I saved up all the cut-offs and planned out a patchwork garment. I gradually got together enough designer fabric tubes, which were formerly my neighbours' turn-ups, to assemble a pair of trousers with horizontal multi-coloured stripes which represented a sartorial collaboration between the six most famous Italian fashion designers. They had embroidered Armani buttocks, Alviero Martini thighs with sandy coloured maps on, pink satin knees by Valentino, an exciting range of lower legs and leather Fendi turn-ups. I then built up a collection of designer buttons with which I embellished them, pearly-queen style. I did once actually wear them, at Hallowe'en.

Another domestic disaster occurred when my washing machine started to malfunction. International road hauling had not been kind to the poor old thing. It had developed a very alarming repertoire of rattles and made groans as if it were occupied by a poltergeist. The laundry I put into it one fateful morning looked fairly clean and just needed to be freshened up but, when it came out, it was coated all over in brownish-black stains which looked for all the world like the skid marks of someone with a serious bowel disease. The sight of Valentino's underpants reduced to this condition haunts me to this day when I see him undress.

This was a laundry disaster far worse than the time I shank all my jumpers into bare-midriff tenager-tops, or even the time I poured loo cleaner into the washing detergent drawer and bleached Valentino's trousers to a very nasty shade of apricot. Not knowing what else to do, I hung the damaged goods up to dry, intending to get a man to look at the machine before attempting to wash them again.

Before I could do any such thing, however, the wind started blowing. Not any old wind, but the Sirocco; that hot, desiccating, merciless desert wind that makes you nearly suffocate and feel as if you have accidentally been shut up inside a tumble dryer. When a broom from my balcony took off and flew over the treetops as if being ridden by an invisible witch, I decided it would be wise to go inside and shut all the windows. From my kitchen window vantage point I watched various packets of washing powder and cleaning cloths hurtle past, and then the detached halves of clothes pegs, and then, some pieces of cloth which looked a lot like Valentino's underpants. I sidled across the room to check the washing line and they had, indeed, vanished... every last pair of them.

Valentino eventually came back from work on his motorbike, almost flying like ET going home. He darted into the garage and told me about the various pieces of wood and plants he had seen flying around in the air on his way through Palermo. He seemed somewhat agitated, I would say. The wind blew for most of the night and was punctuated by extremely loud thumping and cracking noises echoing through the walls of our house, which eventually died down in the early hours of the morning.

I went outside very early the next day for a stroll to the supermarket, intending to replace the missing washing powder. The calm after the storm revealed scenes of devastation wherever I looked. Apart from the astounding number of cleaning products in bottles and handleless mops rolling about the place, there were former pieces of furniture, shattered roof tiles, long and structural-looking planks of wood, whole stiff sheets of roofing felt, and components of what I suppose were once bicycles and scooters. Then suddenly, unexpectedly, there were Valentino's underpants, the whole gregarious flock of them sticking together loyally. They had draped themselves all over the trees in Mrs. Muppet's garden, like the gigantic cactus blooms that spring up in the desert once every seven years after a freak rainstorm. I stopped to gaze upon them in all their glory while I inwardly contemplated the frailty of flowers, and the ephemeral nature of our brief passage on this earth.

I nearly jumped out of my skin when Mrs. Muppet greeted me from behind a thick bush.

"What a storm!" she began. "Our garden furniture all blew away."

"Oh dear," I sympathised. "Yes, it was a very violent wind, wasn't it?"

"Did you lose anything?" she asked me.

I gazed upwards at the wondrous crop of blooms, or bloomers, which the night had brought her. The indelible skid marks were all facing outwards, mucky-side-up, so to speak.

"No," I replied. "Nothing. I lost nothing at all."

I sat back that evening and pondered on the day's events over a gerbil poo infusion, brewed in the cup. Although the pinnies were on and the scrubbing brushes were drawn, deep down I still believed ironing underpants was futile and that dogs should eat whatever they were offered.

Did I have a chance of winning this duel against The Godmother? Could I ever become the fish-gutting, vegetable-frying, pavement-scrubbing, pants-flattening super housewife my darling Valentino must have grown up thinking he would marry?

Of course I could not.

Being a housewife was obviously not my bag. Work was very hard to find in economically depressed Sicily, and there were no investment banks at all in Palermo, but I had other qualifications and other tricks up my sleeves. As Valentino liked to say, I was 'a woman of a thousand resources.' I plonked my cup of tea beside the computer, translated my CV into Italian, and composed a prospective covering letter to go with it which explained that I had a diploma in teaching English as a foreign language and four years' experience teaching in Milan, London and Istanbul, and was looking for work. Once I had looked up the addresses of every secondary school and private English school in the area, I e-mailed it to them all. Then I printed a thick stack of flyers listing some of my other qualifications in business and offering my services as a specialist translator of business and legal documents. Although I had only just started my job search, I felt so good to be doing something I actually knew how to do properly.

Whilst being a housewife was not my bag, losing has never been my bag either. I still needed to get the upper hand in my duel with The Godmother. The only way I could ever win this particular competition was to cheat.

The question was, how?

10

I MEET MARY POPPINS

I had a tense morning one day when I read the local newspaper at the ice-cream parlour. Our local electrical goods shop had just been firebombed because they refused to pay the Mafia *pizzo,* or "protection money," when it was asked for three times in a row. Everyone was talking about it in tense tones, mainly in Sicilian, so Giuseppe Ice-cream filled me in on the details.

The owners lived in a flat above the shop, and both their livelihood and home were destroyed in one night. The four-storey cement building was almost completely razed to the ground and the couple's children were hospitalised. So were several families who lived in other flats in the block, who had nothing to do with the shop owners. Several small children and a baby ended up in a critical condition in intensive care because of smoke injury to their lungs.

The police turned up when the fire brigade had finished dousing the building and the ashes were smouldering over in the early hours of the morning.

"Why did they take so long to arrive?" I asked.

"They were paid or threatened to stay away," said Giuseppe, with a meaningful glance.

I was distracted from a session of evil domestic plotting that afternoon when Valentino got home from work. He plopped a crumpled piece of paper on the table in front of me, in amidst the courgette peelings. I dried my hands and looked at it. I could tell he had brought it from work because it had the crest of the Palermo law court at the top, and because I could only find about seven words on the whole page that I understood.

"Just tell me what it is," I asked him.

"Did you see the name?" he asked.

"No," I answered.

"Mr. Fortunato Mastronzo is going on trial for financial fraud."

"Oh," I said.

"There's someone else going on trial too, who's been doing some kind of financial deals with him," he added, pulling out the second page. "He's called Mauro De Simone."

Valentino took the bag of rubbish out of the bin under the sink and carried it out onto the balcony. Then he let out a loud howl of pain.

"That bloody fossil!" he yelled. "Why does it keep moving around?"

"What do you mean?" I asked.

"Every time I go out on that balcony it's in a different place. Wherever I try to put my foot, that's where it is!"

After nursing his toes with a bag of frozen peas, Valentino telephoned The Godmother. She, in turn, logged on to the Auntienet to research around her home neighbourhood, Brancaccio. This usually included a trip to the butcher's, where there were always long queues, and a long loiter outside the church, where everyone was sure to pass sooner or later.

After a few days she reported her findings. Mauro De Simone had served a six year prison sentence some time ago, and he was also on trial for drug dealing.

"Not drug pushing on the streets," she said, "I mean large-scale importing from South America."

His family had left Palermo when he was a small child, and gone to live in Canada. He had come back to Palermo as an adult, and moved back to Canada for a while after serving his six-year sentence. The Godmother also gave us a list of people Valentino knew who had shady associations with him.

"How do you know these people?" I asked Valentino.

"Primary school," he replied casually. I took some time to digest the news.

"Is he in the Mafia?" I asked.

"Don't know," answered Valentino.

"Do you think the receipts for our house purchase are legally valid?" I asked Valentino.

"I don't know that either," he said.

"And is the registration on the *catastale* real?" I added.

"It must be," he said.

"You're right, it must be" I agreed.

"I hope," added Valentino.

To distract myself from this seriously worrying situation, I focused on my domestic contest with my mother-in-law. I realised that the obvious way to cheat and win was to recruit a secret cleaning lady from the village. There must be plenty of fishermen's wives who would like to earn a little extra money, and would be willing to work under cover to earn it. Sicilians are obsessed with cleaning. What could be better than a Sicilian char woman?

I found out what was better than a Sicilian char woman when I accidentally hired the lady I dubbed Mary Poppins. This was because she entered my house and made mystical, magical things happen in a way I could never understand. She was not just any old Sicilian char woman, she was a Sicilian char woman with an obsessive compulsive disorder. She was so obsessed with cleaning anything and everything that she became ill and needed tablets if anyone tried to stop her, bless her little bleached white, steam-ironed cotton socks.

The first thing she did was to take the light fittings down so she could dismantle and wash them. She said this made sure she could see any particles of dirt or germs and remove them thoroughly. She not only polished my wardrobe on the outside, she also cleaned out the keyhole with a cotton wool swab and then got all my shoes out, washed the inside of the wardrobe, and polished all the shoes before putting them back. When she thought I was not looking, she got my saucepans out of the cupboard and examined them in sunlight and then scrubbed over any specks of contamination that my dishwasher may have failed to remove.

There is no way to express how much I loved this woman. She used toothpicks to gouge fragments of gunk from the kitchen fittings, and from the threads on the screws that held the cupboards up. She brought a metal nail file with her so she could work around the edges of the taps when she was de-scaling them. In fact, when she had finished cleaning the bathroom, I felt guilty doing a pee in it. She polished the backs of all the drawers as well as the fronts and she cleaned the floor by wiping it over with an abrasive sponge and concentrated bleach, on her knees. When I asked her if this hurt her hands, she told me she loved doing it this way because she liked to 'feel the dirt coming off the floor.' When she had washed a room she refused to let me go in there until she had taken my shoes off me, scrubbed their soles, and then restored them to me, decently disinfected. God bless her.

Her house must surely be the cleanest in the world. I expect even the pavement outside it could safely be used to perform open abdominal surgery should the need arise. She worked until nearly nine in the evening and I had to physically remove her from the oven, just to make sure she would be out of the house before Valentino got home - otherwise I would have let her work on, of course. She had crawled almost completely inside it and was screwing the inner panel back on. She had removed it to clean the back of it as well as the visible side and had got distracted on the way, stopping to go over some kind of ventilation panel at the side with her toothpick. When I said I was worried that she was getting over-tired and that I thought it was time to take her home now, and she looked as if she were about to start weeping.

"Stop it!" my conscience told me. "Let the woman finish if she wants to! Can't you see you're upsetting her?"

Eventually I forced her to stop. Her husband had died recently (scrubbed to death?) and her son was almost always out with his friends in the evenings, she said, so going home was lonely. I paid her nearly twice the amount she asked to be paid, and we agreed to see each other again the following week, and every week, for the rest of my life. Hallelujah!

When Valentino came home he was staggered by how clean the house looked.

"Did my mother come over today?" he asked immediately.

"Nope!" I told him. "I've been alone all day."

I did feel a little pang of guilt, honestly I did. But just a little one. I had worked like a slave for years doing twelve-hour days at the bank. I could spend my savings how I wanted, I reminded myself.

"The house looks great," he said, happily.

11

THE MAFIA

I came down off my victorious pedestal rather abruptly a couple of days later.

I had attempted to follow a recipe The Godmother had given me for one of Valentino's favourite dishes. It is a pasta sauce made from chopped aubergines, fresh grilled swordfish and tomato *passata*.

"Now at last you can make him something *genuino,*" she had said, meaningfully. When Sicilians call food *genuino,* they mean it is natural and wholesome. It is the opposite of *porcheria,* which means junk food full of chemicals.

Valentino rolled the first mouthful of lunch around his tongue as if analysing it. I knew in my heart this was not a good sign, but I doggedly remained optimistic.

"What do you think?" I asked.

"Hmm," he said.

"Is that a good hmm or a bad hmm?" I persisted.

"Did you forget something?" he asked.

He was right, of course. It was a bit tasteless. There definitely was something lacking. Valentino went through a list of possible explanations. Did I fry the onions for too long? Did it need more salt? Perhaps I had not heated the tomato for long enough. The simple fact was, The Godmother was a good cook and I was not, am not, and never will be.

I decided my best chance of ameliorating the situation would be to open a bottle of red wine I had to hand. The wine was not only a precaution in case the food worked out disappointing, as expected, but also a plan to help lubricate the conversation I had decide to tackle. I wanted to ask Valentino all about the Mafia and what he really thought about Mr. Lucky Faeces. Engaging in some financial fraud was one thing, but being a signed-up Mafia member was another. I knew Val was very worried, but he tends to hold worries inside him and only talk about proven facts. He is very lawyerish that way.

The first thing you need to know, should you ever visit Sicily, is that you must NEVER, EVER say the word Mafia out loud in public. It is strictly taboo. Sicilians adhere to the old religious belief that you must never pronounce the name of the Devil aloud, as this may summon him and unleash evil forces; and I think they apply the same rule to the Mafia.

When Sicilians go abroad, it seems that everyone makes Mafia jokes around them, or even asks them straight to their faces if they are in the Mafia. It is not just idiots or socially awkward weirdoes who do this, but otherwise intelligent and educated reasoning people. Sicilians do not think this is funny.

I doubt if there are many people who would meet a German and immediately say, "Oh, so you're from Germany, are you a Nazi?" People who regard themselves as normal would probably not learn someone was a Muslim and instantly ask them, "So tell me, are you an Al Qaida terrorist?" I do not know anyone who would try to get to know a Colombian by asking "Now tell me, are you running a drugs cartel?"

Yet people leave their brains behind when they meet Sicilians. The Mafia are criminals. They are serial killers. They are the reason Sicily is so poor that there are better hospitals in most North African countries. Many towns in Sicily have running water no more than twice a week. The streets have potholes big enough to hide a Fiat Punto. Rubbish piles up mountain-high in the streets. The town halls and schools have masonry falling off them and holes in the roofs. And the authorities do nothing about any of this, because they have no money, apparently: the taxes everyone pays are all being "eaten", as Sicilians say... in other words, extorted and pocketed by the Mafia.

I think this is another reason why the Sicilians do not want to talk about the Mafia. Apart from the old historic culture of *omertà*, which is the same thing as the code of silence about playground bullies in primary schools, there is also the fact that talking about the Mafia becomes so damned depressing when you cannot see how to change it. Above all, though, there was the fact that Valentino wanted to protect me from getting too scared.

It was with bold insistence, therefore, that I asked Valentino how much of a criminal he thought Mr. Faeces was.

"I'm beginning to worry," he eventually answered. "I know we've paid in full for the sink and the tiles and other things, but I think we should just back down now."

We sat in silence for a while.

"I didn't know it when we found this house, but the town here is a Mafia stronghold. There are lots of bosses here. There is a princess living in a historic villa here, and people say they keep trying to take her villa and land to make themselves a luxury headquarters. They built a medical clinic on another part of her land with no permission at all. The land is still hers."

"Why would they built a medical clinic? That seems like a nice and altruistic thing to do."

"They built it solely for their own use!" said Valentino. "The police very recently tracked down the boss who had it built and arrested him. He's got cancer. He still controls things from Bagheria, and he has about thirteen houses here. His main house is connected to this clinic by an underground tunnel. He was a *latitante*, living in hiding, so when he needed cancer treatment he popped up in the middle of this clinic through a secret underground tunnel. They arrested lots of his henchmen by tracing letters he wrote. He used a secret code, as they all do, but they said on the news that his knowledge of punctuation was so bad it always betrayed him, so they could always tell which letters were from him."

"So what happened to the clinic?"

"They sequestered it and converted it to public use. You should see it. I've never seen such luxury in my life! The public hospitals here have plaster falling off the walls and lack essential equipment, but this clinic has flat screen televisions set into the walls in all the waiting areas, leather upholstered seats everywhere, and the fanciest medical equipment available anywhere in the world. It's the best equipped oncology clinic in Europe, they say. That's what the Mafia build for themselves, using our taxes, and leaving our children to die in hospitals where they have to lie on the floor in a corridor, without even the most basic equipment."

"Do you see lots of Mafiosi on trial at work?" I asked.

"Sometimes," he answered. "Recently I was sitting in on the trials of the President. You know, Cuffaro went tipping off all the Mafiosi that their phones were being bugged during the investigations into the murders of Falcone and Borsellino. They were the two judges who started the maxi-trials against the Mafia – you've heard of them, haven't you?" he asked.

I had heard of them. They were both killed by the Mafia, trying to stop the trials going ahead.

"This week I've been at the trial of loads of Carabinieri, the ones who arrested Toto Riina - the Mafia Pope, they called him. He was the one from Corleone, who made it famous as THE Mafia town. Anyway, these carabinieri all got major prizes, promotions, rewards and so on for the work they did, but later it was discovered that they cut a deal with all the corrupt politicians who were in with him. They arrested Riina about one kilometre from his house, then the carabinieri waited fifteen days so that the politicians could remove all evidence incriminating *them*, before searching his house. They even repainted all the walls, in case there were fingerprints on them from their visits there. *Che schifo!*" he finished with passion. "How disgusting!"

"Is it true that all the rich people in Sicily are in the Mafia?" I asked.

"It is a fact universally acknowledged that any Sicilian in possession of a great fortune is in the Mafia," said Valentino. I was not sure if he honestly meant it. I had told him he did not read enough, and had then proceeded to buy him a selection of English classics in translation.

"So you can't really make big money through legitimate business in Sicily?" I asked.

"You can, but the Mafia take anything above basic profits," said Valentino. "At least, that's how it seems to me. Anyway, running a business in Sicily takes a lot of nerve."

"Oh yes?" I asked.

"First, you need a lot of certificates of authorisation for this, that and the other. One of them is the Anti-Mafia Certificate issued by the police, which proves you're 'clean.' To get this certificate, your whole family is checked for Mafia connections. If anyone, including first or second cousins, uncles and grandparents, has had any involvement with the Mafia, you won't get this certificate." Valentino paused to take a mouthful of spaghetti.

"That seems extreme," I said.

"It's just realistic. Anyway, it's a crime to pay *pizzo*, extortion money, to the Mafia without reporting it to the police as soon as the gun or cudgel has been removed from the vicinity of your head. If you do report it after paying, you have to hope no corrupt policeman who's seen your official report reveals to the Mafia that you've obeyed the law. If they do, your shop and maybe your home get fire bombed. If you choose not to report it to anyone, you risk going to prison for supporting the Mafia when the tax office asks where those sums of money went."

"So you're damned if you do, and you're damned if you don't," I said.

Valentino twiddled up another forkful of spaghetti artfully and then dropped a great splatter of tomato sauce on his shirt as he put it in his mouth. He had already made the tablecloth look like a battle field, with pools and splashes of tomato and red wine flicked far and wide, and chunks of broken bread lying like severed limbs around the wine bottle.

"Things are improving," Valentino insisted. "Ten years ago it was like a war zone round here. It's much better nowadays."

There's also a third option now, for the most daring, or maybe the most angry. That's to join the '*Addiopizzo*' movement. These people put a sticker on the door of their premises indicating that they're against paying extortion money, and are cooperating with the police in identifying Mafiosi who come asking for it. They're courageous and probably lead stressful lives."

"You know when you said it was like a war zone," I asked, as Valentino poured me some more red wine. He put the bottle down, and I watched the red wine bleed into the table cloth in a growing ring. "What, *exactly*, was it like?"

"Brancaccio, where I grew up, was always among the worst for Mafia activity. They murdered Padre Puglisi, the priest at our church. He went out saying mass in the streets and letting the *mafiosi*'s children come and spend their time with him. He opened a youth club in the church hall with some volunteers."

"What's wrong with letting the children spend time with him?" I asked.

"The Mafia always ban their children from going near church."

"Why?"

"Because of the risk they might learn some morals. But they also neglect their children and leave them at home alone, or roaming the streets all day by themselves. Some of them use their children for drug running and things like that. Brancaccio was a major recruiting ground for new Mafia members because it's a poor area. It's a really bad neighbourhood. Padre Puglisi was taking away their source of recruits.

"He stood up to them by welcoming all children and teenagers into the church, at any time of day or night, and showing them there was a place where people cared about them. For a lot of teenagers in Brancaccio, joining the Mafia is the first time in their lives they feel part of something. The typical Mafia recruit is a boy who never did homework because his parents never helped him or told him it was important, who played truant from school constantly, and who ended up with no qualifications and no job prospects and feeling completely unloved. Padre Puglisi showed kids an alternative to the life their parents showed them and the Mafia found their pool of recruits starting to dry up. So the Mafia shot him. In the back. As he was leaving church."

My mouth hung open and I said nothing.

"At that time there was a kind of curfew. My mother would lower all the metal shutters over the windows at about six o'clock and we stayed indoors like that each evening, barricaded and waiting anxiously till my father got in safely from work so we could relax. It wasn't an official curfew, it was just something that all the good families did to keep safe. The people who went out after curfew were the ones making the problems.

"I remember seeing a dead body in the road on my way to school one morning, a man who had been shot the night before by the Mafia. I basically had to step over it to get to lessons." He took a gulp of wine. "Have you noticed the pet shop down the road, and that weird little shop that sells things for women like balls of wool and reels of cotton and big white knickers...?"

"What about them?" I asked.

"I mean the front of the building, with lots of holes all over..."

"Yes?"

"That was from a fairly big shoot-out. Dead bodies were fairly often found in the streets in the morning. It all seemed fairly normal in those days. It was just the way life was. Nowadays that would cause more of a stir-"

"You bet it would!" I cut in.

"I nearly got shot in a Mafia feud when I was little."

I started choking on a drop of wine that I had accidentally inhaled.

"You have to tell me what happened," I said.

"Well, I was six years old," he started. "I was just hanging around at the entrance to the house."

His mother has a photograph of him at that age, in her living room. He was small and dark in a white vest, with skinny little legs coming out of baggy shorts, and huge brown eyes looking up at the camera.

"It was the afternoon, still hot and sunny and well before the six o'clock curfew that we used to follow. One of the neighbours, an old man who had just retired, was popping out to the baker's for his fresh loaf of evening bread. He asked if I wanted to go with him, so I could buy the evening loaf of bread for my Mother. She gave me the money, and I was so proud being allowed to go out without her. I felt so grown-up! I remember he took big steps and I wanted to take steps as big as him to feel like a real adult, but I had to keep jumping to keep up with him.

"We were coming out of the bakery when suddenly I heard a rapid series of explosions. They were going off all around me, so loud and close that they sounded as if they were exploding inside my own head. I was petrified and froze, rooted to the spot. I had no idea where they were coming from or what they were.

"The old man grabbed me, tucked me under his arm, and started running back towards the apartment block as fast as he could. He was sixty-six years old, and carrying me and two loaves of bread, but I'm absolutely sure he went faster than Usain Bolt. I remember I was crying, and I asked him what the noise was. He acted calm. He said some naughty big boys had been setting off fireworks in the street, but there was nothing to be scared of.

"It was a miracle that no stray bullets hit either of us. I gradually realised what really happened as I got older and overheard adult conversations. I asked the old man about it a few years later and he told me several people had been killed that afternoon."

"Were you allowed to go out and buy the bread again?" I asked.

"Not till I was about sixteen!" laughed Valentino.

Now I realised why The Godmother had such a major network of informers in Mafia-related affairs. She lived in the thick of it.

"The children in Brancaccio recently held a protest march against paying *pizzo*," Valentino went on. "The idea of doing something like this when I was their age would have been completely unthinkable. It won't make the Mafia stop what they're doing, but the protest will change the mentality of the children: that's its real purpose. Things have changed a lot nowadays. You've got nothing to worry about."

"Not everyone has nothing to worry about, though," I insisted. "What about our local electrical goods shop?"

"Most people who run a commercial business get visits from the Mafia," said Valentino. He tore the remaining hunk of bread in half meaningfully. "That's why I do my low-paid, boring civil service job for a pittance."

"How much do they usually ask for?" I wanted to know.

"I've heard people say they usually ask for about ten percent of the shop's takings. But they don't exactly ask to see cash flow statements, they just guess how much the shop can afford, then make threats. That's why some shops go out of business; they ask for too much, more than the shop can afford, and when the shopkeeper says that's too much, they get threatening, and the shopkeeper has no choice but to close the place down."

Sicilians who are threatened by the Mafia and make a real stand against them are in great danger, because the police and the state in general does not seem able (or willing) to protect them. They do not have anything like the witness protection programme which we see in American TV shows.

The Sicilians live permanently in one of those situations we all know, where everyone is thinking the same thing, but nobody wants to be the one who opens their mouth and says it.

If you want to know more about the Sicilian Mafia, here is a word of warning. I have read more garbage written about this topic than I have on any other subject, ever. Anyone who claims to have the "inside story" is simply lying; if they did know anything secret, they would immediately get killed for writing it.

A few days later, Valentino came home from work too agitated to hide it from me.

"What's wrong?" I greeted him.

"I've got three translations for you to do," he answered. I could tell how distracted he was because he did not even kiss me. "There are two summonses to be sent to America, and the initial documents for an adverse possession."

I scanned through the papers he handed me, and roughly calculated that I had about two thousand euros worth of translations to do. I would e-mail out a formal quote tomorrow.

"Great," I said, "but what's wrong?"

He looked into my eyes, but said nothing. "I asked a friend to double check the listing of our house in the Land Registry."

"And?"

"The good news is that the building really does legally belong to us."

"There's bad news?" I asked.

"Yes," said Val. "The bad news is that it isn't a legal human dwelling."

"Well then, what is it, legally?"

"A slaughterhouse."

I phoned my sister Susy in a state of hysteria. My ultrasonic outburst was ruined by bad phone reception.

"Oh my God!" I wailed, hyperventilating. "I've sold a fantastic investment in London and sunk all my money into a slaughterhouse in the heart of Mafia country that's probably getting dead bodies piled up in secret tunnels underneath it even as we speak! Why? Why would they do that?!!! Oh my God!!!! I'm going to be framed for murder and then buried in my own basement.... that I don't actually have personal access to!!!!!!!!!"

"I'm sorry, you cut out there," came Susy's voice intermittently when I was at the fourth exclamation mark. "Can you repeat the bit from 'sunk all my money' please?"

I repeated it, with additional exclamation marks.

"I heard you up to 'secret tunnels'," Susy cut in again.

I went out onto the kitchen balcony hoping for better reception, and experimented with various positions. By the time I had repeated the same rant five times, at both ends of the balcony and, for one rendition, bent over double with my arm extended out over the balcony, my hysteria was losing steam. I discovered the best spot was right in the corner where the ammonite fossil sat. I moved it out of my way and leant over the railings while I filled my sister in on all the news we had so far on Mr. Faeces.

After I had finished and put the phone in my pocket, I decided to load up the washing machine. I wanted to clean up the table cloth that Valentino had anointed with red wine, before it dried out and the stains set in. As I emerged back onto the balcony with the mucky bundle, reflecting that The Godmother actually was getting to me a little bit, I stubbed my toe on the fossil in its new location.

With an anguished scream I dropped the table cloth and ran inside to nurse my toes with a bag of frozen peas. We never actually ate peas from the freezer. The third freezer drawer was just our First Aid cabinet.

"Bloody fossil," I muttered under my breath. "Bloody red wine. Bloody washing machine. Bloody slaughterhouse."

12

VALENTINO GIVES ME MY FIRST SICILIAN DRIVING LESSON

After I had been living in Sicily for several months, doing translations and teaching English lessons at home to a few lawyers and doctors, Valentino was shocked to realise that I was afraid of driving to the next fishing village.

"You used to be quite happy to nip all around central London by car, at the drop of a hat. It's easier to drive in Sicily," he challenged me.

"No, it's not. It's different here," I said. "There are different driving rules."

"What do you mean, different rules?" he said. "There aren't any driving rules here. That's why it's so easy."

A few days later an English friend mentioned, while we were chatting on the phone, that her husband was attending a week-long, full immersion 'defensive driving' course. This would teach him how to cope with getting into a skid on ice or snow, and other potential road hazards. I suddenly realised that, to prepare me for driving in Sicily, what I needed was a full immersion course in 'aggressive driving.' I suggested this to Valentino and he happily offered to teach me himself.

"You won't find a better instructor than me for that type of thing," he promised. "Next time we get the opportunity on a suitable piece of road, I'll put you behind the steering wheel and teach you to overcome your fear. The secret is to make everyone else afraid of *you*."

A suitable piece of road cropped up, as chance would have it, the very next day. Valentino was driving along, deep in discussion as always.

"Everyone agrees Sicilian vegetables are the best in the world," he was telling me grandiosely, emphasising the fact that his opinion was wholly undisputed by taking both hands off the steering wheel to gesticulate elegantly while guiding our Silver Fiat Punto round a sharp bend with his knees. "What vegetable has England got that's better than the Sicilian version?"

I gripped the sides of my seat with white knuckles and tried to think of some English fruit or vegetable that was better than its Sicilian counterpart as we sped past a series of industrial buildings on the outskirts of Palermo. We rolled along beside a sprawling thicket of prickly pears, like dozens of green dinner-plates stacked miraculously edge to edge into a towering mess eight feet tall and bristling with four-inch thorns. They were studded around the edge of every succulent, cactus-like outgrowth with magenta and yellow fruits which would flow with syrup as sweet as honey when they were cut open.

"Look, those are roadside weeds and they make fruit that tastes like ambrosia," said Valentino.

"Potatoes," I said. "I think English potatoes are a bit better than Sicilian ones."

"And you can keep them," said Valentino, leaning over to give me a peck on the lips while keeping one eye on the road ahead. "I prefer pasta."

Suddenly the brakes squealed and he slewed the Punto diagonally across two parking spaces, to maximise the benefit of the shade cast by a large date palm. He used the kerb to bring the vehicle to an abrupt halt, stalling the engine.

"Look how they've painted those lines! What kind of an idiot would want to park their car in that tiny little rectangle?" he scoffed in genuine amusement. "Right, now we can swap places and start your driving lesson," he announced, his slim, athletic frame already half out of the car.

He dashed around to the passenger seat while I emerged more slowly into the suffocating heat. Gusts of the desiccating Sirocco wind blew my thin cotton skirt into a nappy shape around my upper thighs and plastered my hair over my face. It had already deposited a thin layer of red dust, blown up from the Sahara, all over the car bonnet. Once I had clambered behind the steering wheel I slammed the door shut with relief and turned up the air conditioning.

Valentino had insisted that, like everything else I ever tried, I was sure to be magnificent at driving in Sicily.

"It's easier than driving in England," he told me. "How can it be harder? I know I said there are no rules but, seriously, there are very few rules to follow."

"Exactly," I insisted.

He looked across at me with that silent laugh forming on his face. With his dark skin and chuckling eyes I could easily imagine him as a dashing pirate springing about a ship's deck, brandishing his sword with a flourish. Unfortunately he often ruins the effect by wearing his colour-blind choice of clothing, or what I call "garments for the hard of seeing". Today's outfit was a carnation pink Palermo football shirt and red trousers. I had lived in Sicily for over a month thinking that Palermo had a huge 'out' gay community before I realised that all these men dressed in pink - some of whom had pink mobile phones and even pink cars - were just passionate football fans. I made a mental note to start hiding some of Valentino's worst garments where he would never find them. In Harry Potter's bedroom, for example.

"First you need to get back onto the road," he told me. "No, no no no! Don't use the indicator!"

"Why not?" I asked. "I need to pull out."

"You can't use the indicator willy-nilly," said Valentino patiently. "Don't give away too much information to the other drivers. Never use it when you're trying to pull into a stream of moving traffic. Why on earth would you warn anyone that you intend to pull in front of them, cut them up completely and then never actually get above fifteen kilometres an hour because your granny in the back gets scared?"

"Those are the kind of drivers who indicate to pull out?"

"Yes! If you do that, you'll instantly find that every car passing you is no more than three centimetres from the car in front of it. Are you sure you've already got a driving license?"

I anxiously pushed some sweaty strands of hair away from my forehead. "Now you see why I need extra lessons before driving here. It's very different. I've never run anyone over before, and I don't intend to start now."

"Listen," said Valentino, "you need to learn judicious use of those flashing orange lights. The idea is not to give away any information which could give the other driver the advantage. A classic beginner's mistake is to loiter near a parking space with the lights flashing. This alerts everyone in the neighbourhood to the fact that there's a parking space available and, of course, they'll devise a means of getting into it, before you do, which your simple, innocent mind could never conceive of. While on this subject I must warn you that you should never, ever, I repeat *ever*, pause to let a car out from a side road or parking space in front of you. The driver will consider you weak and possibly of a mentally unstable condition, and he'll warn other drivers about you. Absolutely nobody will ever thank you at all for your considerate behaviour, and eventually there's a danger you may become bitter and twisted and develop wrinkled brow lines."

I pulled a face at Valentino and nudged the grey Punto closer and closer to the constant stream of traffic until I had inched out so far that the driver of a white Fiat Cinquecento opened his window and deftly flipped his wing mirror down against the car door to allow his vehicle to slither through the tiny gap without slowing down. Finally we edged out an inch further and, at last, the space was just too small to allow a Fiat Doblò, the compact Italian version of a people carrier, to squeeze past. Three small children and a dog pressed their noses against the window to stare at me while the driver peered past his portly wife and glared. Having resentfully acknowledged my victory, he sat back and showed the toddler on his lap how to operate the horn while waiting for me to pull away.

Valentino congratulated me as I jerked the Punto out in front of the Doblò. We passed a row of shops and drew up behind a line of cars waiting at a crossroads. A swordfish was displayed outside the fishmonger's on a bed of ice. I always find swordfish distracting because I feel so sorry for them. They have huge, beautiful eyes that often look as they are still alive and full of pathos. Suddenly a red Fiat Seicento behind us pulled out onto the wrong side of the road, drove past all the waiting cars, jumped the red light and turned right in front of us, accelerating away with a squealing of his brakes.

"There," commented Valentino, "that was a good example of the trickiness of indicator use. Sometimes the indicator is not used, simply because the complexity of a driving manoeuvre makes it impossible to decide whether the left or right indicator is appropriate. For example, should that driver have indicated left to let people know he was pulling onto the wrong side of the road, or right, as his ultimate intention was to turn right?"

"I suppose he should have indicated right," I ventured, wondering whether this were a serious teaching point or just another of Valentino's jokes, "as that's where he was going in the end."

"The dilemma has still not been resolved," announced Valentino enigmatically, "and, to avoid traffic accidents by confusing or misleading people, it's better simply to use the horn abundantly and also turn up your car stereo as loud as possible while performing this manoeuvre, to make sure everyone knows where you are and keeps out of your way. You could even hit the hazard light button too, if you want to be extra cautious. That way, you'll have both your left and your right indicators flashing, so all eventualities are covered."

"Well," I asked, slightly irritated, "why do Sicilians use their indicators on the motorway the whole time?"

"When you get into the outside lane of a motorway or state road," explained Valentino, "you must activate your left hand indicator until you intend to cut in on someone. Maybe this is to let them know you're not intending to pull in yet, so they can safely overtake you on the inside. I fear the roots of this tradition are lost in the mists of time, like the origin of Father Christmas."

"Or the explanation of why Sicilians keep giving you handmade lace doilies to put under your lamps and fruit bowls?" I added.

"Or why English people think they need a cup of hot tea when it's thirty-seven degrees outside?" added Valentino, grinning again cheekily.

Our Punto suddenly rocked from side to side in the slipstream of a lorry of olive oil which thundered past no more than two centimetres from the car door.

"Sicilians aren't exactly good at lane discipline, are they?" I commented, irritated and unnerved. "But I suppose that's logical, because in Sicily there are no lanes. There are no lines on the road at all! No dotted lines down the centre, no double white stop lines, no solid white no-overtaking lines, nothing to mark out whether you are still on the road or veering wildly into some supermarket's car park."

"They do paint them on when the roads are new," explained Valentino calmly, "but it all gets washed off the first time it rains. The white lines are the key to everything, you know, the difference between England and Sicily."

Valentino often compares England and Sicily and his observations are usually very astute. He is so quintessentially Sicilian that I often wonder where he gets his insight into English culture. His only available object of study is me. I suppose that means I am quintessentially English.

"You English people believe in inflexible, precise rules that everyone should follow, like painted white lines. We Sicilians regard rules as being for everyone else, not for us personally. We despise authority. We've had nearly three thousand years of being invaded and ruled by foreigners whose objective was to steal everything we had: The Greeks, the Romans, the Arabs, the Normans, I can't even remember who else but practically everyone in the world has had a go at ruling us. Just when one group of conquerors was starting to be assimilated and find ways to integrate with the Sicilians, another nation would invade, so the people in authority have always been the foreign outsiders, the conquerors, the enemy. Since we regard authority as the enemy, the more rules we can get away with breaking, or bend to our advantage, the more heroic and patriotic we feel. I'm afraid that's why the Mafia still has a place in our society and will always flourish in our culture.

"We make up our rules as we go along, based on the belief that might is right. Look at that driver there. Basically, where our lane finishes and his lane begins is a matter of personal assertiveness. Whether I stop at a crossroads and wait for a break in the traffic crossing my path, or shoot out in front of it, or trickle out subversively until I create a gridlock-style four-way traffic jam, is purely determined by my level of inner courage. That's what you need to develop, sweetheart."

I swerved suddenly to pull out of the way of an approaching white and rust-coloured Fiat Cinquecento with no front bumper, no headlights and a bonnet crumpled beyond recognition. The sudden sideways movement of our car made the black plastic rosary beads, draped around the rear view mirror by the Godmother, swing wildly and make a ticking noise as they tapped against the medallion of Saint Rosalia, hermit nun and patron saint of Palermo, which hung in their midst.

"The key to becoming a relaxed driver in Sicily," Valentino continued, "is to master the art of seeming more crazed and dangerous than other drivers. This will warn them that they had better get their vehicle out of your way, because you certainly don't look like getting out of theirs. First, practise making demented faces in the bathroom mirror before leaving the house. The more of your teeth you can show at any one time, the better. Taking both hands off the steering wheel as you approach another car and waving them over your head, whilst screaming at the top of your voice, is also a good manoeuvre to work on. It helps the other driver focus his mind. A different crazed driver manoeuvre, ideal for beginners, is to play some exquisitely beautiful opera, by Giuseppe Verdi for example, and to pretend to be conducting the orchestra while you drive along. Watch this." As he spoke Valentino turned on the stereo, instantly filling the car with the strains of *O Sole Mio* to which he sang along, remarkably tunefully, conducting the orchestra as I guided the car through the increasingly chaotic traffic. "Accompanying the music by singing at the top of your voice will help you to produce a range of facial expressions which could appear alarming to other road users. Some very advanced users of this technique are capable of jiving to dance music from the 1950's and actually duck-walking into the passenger seat and back whilst overtaking on a motorway. Turn left here. We're nearly at Toto's bar."

I swung left without waiting for a break in the traffic.

"Very nippy. Well done," Valentino congratulated me, over the noise of squealing brakes all around us and the opening strains of a rousing chorus from *The Marriage of Figaro*. "Once you know how to appear demented, the next step is to demonstrate greater aggression than the other road users. Everything you must do to this end will be counter intuitive. Native Sicilian drivers will try to intimidate you at every step of the way, and you must face them down."

For the moment I needed to concentrate on avoiding oncoming vehicles, most of which seemed to be closer to my side of the road than their own. We were now in central Palermo and the traffic was constant, the run-down buildings crammed into narrow streets where they seemed to jostle with each other to retain their space along the roadside. Valentino told me to turn down a street which gradually narrowed until the balconies on each side almost touched overhead. A series of them were wrapped up in the dark green netting used as a safety measure on buildings which are no longer structurally sound, when large chunks of masonry start to fall from their balconies onto pedestrians below. Whilst intended as temporary, many buildings remain dressed like this and fully inhabited for years without any work done to restore them to a safe condition.

I rounded a curve and was faced with the apparition of a dusty white Fiat Punto, battered beyond all recognition and with nothing to lose, approaching me at several times the legal speed limit on my side of the road. Succumbing to natural instinct, I pulled as far into the kerb as possible and applied the brakes while the white Fiat Punto demonstrated the superiority of Italian engineering by accelerating almost to the speed of light, or so it seemed, in mere seconds. We came to a stop with an ear-wrenching scraping noise as the right hand side of the Punto scuffed along the wall of the old block of flats built, like so many in Palermo, directly onto the road with no pavement as a buffer zone.

"You handled that situation wrongly," said Valentino calmly as the car came to a halt.

I glanced across at him and realised that, peering straight in through the passenger window, was a miniature statuette of the miracle-performing monk Padre Pio, set into a niche in the wall of the building and flanked by vases of plastic flowers, badly faded in the relentless Sicilian sunshine. He held a set of translucent red rosary beads draped around his little cement left hand and gazed down upon me benignly, as if feeling satisfied he had performed yet another of his world famous miracles fast enough to save my life.

"I'm so sorry, Val," I said, dreading to think what the side of the car might look like. I imagined I must have peeled away half the bodywork like a tin of corned beef opened with a key.

"What damage?" asked Valentino, bewildered for a moment. "Oh, you mean that. That's just normal wear and tear. You can't expect to drive a car around without it showing signs of use. No, I mean that you shouldn't pull over when another driver is on your side of the road. You should use the puffer-fish tactic, making yourself appear as large as possible. Always charge into small streets like a bat out of hell, and aim to get to the other end before any cars appear. Pull right into the middle of the road, or ideally a little onto the wrong side of the road, to emphasise to any on-comers that you are not a getting-out-of-the-way kind of person." Valentino turned up the volume of the *Chorus of the Hebrew Slaves* on the stereo.

"Motivate that orchestra at the same time, if you have the nerve," he added, closing his eyes to drink in the loveliness of the music. As I peeled the car from the side of the building and glided out into a broader street, Valentino waved his hands majestically to demonstrate what he meant.

"Look, there's a parking space right in front of the bar. Quick!" Valentino reached out and spun the steering wheel around beneath my fingers to wedge the car between two other grey Puntos. "Sorry to do that, but I was sure you would miss it," he explained apologetically as I turned off the engine.

In Toto's tiny bar we leant against the cool marble counter and waited for the only other customer to finish his coffee and leave before we were served our usual espresso and large mug of tea with milk. Toto came around the bar to greet Valentino and me with friendly kisses and complain that we did not visit him often enough. Valentino told him having a wife was very time consuming.

"The best way to spend your time," said Toto.

"The only good way," replied Valentino. "We were talking about the wonderful produce of our beautiful island," began Valentino as I took the first, soothing sip of my tea. I added a full sachet of sugar, the traditional English therapy for someone who has been in a car crash.

"The best in the world," pronounced Toto. "Why do you want that awful tea when we have fresh oranges?"

I had never considered asking for an orange juice. I suppose the fruit arrangement was so artistic I assumed it was just for decoration.

"Look," said Toto, opening one of the refrigerators behind the counter. It was packed from top to bottom with racks of oranges. "Leave that tea, and get your mouth ready for a treat."

He produced an orange juicer from behind the counter, slashed about seven fruits in half with a knife like a scimitar and ground them mercilessly onto the plastic hub until he had enough juice to fill a tall glass. The juice was so sweet and tasty it made me salivate like a bulldog.

Valentino started another eulogy with Toto but was interrupted mid-flow by his mobile phone ringing. He launched into a highly animated conversation in Sicilian, of which I understood not a word. I silently sipped my orange juice while wondering why Valentino felt it necessary to gesticulate frantically to someone who could not see him. He had gradually raised his voice until he was shouting and suddenly, at the climax of what appeared to be a dangerously heated argument, he forgot which hand was holding his telephone, made a dramatic gesture to emphasise his point and flung the delicate piece of equipment across the room where it hit the wall, making the battery fall out. He crossed the café in two steps.

"Oh good, it still works," he commented as he fitted it back together, looking immensely relieved. "We'd better get going." He slipped some money across the counter and kissed Toto again, pausing at the door to let me out first into the roasting hot breeze.

"Don't you need to call back and finish the conversation?" I asked before walking out.

"It was only my Mum wanting to know how we'd like our pasta today," he explained.

Back in the car, I backed out of the parking space gingerly and managed to take advantage of a momentary break in the traffic to swing into the middle of the road, narrowly missing a white Fiat Uno whose driver hooted at us irately and held up his hand at Valentino, raising his index and little finger to represent the horns of the devil.

"*Cornuto!*" he mouthed furiously. "Horned devil!"

As I chugged happily along the road, singing along to 'Nessun Dorma' with Valentino, I allowed my mind to wander through my list of Great Meals I had Eaten in Sicily. Valentino was right. It was hard to think of better food anywhere in the world. Sicilian fruit and vegetables just had *more taste*.

"Look out!" yelled Valentino, showing genuine alarm for the first time since I had been driving. "Oh God, I think you ran over that man's foot!"

He yanked hard on the hand brake, which slowed the car down, and leapt out of it before I had brought it to a complete stop alongside a white van loaded from floor to ceiling with artichokes. The short, paunchy man had dropped a crate of artichoke heads, which had rolled into the road and under his van. He was perched on the back step of his vehicle, clutching his left foot in his hand and shouting at the top of his voice. Although I did not understand Sicilian, I had no need of a translation of the stream of expletives and expressions of pain filling the swelteringly hot, dry wind which buffeted us from all directions. The man looked ready to kill, like a wounded lion half out of its lair. Valentino looked down at him and suddenly delivered a sharp slap to the man's head, which made me let out an involuntary gasp of shock. Whilst I felt reassured that Valentino was utterly loyal towards me, I thought it was hardly appropriate to intimidate the man with further physical violence. Before I could speak out, the man had hopped to his one sound foot and was inexplicably hugging Valentino, laughing through the tears he was struggling to hold back.

"This is just awful," I said, holding my skirt down as it flapped noisily in the wind. "Shall we call an ambulance? I don't know how to say how sorry I am."

"No, no, it's fine. He's my cousin Calogero," smiled Valentino, clearly delighted to have bumped into his cousin so unexpectedly.

"But I still ran over his foot," I said, with a tense anxiety which was heightened by the violence of the Sirocco blowing the artichokes strewn across the street in ever wider circles.

"He deserved it," judged Valentino decisively.

"How could he possibly deserve it?" I asked indignantly. "It must be agony."

"When we were little children he once put chicken poo in my spaghetti and I got terrible gastroenteritis. Now we're even."

I smiled at the injured purveyor of chicken poo in a way which I hoped conveyed my sincerest apologies. How could I have let my mind wander so far I would drive over a man's foot?

"Actually, we're still not fully even," mused Valentino. "Calogero once made me break my leg as well, by poking a stick through the spokes of my bicycle wheel, and I've never paid him back for that. It was a very complex fracture near the knee. I had to stick his head under my armpit and use him as a crutch for six weeks."

"Keeping my head in your armpit for the whole of August paid me back more than enough," said Calogero through clenched teeth. The two cousins broke into peals of laughter that made several

113

passers-by turn to smile, amused without even knowing the joke.

"Get me to the hospital for pity's sake," protested Calogero suddenly. "This is agony."

We helped Calogero into the front passenger seat of the car and Valentino gathered up some of the dancing artichokes and piled them inside the van, being careful to avoid splinters from their viciously barbed leaves.

"You know it'll have to be set in plaster," he teased Calogero, like a naughty schoolboy. "You'll sweat like a pig and your foot will stink."

"I'm so sorry," I apologised again to Calogero.

"Don't worry," he replied. "Valentino, what's your Mum making for lunch?"

"Spaghetti with squid ink sauce," Valentino answered. "Ring her up to say you're coming, too, and let her know we'll be a bit late because we're stopping off to collect some plaster of Paris on the way home."

And the two cousins broke into laughter again, although Calogero may actually have been grimacing in pain rather than truly laughing. I could not be sure. I just watched the city jostle past and looked back at one last, battered artichoke chasing the car madly as it flew along erratically in the searing gusts of the Sirocco wind.

13

A BIT OF TOURISM IN BAGHERIA

Valentino and I went to a summit meeting with the neighbours, out in the street between our houses. We decided to band together and make one last, united attempt to get Engineer Mastronzo to finish the details on our houses, and arrange the paperwork for them to be legally registered as houses rather than slaughterhouses, and then hire a lawyer if that failed.

One of the neighbours was a policeman, a *poliziotto*, and another was a *carabiniere* – a member of the military police. The police in Italy are equipped with an awe-inspiring array of firearms, bullet proof vests as standard issue, and uniforms with some seriously shiny bits. *Carabinieri*'s hats have a 3D sculpture in silver of a ball of flames on them, they have boots that go right up to their knees, and they actually have hand grenades as well. Our law-enforcing neighbours decided to visit Mr. Faeces in full uniform, including their firearms.

If their method of persuasion failed, Valentino was to select a lawyer to represent us all instead.

The Godmother wanted to help us, but she decided to appeal to a higher authority than anyone else was using. The Auntienet could not solve this on its own. The Godmother decided to involve God.

She mustered her prayer group, a formidable posse of about twenty old ladies and a few men who met on a weekly basis for an afternoon of about four hours' solid prayer, followed by cake. Amid the flailing rosary beads she presented our situation, and immediately they were on the case. They decided that an appeal to help us out of our plight would be added to the agenda of their next pilgrimage to Baby Jesus of Naples. They regularly make coach trips to a church near Naples where a statue of baby Jesus has been known to grant miracles of all varieties. We were certainly valid candidates.

Once I had established there was nothing more to be done, for the time being, I needed some distraction. I had become well known around the village and had established that it probably had few further novelties to offer, so I decided it was high time I ventured further afield to explore the nearest town, Bagheria. The locals labour under the monstrous delusion that it is a tourist town and bill it as "City of the Villas". They are oblivious to the simple facts that, firstly, there are no tourists here; secondly, that the villas are of no interest because they have all been turned into schools and offices with facades disfigured by air conditioning units, or are private residences not open to the public, or have simply fallen down (even though still inhabited); and, thirdly, that if any tourist did accidentally wander here, they would be frightened out of their wits by the appearance of the local population.

Despite knowing all this, I remained doggedly convinced that a closer look would reveal hidden treasures. I yearned to discover little gems of side streets lined with enchanting curio shops, cafés offering exquisite delicacies, and perhaps even an intact villa to look at. I persuaded Valentino to venture into deepest, darkest Bagheria one Saturday when I discovered in my guide book that the town does, indeed, have one solitary villa open to the public. This villa, whose real name is Villa Palagonia, is known locally by the mysterious name of "Villa of the Monsters" because of the armies of strange sculptures that line its perimeter walls, all carved out of porous volcanic tufa. The caricature sculptures portray bizarre creatures, deformed little men, goblins, and ugly hybrid manimals.

As Valentino negotiated the Bagheria traffic in his own inimitable style, I observed the locals from the rolled-down car window. Some members of the public in Bagheria manage to inspire fear and amazement simply by wearing a hostile expression and stubble you could use for scouring saucepans clean. Other vintage specimens have missing teeth and ragged hair. The scariest of all, however, are those who use cutting edge fashion as their weapon. Whilst Valentino was overtaking a little open-topped pick-up truck, customised with curly wrought iron bumpers and a matching twiddly radiator grille welded on, and shedding onions as it turned each corner, I spotted a woman who could not have been under eighty years of age and ninety kilogrammes of weight in a Barbie pink velour tracksuit, like the ones Britney Spears wears when she is fat. I think everyone in the world knows that old Sicilian ladies are supposed to wear black dresses and shoes with bunion-shaped curves on the inner rim. When threatened, they can twirl rosary beads the way Bruce Lee brandished nunchakus. They do not need to use decoy tactics as well, such as disguising themselves as Hollywood starlets having drug-related psychological meltdowns. I stuck my head right out of the window to have a good look at her as we sailed past, gazing in awe at her lilac sequinned handbag clutched in hands ravaged by arthritis.

Valentino let out a string of loud expletives in Sicilian. "These drivers are the worst in the world!" he shouted furiously. "I thought we drove like pigs in Palermo, but look at them! They have no mercy! They drive with their eyes closed! In Palermo we're considerate and we only double park. Just look at that!"

I looked, and realised we were not actually in a four lane traffic jam, but were actually inching our way along a street where the cars were triple-parked. I must admit that the street was attractive. The upper storeys of the buildings had wonderful carved stone balconies with statues flanking them and intricate baroque sculptures adorning their supports. The window frames were masterpieces of masonry, and the pavements either side of the road were lined with orange trees laden with bright fruits gleaming among the leaves.

The shops were full of clothes, all of them. I counted over twenty shoe shops in that one street alone, and all the rest sold apparel, apart from one estate agent (which was closed) and a shop offering wedding list services. One might be forgiven for thinking, therefore, that the locals would have a great interest in fashion and style. The fact is, they have fashions here that never have existed, and never will exist, anywhere else in the world. Some memorable examples I spotted that day, in vast quantities, were tartan hipster Bermuda shorts worn with fishnets underneath and plastic stilettoes; gold and silver trainers for all ages and both sexes; and everywhere, on everyone, spectacularly skin tight T-shirts with bizarre slogans written on them in incorrect English.

The single most terrifying fashion blunder committed by almost the entire younger female population of Bagheria is the bare midriff. The bare midriff concept, I should hardly need to point out, was conceived as a means of displaying a tantalisingly sexy flash of bare skin on a slim, shapely girl. It has been reinterpreted in Bagheria. Here, it is regarded as an outlet, a sort of emergency pressure-valve to release surplus stones (or tons) of blubber when overeating has reached such perilous proportions that the hipster jeans are groaning at every stitch, the muffin-top has flopped down so far under its unsustainable weight that the waistband is completely concealed, and the T-shirt is simply unable to expand any further widthways around the newly enlarged girth, so it suddenly snaps upwards and settles, in a ruched format, inside the dark, damp groove between the uppermost roll of belly fat and the monumentally sized bosoms. The number of breath-taking, heart-stopping, jaw-dropping teenage girls to be seen waddling around Bagheria and bouncing against the lampposts in this condition is, in my opinion, a contributing factor to the record-breaking rate of traffic accidents occurring each year.

Approaching the villa, we first passed through the original gateposts. Since the town of Bagheria has invaded what was once the garden of the villa, the arch of the gateway now stands far away from the villa itself, along a busy shopping road lined with cafés, ironmongers, greengrocers and those baffling shops, exclusive to "developing" countries, which sell nothing but greasy old metal components extracted from used cars, broken washing machines, unusable Sicilian-style irons, farming implements and anything else mechanical and capable of going rusty.

We passed one example, called "*G. Fricano e Figli – NON TEME CONCORRENZA*" in a very messy hand-painted sign. 'Concorrenza' was all squashed up at the end because he was running out of space. The phrase means "G. Fricano and Sons - DOES NOT FEAR COMPETITION" so evidently he stocks second-hand greasy metal things that the other shops simply cannot obtain.

As we approached the villa, we entered a melée of narrow residential streets festooned with dented cars and laundry strung up from the lamp-posts like a Middle Eastern Bazaar. All the streets were one-way, so we got lost countless times and crept up on the villa in a circling movement, spiralling gradually inwards. The so-called "monsters" sat all along the perimeter walls. We kept spotting stone dogs playing violins and donkeys riding upon women with three tits, glimpsed between fluttering pairs of humungous knickers.

They stood, eroded yet still ugly, and gazed down forlornly upon the neighbours and their threadbare laundry. A line of sopping wet sheets which shrouded the windscreen provoked more Sicilian from Valentino as he activated the windscreen wipers. Eventually we reached the second pair of gates, flanked by statues of ugly, squat-legged goblin-like beings about nine feet tall, tightly wedged between a ticket booth and a ladies clothing shop.

I was unable to resist the temptation to pop into the shop, just to see what it would be like. Mostly it contained footwear with six inch heels thinner than pencils. The assistant was a paunchy, middle aged man wearing a purple t-shirt bearing the unforgettable legend, "mysterious seducer." He was selling a pair of golden trainers to an elderly lady in a lycra top with a picture of Tweetie Pie in sequins, and the words "This year I always am full of kiss" embroidered alongside. In my haste to escape I almost bumped into a round-shouldered granny using a Zimmer frame, sporting a tracksuit with "First-World sexy sequin girl" written across the back in very shiny metallic letters - but not sequins, oddly enough.

The man in the ticket booth looked quite sporty and wore a tracksuit with "UPPERCUT SCHOOL OF BOING" on the back. Whatever could that mean? My mind was flooded with wondrous images of prize athletes holding kick-boxing tournaments on trampolines. Could Jackie Chan have invented a new martial art? Kung Fu performed upside down while bungee jumping? The bouncy fellow greeted us in very bad English and slapped two tickets and two information leaflets onto the counter. They bore a little union jack on the corner, which I naively thought meant they would be written in English. Later I would realise how wrong I had been. Valentino asked for a replacement in Italian, and off we went, ready to explore.

We walked in through the gates and saw the beautiful facade of the villa at the end of a broad, sandy path lined with flowering oleanders, orange trees, cacti, and a variety of spectacular flowering trees laden with huge and beautiful pink, red and yellow flowers. We decided to explore the garden before entering the villa, and wandered along a path to the right which followed the circular perimeter wall. After turning the curve we were faced with a row of what looked like private back gardens. There were plastic slides and see-saws, abandoned tricycles, a few parked cars and the ubiquitous Sicilian laundry hung up to dry.

"Che schifo" said Valentino without hesitation.

This literally means "How disgusting." Sicilians say it very often. Among Italians, the liberal use that Sicilians make of this phrase is regarded as rather a cliché. Sicilians use it to express their disapproval of anything they feel is unsatisfactory. They say it with great passion and feeling, none with more passion and feeling than Valentino.

"Che schifo," said Valentino again. "Che vergogna. How shameful! Che schifo!"

I had hardly anticipated a National Trust style monument with original furniture and a gift shop selling perfumed soaps and souvenir pencil sharpeners, yet I must admit that, considering the exorbitant entrance fee, I had hoped for something a little better presented than this. The villa and its gardens had obviously once been a little spot of paradise, and still had immense potential to be presented to tourists as a fascinating and thoroughly satisfying place to visit, despite its decrepit condition.

We hastened around the other side of the garden and admired the view of the villa from the back – or was if the front? It seemed to have two fronts, each completely different from the other yet equally beautiful and imposing. One can easily get from one side of the villa to the other by walking under an archway that passes through the centre of the buildings.

"Look out!" yelled Valentino as I wandered into the shadows. "Don't get garrotted by the washing line!"

The aristocratic heirs of this villa still lived in it, evidently, and there were a few noble panty-girdles and baronial-looking jeans with balloon seats drying under there on a neck-height string. We admired the stone plaques lining the walls in this shady archway beneath the building. They were life-size stone relief portraits of various members of the family who had built the villa and a variety of different coloured types of marble. Some looked like priests, some were in armour and some were in magnificent robes.

The side of the villa which we later discovered had indeed been the original front featured a symmetrical, double stone staircase which curved upwards in a semi-circle on each side and met at the top to form a balcony outside the main entrance, which was an imposing door on the first floor. The frontage was concave, which meant that, from the windows flanking the door, one could look out and spy upon whoever was approaching, without being visible to them. The entire ground floor had once been given over to the servants. The aristocrats entered by going upstairs to the upper entrance.

"Read something out of the leaflet," Valentino told me. "Let's learn something about the history of this place."

"The double flight of stairs is very unusual" I read out, *"realised in calcareous stone. The villa has an extraordinary unitarian planimetrical design, with all its elements developing and reacting in respect to the barycentric axis of the avenue."*

"What?" said Valentino.

"Don't you know what that means?" I taunted. "You dunce!"

"Well, go on, what *does* it mean?" he retorted.

Valentino consulted the Italian version. Eventually we deduced that "unitarian" was not referring to the Unitarian church, but rather that the design was harmoniously balanced. Planimetrical apparently, to the translator, means well-proportioned, and barycentric means having line symmetry.

When we stepped inside the heavy door, we found ourselves in an oval-shaped hall painted with frescoes of some of the twelve tasks of Hercules.

To either side of us, identical doors led off into each wing of the villa.

"Well, this is very barycentric, isn't it?" said Valentino.

Indeed it was.

The room was light and airy, and absolutely beautiful. Hercules' tasks were depicted as white marble statues, painted in trompe l'oeuil style, set among stone balustrades, columns and arches against a background of trees and rolling countryside, painted with exquisitely delicate flimsiness as if everything were almost floating in the air.

Directly ahead of us was a small chamber, its walls painted with the most delicate pictures of tiny birds, delicate garlands of leaves and flowers, fine ribbon bows floating in mid-air, and other motifs all taking their inspiration from ancient Pompeian wall paintings. Through a pair of locked glass doors we could see part of a curving corridor which followed the length of the building. The ceiling was made of antique mirrors, now dark and smoky. The floor was an intricate pattern of inlaid marble of various colours, in its polished and multi-coloured prime no doubt a splendour to behold but now a heart-breaking mess of holes and dislodged or shattered inserts too dangerous to walk on. The walls were a mix of tiles in marble and mica, that unique natural substance which is able to trap light from the sun or candles and give off a phosphorescent glow long after the room has sunk into darkness. The state of utter neglect was so depressing that I turned away and tried to trick my mind into believing I had actually seen it in its original magnificence.

To our left, the door led to the private part of the villa still inhabited, and this was locked. To our right lay the main room of the very small part of the villa actually open to the public, the Hall of Mirrors. At that time, mirrors were the most expensive items one could possibly use for interior decor, short of using solid slabs of pure gold. It is strange nowadays to realise that the varied and exotic array of high quality marble in unusual colours, which faces all the walls lining this hall of mirrors, would have been downright economical compared with the mirrors all over the ceiling. A method of backing a plate of flat glass with a thin sheet of reflecting metal, an amalgam of tin and mercury, was first developed and came into widespread production in Venice during the 16th century. Up until this time, a mirror has simply been a very polished piece of shiny metal. It was not until 1835 that the use of metallic silver was invented in Germany, and until then the Venetians held a virtual monopoly in the business of mirror production. Legend has it that the government of the Venetian Republic hired professional assassins to track down and poison the Venetian mirror makers who had been lured to Versailles to make the Palace's famous Hall of Mirrors in the 17th century, so keen were they to protect the Venetian mirror monopoly.

Therefore the decision to cover the entire ceiling of this hall with mirrors was a deliberate display of immense wealth and ostentatious extravagance. This was a period in Sicily's history when the barons were filthy rich, and the order of the day was to flaunt what you had. Ships from all the seagoing European countries would stop off in the bay of Palermo and fill their holds with Sicilian oranges and lemons, to stop their smelly sailors (or pirates) from getting scurvy on the high seas. On their way back from trading raids in Asia they would stop off again. By this time they had usually been drinking their own piss for a few months and were so scorbutic they had seeping wounds and wobbly teeth. Their holds were crammed with gold doubloons, however, pieces of eight and literally heaps of curry powder, barrels of tea, spare parrots and other exotic treasures. They would pay whatever price was asked for a tankard of freshly squeezed homemade organic lemonade. The Sicilian barons who owned the citrus orchards became fabulously wealthy. They deserved it, of course, for ensuring that sailors all over the world received a nutritionally balanced diet.

The Count of Gravina, and Seventh Prince of Palagonia, however, the owner who oversaw the interior decoration of this villa, was not merely content with a vulgar display of wealth. He wanted his room to be extraordinary as well. The mirrors covered the ceiling, following the curvature of the cornicing and hugging the upper level of the walls all around the room. They were deliberately mounted at subtly varying angles, so that, as you walked around the room, you saw yourself reflected dozens of times. There were not only reflections of yourself in the mirrors, but reflections of your reflection, and reflections of that reflection. Every little movement you made was magnified into the flickering of a crowd, a shimmering horde of ghosts mocking your movements.

The mirrors are now badly tarnished, which in some ways adds to their aesthetic appeal, but this deliberately unnerving effect must have been far more impressive when they were new and reflected perfectly. This strange visual trick, however, was still not enough for the seventh Prince of Palagonia. The mirrors were also painted. Exotic birds perch high up in the room, painted on the glass of the mirrors. Shells and flowers and other delicately painted adornments embellish them further, and bordering the entire room are branches of red coral, spreading out from the rims of the mirrors in a way which looks disturbingly like blood seeping through, as if oozing from behind them.

The walls are faced with slabs of marble in dark, blood reds and maroons and other exotic colours, gathered from multiple sites around Italy and beyond. Among them are panels of glass, painted from behind to like marble. This again was another deliberate sign of ostentation, as this newly invented fake marble was, at that time, far more expensive than the real thing.

Somewhat above eye level, each panel surrounding the whole room bears a relief sculpture of an ancestor of the Gravina family. When I say relief sculpture, I use that term because I do not know what else to call them. Maybe I should describe them as wall-mounted statues. They are life-size, and they look like marble sculptures of people trying to clamber out of the stonework, as if frozen in some scene from a horror film where victims are entrapped and trying to escape from an alternate dimension. I found them fascinating and wonderful, yet also disturbing.

Valentino did not like them at all.

"Che scifo," he said. "These are creepy. And they are not very planimetric either, are they? What kind of lunatics would want to have a room like this in their house?"

Stories about the family that originally inhabited this villa abound. Many are probably apocryphal, but they are highly entertaining. Construction of the villa began in 1715, on behalf of Don Ferdinando Gravina and Crujillas, Fifth prince of Palagonia, peer of the realm, and Knight of Toson d'Oro, which was apparently a prestigious honour bestowed by the king of Spain. Despite his grandiose titles, he was a benevolent man who made great contributions to the poor house of Palermo and other works to help the poor. He already had other palaces, including a highly forbidding-looking prison type home the other side of Sicily, the Palazzo Gravina Crujillas in Catania.

Perhaps hoping for an equally forbidding summer residence in Bagheria, he hired a man with the title of Military Engineer as his architect. His chosen man also happened to be assistant architect to the Senate of Palermo, and a Dominican Friar to boot. His name was Tommaso Maria Napoli. One might think he was too busy piously constructing military earthworks, in his monkly habit, to actually design the summer villa. Perhaps he was, for an assistant was also hired, another greatly esteemed Sicilian architect, Agatino

Daidone. Maybe that is why the villa has two completely different fronts. Maybe they could not agree whose design to use, so they just used both of them, stuck together.

Work on the villa proceeded at Sicilian speed. Whenever you see a Sicilian man working in a hole in the road, there are at least twelve others standing around watching him, and providing constructive criticism to egg him on. I presume Villa Palagonia was constructed in a similar manner. A full twenty-two years after it was started, in 1737, Don Ferdinand was dead and his son, Ignazio Sebastiano Gravina, began work on the lower floors which surround the villa. Finally, his son, grandson of the founder of the villa, Francesco Ferdinando Gravina e Alliata, was ready to get cracking on the interior décor in 1749.

This is where the story of the villa becomes exciting, because this Seventh Prince of Palagonia was quite a nutter. It is hard to determine whether he was simply a very rich, delinquent eccentric, or whether he was an evil psychopath. He was the mastermind behind the hall of mirrors, which was allegedly designed to torment his young wife and drive her to utterly lose her mind through fear of its spookiness.

He gradually proceeded to have the entire perimeter wall topped with gruesome sculptures. These statues represent humanoids with animals' heads, imaginary animals, partially humanoid figures, statues of ladies and knights portrayed as deformed dwarfs, clownish musicians and various other caricatures. Some said they were cruel caricatures of Francesco Ferdinando's wife's various lovers and any other person who had offended him. Others said he was simply a lunatic wasting extraordinary amounts of money on ugly and pointless "art". Whatever people thought, the locals started calling the place the "Villa of Monsters", and that name is still used today. To this day stories of what a bad man he was, probably apocryphal, circulate around Bagheria.

His style of interior décor made the villa famous throughout Europe for its *avant garde* style, and mix of decadent opulence with daring modernity. His inimitable character remains stamped and deeply felt throughout this rather demented residence. It was visited by anyone who could get themselves an invitation to enter the freaky place on their aristocratic grand tour of Europe. Visitors included the early travel writer Henry Swinburne; Patrick Brydone, who was in Sicily because of his passionate interest in lava flows which later led him to realize the earth is far older than had hitherto been realised; English architect John Soane, upon whom the villa made a profound impact and who subsequently designed the Bank of England; the Count de Borde, about whom I can find nothing interesting to say, so I do hope he was not bored; the artist and travel writer Jean-Pierre Houël; and Alexandre Dumas, whom many people know as the author of the Three Musketeers but whom fewer people know was the grandson of a French nobleman and a Haitian slave, who once remarked to a man who insulted him about his mixed-race background: "My father was a mulatto, my grandfather was a Negro, and my great-grandfather a monkey. You see, Sir, my family starts where yours ends"; and illustrious German multi-talented politician, writer, and sausage-eating bore Goethe, who went on to write that "To have seen Italy without having seen Sicily is to not have seen Italy at all, for Sicily is the clue to everything".

When Goethe visited the villa, this trickster, Ferdinando Gravina e Alliata, gave him a joke chair to sit on. He had played the classic schoolboy trick of partially sawing through the legs, leaving the chair apparently intact but ready to collapse into sticks when Goethe lowered his sturdy Teutonic buttocks upon its seat. Apparently Herr Goethe was not amused. Goethe's comment on the villa was a sense of repugnance at the sight of the gruesome statues, and the valid comment that the count should have wasted less money on such pointless creations and spent more of it helping the poor, like his grandfather.

On our way out of the villa we stopped to ask the Uppercut School of Boing why it was in such a decrepit condition, with see-saws and laundry everywhere. He explained, somewhat huffily and defensively, that the villa had gone through various odd lines of inheritance since various owners had died without children, and eventually came into the possession of a nun. She decided, in her wisdom, to split it up into no less than fifty separate apartments and sell them off separately. The fifty owners of the villa can now no longer agree on anything. They quarrel over which repairs to carry out, who should do them, who should pay for them, which parts of the villa to open to the public, when to open them to the public, if at all, who can hang their laundry where, who can go where, and what should happen to the villa in the future. Essentially, a monument so important that it should have been sequestered and run by the government, as a piece of national heritage, is gradually being squabbled into rubble.

Valentino and I drove home from the villa in excited discussion about whether it was a good thing to spend all that money on freaky art or not. Entering the village we spotted Giuseppe Wheelbarrow on a street corner. I made Valentino stop in the middle of the road and block the traffic so I could chat with Giuseppe: I was enthusiastically embracing the Sicilian way of driving.

When I told Giuseppe where we had been, he put down his wheelbarrow and laughed.

"We don't need more ugly faces round here, do we? We've got enough of them walking about already. Look around you!"

I laughed, and off he trudged, his barrow overflowing with unidentifiable metal objects. Perhaps they were destined for G. Fricano and Sons, the men who do not fear competition.

14

THE MEDITERRANEAN DIET

One bright, sunny morning a few days later, The Godmother came over. Ostensibly she wanted to get a bag of organic lemons from my neighbour who has lots of trees in his smallholding, deliver me a new string of rosary beads, and hang an additional, larger crucifix in my sitting room, to remind me of her. As soon as a pained, tortured Jesus almost a foot high looked down despairingly upon whomever sat on the sofa, she turned to the kitchen, and I realised she had ulterior motives.

"What is this *shiperspi* you made Valentino yesterday?" she asked, smiling deceptively.

I got her to repeat it several times before I realised she was saying shepherd's pie. That was when I realised the main purpose of her visit was to check up on what I was feeding her son. Valentino had, apparently, let slip some of the things I had given him to eat, and she was displeased. I was giving him foreign muck from England.

I got the leftover shepherd's pie out of the fridge and served her a portion, which she eyed up suspiciously. She literally wrinkled her nose at it. She tasted a small sample, deliberately making a show of putting a tiny amount on the end of her fork. The Godmother is not someone who ever eats tiny forkfulls of anything. She was pointing out that eating a normal forkful could be hazardous.

Now, by some extraordinary fluke, this shepherd's pie happened to have turned out to be an absolute winner. It happens to me about three times a year that something I cook is, inexplicably, marvellous. My inedible disasters the rest of the time more than make up for it, of course. On the same magnificent day as the delicious *shiperspi*, I happened to have baked two fabulous cakes as well.

"It's quite tasteless," said The Godmother, plonking her fork down definitively, to announce that she certainly would not be eating any more of *that*.

I offered her some of the orange cake, which Valentino had already almost finished as he liked it so much. I put on an apron as I was also clearing and doing some washing up at the same time. I had made the apron from some traditional block-printed material I had bought in Provence on a holiday to France a few years earlier. It was beautiful and unusual and nothing like the aprons The Godmother wore, which were like dresses covered in luminous cabbage flowers, slit down each side with frills which went all the way around her armpits.

"Where did you get that?" asked the Godmother.

"I made it," I answered.

Sewing is the one domestic activity which eludes The Godmother. She cannot even thread a needle.

"Oh, so you saved two euros," she commented. "You can buy those in the local market."

"Do you like the cake?" I asked.

"It's rather gritty. And bitter. Look how I'm eating it," she commented, grimacing several times, to make sure I got a good look at how its grittiness and bitterness made her grimace theatrically.

"I know," I suggested. "I've got a cake that my neighbour Carmen made. Would you like a slice of that?"

"Yes, please," said The Godmother.

When preparing the cake, I had divided the mix in half and added freshly grated orange zest to one, and lemon zest to the other. I cut a large slice of the lemon cake, and served that.

"Oh, tell Carmen that her cake is delicious!" said the Godmother in delight, and ate the lot. "You see, there's no comparison with our food. Our food is all *genuino*. You can tell it in the taste. They call it the Mediterranean diet."

I had no idea what kind of artificial ingredients she thought I had sneaked into the orange cake. The Sicilians believe passionately that their food is healthier than any foreign comestibles could possibly be. Fish from the Mediterranean, one of the world's more polluted seas, which in parts is little more than a colossal open-air septic tank, is the only fish safe to eat in their opinion. Vegetables grown on Sicilian soil are organic and pure and natural, whilst imported ones probably cause heart disease, cancer, and maybe even piles as well.

"Yuck! Your English fish and chips are so unhealthy!" they will exclaim. "How could you ruin fish by frying it?"

Sicilians eat immeasurably more fried fish than the English do.

Almost every Sicilian household has a deep fat fryer specifically for the purpose of frying prawns, octopus, cuttlefish and any other tiny fish caught prematurely from their over-fished waters. They fry potato croquettes, rice balls and slabs of chick pea paste as well. Yet they have bought into the myth of a "Healthy Mediterranean Diet," which people throughout the western world are urged to emulate for the sake of their arteries. I am not saying the Mediterranean diet is not nice – it is absolutely delicious – I am just saying it is not particularly healthy.

All the Mediterranean Diet mythology originated, of course, from the British middle class dream of retiring early and going to live on one's own vineyard in Tuscany. Britain is full of men who fantasise about becoming a Mediterranean Man, who comes home from work at midday for a delicious lunch eaten under the grapes hanging off his pergola, sloshes down a couple of glasses of his own red wine (no more Chateau Cardboard vintage for him!), and spends the rest of his lunch break bonking his wife in seven different positions like a true Latin Lover. Then he heads back to work for another three hours of lazily chatting in fluent Italian, French or Spanish with his vineyard employees about how picturesque the lemon orchard looks at this time of year.

British newspaper *The Telegraph* has printed a truly staggering barrage of articles, proclaiming that the Mediterranean diet is so healthy it just might keep you in business as a gigolo well past your 100th birthday, whistling while you work for the sheer joy of having clear arteries and gallons of cholesterol-free semen. Their various claims include: Mediterranean diet can help women get pregnant; Mediterranean diet extends life by up to three years; Mediterranean diet as good as statins; Mediterranean diet can reduce risk of depression; Mediterranean diet cuts risk of heart disease.

I have looked into the research behind this diet. These facts that all the "studies have found" were based on a study of about six people, in most cases. Five of them were still taking their statins and Viagra during the Mediterranean Diet experiment anyway.

This is not the only fallacy. The food you are told to eat on the Mediterranean Diet is not even what Mediterranean people actually eat. It is what north Europeans and Americans like to imagine they eat.

The American "Dr. Oz Mediterranean Diet Shopping List" contains foods so far removed from the real Mediterranean diet that not only are they unobtainable here in the Mediterranean, but it is also impossible to find anyone here who knows what they are. He advises such items as whole wheat tortillas and hanger steak – even

I don't know what they are. He recommends kale, which doesn't grow in the Mediterranean. He advocates canola oil; when I asked for canola oil in my local supermarket a few years back, they suggested I try the hardware store. Oz even dares, I said DARES, to suggest whole wheat pasta.

I once served whole wheat pasta to Valentino, my very own Mediterranean Man.

"What the heck is this muck?" would be a loose translation of his reaction. He didn't eat it. He wouldn't even taste it.

The most staggering inclusion of all in the Dr. Oz list is chilli powder. I dare you to give an Italian something with chilli on it: they will never speak to you again, and they will bring up their children and their children's children to kill your children and their children upon sight in a spectacular vendetta that lasts unto the seventh generation and beyond. I am pretty sure the origin of the endless feud between the Montagues and the Capulets of Verona had something to do with chilli.

I freely admit that the Mediterranean diet is absolutely delicious, without a doubt, but it is not healthy. The real Mediterranean diet is about as healthy as a Big Mac with a side order of fries. What the real Mediterranean Man eats is stir-fried paella and potato omelette swimming in butter in Spain; pasta, pizza, lasagne and flab salami in Italy; and in Greece, moussaka, and strange lumps of lamb that taste of armpits. The level of obesity and type-two diabetes in Italy is simply shocking. That is what happens if you dedicate your life to being a devout Pastafarian, and eat a diet that is 90% carbohydrate, 40% fat and 20% caffeine. It sometimes seems that anyone in Sicily the wrong side of fifty is diabetic.

Not only this. High blood pressure has reached epidemic proportions, for lashings of salt are indispensable to the authentic Mediterranean diet. On the fantasy Mediterranean diet, butter is replaced with healthy fats such as olive oil. All Sicilians know olive oil is so healthy that the more of it you can eat, the better. In my mother-in-law's household, they are so healthy that a one-litre bottle of olive oil never lasts more than a week. Red meat should also be limited to no more than a few times a month on the doctor's version of the Mediterranean diet. My mother-in-law, like all sensible Sicilians, limits red meat. She limits it to no more than a few times a week. About four or five times a week.

Of course I said none of this. I just said,

"Would you like another slice of Carmen's cake?"

She would, came the reply, and she ate all of her second helpings too.

While she was munching away, our neighbour the *carabiniere* shouted for Valentino from outside the kitchen window. I went out onto the balcony. He was in his uniform, the buttons, epaulettes and cap badge of which shone so brightly in the sunlight that is hurt my eyes to look at him.

"He's still at work," I called out, shielding my eyes and squinting down at the neighbour. "Shall I give him a message?"

"Could you tell him, we need him to get a lawyer to deal with the Engineer Mastronzo? I've just got back from a second visit, and it's nothing doing. Our only hope now is to go the legal route."

"Oh that's bad," I said. "OK, I'll tell him."

As I turned to go back inside, I stubbed my foot on the ammonite fossil so hard I actually kicked it across the balcony.

"FFFFfffffffffffff!" I snorted, bending over double. I hopped along the balcony, clutching the iron railings.

"Aiiiyeeeee!" yelled The Godmother behind me. "Ow, my bunion!"

She had followed me out onto the balcony and stubbed her toe on it, too. She promptly picked it up and used it to wedge the door of the cleaning products cabinet closed. That was a good idea. The catch had gone funny and it blew open in strong wind. At last we had an actual use for the fossil.

A few days later, The Godmother dropped in on us unannounced. She started unloading bags, massive Tupperware containers, and saucepans with their lids tied on with string, from her car. It was like a Red Cross food parcel airlift. Carmen happened to be outside and offered to help us carry them into the kitchen. I liked her shoes, which were essentially two vast blocks of pink perspex strapped onto her feet with about twelve yards of glittery string.

"My mother-in-law loved the lemon cake you made the other day," I told Carmen, winking heavily behind The Godmother's back.

"Ah yes, it was my grandmother's recipe," Carmen said, catching on immediately. She intuitively understood the mother-in-law situation. She had once told me how her mother-in-law had insisted upon having the key to her house when she was first married. One day, Carmen and her husband were having sex on the living room floor and her mother-in-law walked in on them, unannounced. Carmen noticed but her husband didn't, so she pretended not to see and put on quite a loud show, apparently, keeping her eyes closed until her husband shouted "Mizzica!" at the top of his voice, and rolled off her. Apparently the key was returned a few days later.

When we reached the kitchen, The Godmother began unpacking

the ready-meal food parcels and telling us what each one was. Whilst I was grateful that she had saved me so much work, and I had no doubt it would all be delicious, it was not lost on me that her sole purpose was to point out that her son would only get fed properly if she were the one to feed him.

One of the saucepans contained Valentino's favourite sauce, the one made from chopped aubergines, fresh grilled swordfish and tomato passata. We decided to have this for lunch, and invited Carmen to join us. Her husband was away on a business trip so she would be lunching alone otherwise.

Carmen loved the sauce – which was delicious, as it should be – and asked for the recipe. I already knew this recipe, of course... except that I didn't.

When hearing The Godmother tell Carmen the recipe, I learned that it included white wine, nutmeg and a few cloves of garlic which are removed before serving. The Godmother had not included those ingredients when she taught me the recipe. She had deliberately ensured that I would not be able to make my husband's favourite meal as well as she did. She was cheating too! She may be mad on cleaning things, but she liked to fight dirty. She had started cheating before I had. In that case, I would have to redouble my efforts and make sure I cheated *more.*

Valentino's colleagues had been trying to serve Mr. Lucky Turd the Engineer his papers for several days, but could never catch him, when Valentino came home from work with another crumpled and folded sheaf of papers. A colleague in the office had been stamping and otherwise decorating the papers with ceiling wax, and had made him a secret copy: Lucky Faeces The Engineer was on trial for assisting drug dealing activities for a couple of Canadians called Mauro De Simone – the one The Godmother had already found out about - and Michele Calò.

Drug dealing! This Engineer was a thoroughbred, international crook. With names like those, the Canadians must have origins in Sicily. We asked the Godmother to log on to the Auntienet and try to find out as much as she could about them.

15

A BRUSH WITH THE LAW

Valentino came home from work one day and told me they needed an interpreter for a trial relating to a rape case.

"So, no trials yet involving a Mr. Faeces guilty of selling people a house that's really a slaughterhouse?" I asked.

"Not yet," said Valentino. "It takes a bit of time."

"And the drugs trial?"

"Coming soon."

They wanted a mother-tongue English speaker because the usual interpreters, who were all Sicilian, could not understand what the witness was saying. He was an "extracomunitario," which means "person from outside the European Union." I was told he had an extremely strong "extracomunitario" accent. What does a "non-European Union" accent sound like, exactly? I was keen to find out.

They needed someone tomorrow. Uncle Pasquale, who just happened to be the person who manages the official list of interpreters for trials, had told Valentino that the pay for such work could be very generous, and we both reasoned that this could be an ideal opening for interesting and more lucrative work which would suit me perfectly. We allowed ourselves to get excited about the glittering (part-time) career which seemed to have laid itself at my feet.

My sister Josephine, who has a degree in Italian, and had just finished working for a year as a professional translator in Milan for a firm of lawyers, instantly mutated into "Disgusted of Essex" when she heard that they were using me as a court translator. She said that only in Palermo would they use someone with no formal language qualifications or training as an interpreter, just because their husband's uncle is in charge of the official list of translators and they cannot find anyone else who can understand an alcohol-crazed Central African who spits when he talks. And of course she was completely right. Nowhere else in the European Union would the ability to speak one and a half languages qualify you to work as a simultaneous interpreter. But who was I to quibble with abysmal standards and perversions of justice? I wanted a job.

The next morning I dressed in a black trouser suit which I felt made me look highly serious and professional in a courtly kind of way, and went to work with Valentino. He had arranged to be on court duty that day, by swapping positions on the rota with one of his colleagues, so he could take me to the courtroom himself, keep me company, and give me moral support.

In the car on the way there, I tried to get Valentino to teach me the basic terms that I would need to know, such as "accused", "defendant", "state prosecution", "witness," "co-respondent shoes" and so on. Lots of words are used in trials which do not occur in legal documents, and you cannot stop a live trial to look something up online. For some reason which utterly evades me, and which I am still determined to get to the bottom of, he insisted that words like this were highly unlikely to crop up during the trial. He has worked in court for years. How on earth can he have managed to avoid listening to anything anyone says for so long?

Eventually I had to drag the words out of him by resorting to a semi-hysterical screaming outburst, where I threatened to grab hold of the steering wheel and run us off the road into a large wheelie-bin.

We arrived unharmed and, having watched Valentino park the car in a space the right size for a motorbike, I sauntered into court trying to look as if I were not terrified. The whole court building is deliberately designed to make you feel like an utter nobody. The ceilings are so high you can hardly hear the echo by the time it bounces back at you, or else you have got bored of waiting and wandered off. The doors are solid metal and look as if they are capable of resisting heavy explosions and gunfire as well as amputating your finger if you are gauche enough to slam one in them. The guards wear military style uniforms and look at you as if you are about to go to prison for twenty years and deserve it, too. So there.

We went to the administrative offices first, which felt less intimidating as the rooms were wallpapered with hand written notices held up with sticky tape. I was introduced to about twenty people and kissed all of them. I was most relieved to be presented to the judge as well. He seemed fairly approachable, so I asked him about the English skills of the witness and whether I could speak to him before the trial began, to get an idea of how comprehensible he was. The judge said I was welcome to do that but he did not think it would particularly help me, or be necessary.

Why would it not help me? I became suspicious.

Eventually we went into the courtroom where the trial was to take place. The chamber was about the height of three houses and the walls were covered with flooring, to maximise echoing and the incomprehensibility of everything said by everyone. One wall was parquet, two were marble paving slabs and the last one was gravel.

I was most surprised to find that there was no jury. Valentino told me that Italian trials only use a jury for murder cases. The barristers wore academic gowns like the ones we wore for graduation from university, except that their shoulders were embellished with elaborately knotted silvery ropes and heavy tassels which looked exactly like some de-luxe curtain tie-backs I saw recently in Homebase. It was eight degrees centigrade and the building had absolutely no heating whatsoever, so everyone had their overcoats on underneath, except for the main judge, who had an anorak with fur round the hood. So much for my natty trouser suit: I should have worn a skiing jacket, a woolly bobble hat and perhaps a couple of reindeer skins as well.

Before the arrival of the defendant, I had to wait over an hour while the three judges and the lawyers asked to postpone the hearing of one case after another. The average trial in Sicily takes four years and now I knew why.

One of Valentino's cousins, who is a Carabiniere (a military policeman) was accused of having a nicked stereo in his locker and, by the time he was proven innocent, he had been suspended without pay for a truly unbelievable four years. The amount of compensation they had to pay out for this rather stressful period of his life has basically set him up for life. This shocking insight into the excruciatingly slow-motion machinations of the Italian legal system made me despair for our house situation. Until this point I had pinned all my hopes upon our barrister, but now I feared it may never get sorted out at all.

After all this delaying and faffing, with the female lawyers getting things in and out of their Fendi handbags and Giorgio Armani briefcases and adjusting their Gucci scarves, and of course sometimes caressing their metallic curtain tiebacks, Valentino eventually told me that we were still waiting because they had forgotten to bring the accused out of his prison for the hearing. We would just have to wait until he arrived. I had missed this announcement completely, probably because I was falling asleep through the intolerable boredom. Or was it a hypothermic delirium?

At least Valentino had located the witness by this point, but had reeled backwards when taking down his name. His eyes were so bloodshot it made me wince to look at them. Val said that he did not want me to go and talk to him, as he reeked of alcohol and seemed like quite a low-life. He also had a fairly strong body odour which Valentino astutely discerned I would find distressing. Alas, I still had no idea what an *extracommunitario* accent sounded like. I waited on the bench alongside a large assortment of designer bags, shivering miserably and trying to stave off pneumonia by using my hair as an improvised balaklava helmet.

Eventually the supposed crook arrived and was put into a cage to one side of the court room. This was the grand climax of the day. He sat there loudly snarling and grimacing through the kind of stubble you could use to strike matches on. He looked appropriately menacing and evil at all times, occasionally clutching at the bars as if he were planning to rip them from the floor and use them to massacre the lot of us.

Meanwhile Valentino escorted the witness up to the front bench and helped him remain vertical at all times, but left him to his own devices as far as placing one foot in front of the other was concerned, and I was told to follow. I was given a sheet of paper to read out and obliged, thus, to swear an oath to translate the truth, the whole truth, and not make any mistakes or God help me. At least I think that is the oath I swore. I only understood it in parts. Luckily my microphone did not work when I was reading it out so, if I mispronounced anything, nobody heard. I may have inadvertently turned it off myself, as I was so nervous my hands were shaking.

The victim of my interpreting efforts was a Zairean who said he had witnessed the rape of a Zairean woman at the hands of the aforementioned North African in the cage. The mixture of booze and BO smelled so pungent while I was relaying his place and date of birth in Italian that my nose started running uncontrollably and I felt dizzy. Now I was able to conclude that a *Non-European Union* accent is basically an incomprehensible blend of Zairean pidgin, alcohol-induced slur, and an abundant use of words from Tshiluba, Kikongo, Lingala and some of the other 250 official languages spoken in Zaire. How could the judge have thought it would *not* help me to be aware of this in advance?

"That man," he said, pointing with his whole arm at the caged menace, "tiffed ma mobblefon."

"I beg your pardon?" I said.

"He did tiff ma mobblefon," repeated the man, lowering his voice confidentially.

"Your what?"

"Mobblefon."

"Oh! Your mobile phone!" I squealed, delighted I had decoded something. "What did he do to it?"

"I thought she spoke English," muttered one of the lawyers under his breath from behind me. His words echoed loudly from the marble paving slabs and the parquet wall.

"He tiffed it," said the Zairean. He was swaying slightly and his eyes seemed to be getting even redder.

"What?"

"Tiffed it!" he repeated. I do not know who was more desperate by this time; him, me or the judges.

At this moment we were all distracted by the stubbly rapist who, grunting and pulling harder than ever before on the bars of his cage, unexpectedly released the loudest, flappiest fart I had ever heard in my life. I suspect it may actually have been a *luffione*. It reverberated off the marble paving slabs all over the opposite wall and then echoed to and fro for several seconds between the gravel walls, until it finally tinkled away into methane-scented silence.

Every single person in the room had forgotten what they were saying or thinking. We sat in stunned silence, avoiding eye-contact.

"Do you mean thieved?" I exclaimed, with a sudden flash of inspiration. "You mean he stole it?"

"Yes!" shouted Mr. Zaire. His eyes were like two stewed tomatoes by this point.

The dialogue stumbled along like this for a while, my hands still trembling like leaves, and then the Sicilian barristers started using legal terms which I did not understand so things took a turn for the worse. Luckily the barrister for the prosecution soon realised it was better to avoid technical vocabulary where I was concerned, and very kindly phrased his questions in everyday terminology.

However, I still had to cope with the fact that both he and the barrister for the defence were seated behind me, and using appalling microphones which were certainly manufactured by the same company which produces the ones they use on the London Underground. Maybe that is why Valentino thinks they never use words like "witness" and "prosecution" in court. Maybe he just cannot hear them.

Meanwhile the accused in his cage was still clutching the bars and snarling and growling through his teeth, and also falling silent to concentrate on releasing smaller bursts of flatulence from time to time.

At this point the judge obviously felt a particularly fierce draught of cold air, or possibly smelly air, as he pulled his anorak hood up and zipped it to the neck. I do not know how the defendant felt but, personally, I would be very uncomfortable with the knowledge that my fate and perhaps a lengthy prison sentence would be decreed by someone dressed like Kenny from Southpark.

As if all this were not already enough to make me have an apoplectic fit of panic, I also had the utterly infuriating experience of the defence lawyer behind me (whose curtain tiebacks were all unravelling, by the way) translating everything in tandem with me, whenever he knew how to. So I would start translating what the witness had said, and would have a kind of buzzing from behind me of this idiot saying, in broken English, something slightly different yet vaguely similar to what I was planning to say. I found it impossible to translate like that and I came to a complete halt. When Judge Kenny asked what was wrong, I was so irritated that I exploded with venom:

"There's an echo in this room, coming from behind me, and I can't concentrate!"

He did not understand my point at first, but the two other lawyers on the panel beside Judge Kenny reflected for a moment, laughed, and told him what was going on. Italians are unused to sarcasm, and regard it as ingeniously subtle and witty. At this point Judge Kenny told Fraying Tassels, in no uncertain terms, to remain utterly silent. Which he did.

Thus we proceeded. After this, the next major fly in the ointment was the fact that all these characters had met each other in a doss-house run by someone called Father Nino, and somewhat inconveniently I did not know the Italian word for "doss-house." It was so frustrating that the barristers managed to ask question after question without ever using the word doss-house, to help me out, whereas Mr. Zaire used it about three times in every sentence. I think Mr. Zaire hated the place, as his poor bloodshot eyes would illuminate like burning red embers when he talked of it.

Judge Kenny was still inside his hood, so I was unable to gauge whether he had realized I was in trouble.

I called it a "*rifugio*" in Italian, desperately hoping that this would be all right even though the only context in which I know, for certain, that one can use this word in Italian is those little log cabins where hypothermic mountaineers can shelter from the snow to stave off death from exposure. This word probably came to mind because I was beginning to feel hypothermia and a touch of pneumonia coming on. It is very unfair to suffer brain-freeze without actually having eaten any ice-cream. I just hope that I have not left Judge Kenny with the impression that all these illegal African immigrants love mountaineering and reside in a hut maintained by a missionary priest at high altitude.

As we delved deeper into the sordid mystery, things became gradually more confusing. The Zairean seemed to change his mind about the turn of events whilst he was narrating them. At first, he was good friends with the lady in question but later on he did not know her very well, as she was a respectable lady married to someone else. He said rather a lot of words about her in... ooh, perhaps Swahili or maybe they were Tshiluba, which he definitely did not intend me to translate. He appeared to be very frustrated. Also, he initially only knew the defendant by sight but later on was led to admit that they were regular scrapping partners in the doss house, or Alpine mountain refuge, whichever you prefer, and Padre Nino's main activity was pulling them off each other and mopping up the blood.

There was also a most strange turn of events when he set the scene of himself and his lady friend, or rather vague acquaintance, taking a walk in the park together and then, at the moment she was set upon by the stubbly flatulent defendant, he seemed to stand by and watch up until the point when she was corporeally violated and, once he had ascertained that penetration actually took place, he ran away. Then he hooked up with her again afterwards and escorted her to the police station to make a statement, fifteen days later. When the defence lawyer asked him why he had not tried to help her, he dithered somewhat and then stated that he had been scared, although, with his history of regularly fighting the stubbly Moroccan, one might think he would only have been going over old ground. And he certainly knew where to find Padre Nino to get the blood mopped up in the mountain refuge.

These critical questions were left hanging in the balance, my impression being that the lawyers were all weary of hearing different versions of the same story and simply gave up prompting further variations. I think they were also tired of sitting in a room which smelled ever more strongly of old boiled cabbage.

A couple of weeks after this deeply traumatic event, Valentino received feedback that Judge Kenny was fully satisfied with the way I translated, and that for the work I had done for those three and a half hours I was be paid the princely sum of fourteen Euros. That is about enough money to buy a hot water bottle, or one single metallic trim curtain tieback, or perhaps about two square inches of a Gucci Scarf. Apart from the boredom and risking death through exposure, I had undergone the most stressful three hours I had ever experienced in my working career.

Valentino checked the pay scales for that type of work and, if the judge had taken into account that I had been summoned to translate as a matter of emergency, and that I had been there at their service for three and a half hours, rather than the one hour in which there was actually a stubbly defendant to hear the evidence, then I should have been paid sixty-five euros.

Judge Kenny sent an enquiry some time later via Uncle Pasquale, wanting to know if I would be interested in doing another court interpreter job. I told Uncle Pasquale that judge Kenny could take his court case and stuff it right up his anorak as far as I was concerned.

16

WE GET MARRIED FOR THE SECOND TIME, CATHOLICALLY

We wanted to arrange a church wedding as soon after the civil wedding as we could. Unexpectedly, we felt strangely in limbo being civilly married but not religiously married. We managed to set up the whole event in less than three months, so we were ready to be married in the eyes of God in early March, which was nothing short of a divine miracle, frankly. Getting through the Catholic bureaucracy, which was involved in getting married, dominated my life for those three months. For Valentino to marry me, a foreign heathen, in a Catholic church, we first needed permission from about ten men in funny hats and dresses. I learned that, in the Catholic hierarchy, the more powerful the man, the sillier the hat. We were slowly passed up the line of command and it became ever harder for me to keep my respectful-looking face on, yet somehow the power of love got me through.

After this we had to attend a pre-marital sex education course run by a celibate Catholic priest, which was hardly necessary in my case. ("Erm, I think you'll find ACTUALLY that...") In all seriousness, the premarital course was interesting as I learned a lot about the bible and about Catholics that I may otherwise never have found out. For example, apparently it is all right to enjoy sex, indeed it is actively encouraged. But only with your husband. And only if you want a baby to result from it.

The serious content of the course was an examination of what each partner thought marriage means. We were encouraged, as couples, to contemplate our personal means of resolving disagreements and to talk about whether we think we have reached the most effective way of doing so. Some of the rules of a Catholic marriage were laid out clearly. When a couple marries, they become a family. Their parents and the rest of their previous family are now their relatives, but no longer their immediate family unit. This means that the opinions or needs of your spouse absolutely always come before your mother, for example. Married couples make decisions together. They must make all choices that have an impact on the family, together. Mothers-in-law have to butt out.

In Italian there is no specific expression for being sexually unfaithful. The only word Italians use is "betrayal", and they use it to mean not only an errant act of sex but also other types of betrayal, such as spending every evening at the pub and leaving your wife at home with the children, or spending half a day at the hairdresser's and letting your husband come home and find no dinner ready, or talking to your mother or sister about intimate matters that should only be discussed with your spouse.

I found the course thought provoking and, in fact, I spent the whole time realising how lucky I was to have found Valentino, and feeling more and more certain that he was my lifetime soul mate. This was a relief since we were, of course, already married. Two couples on the course with us split up as a result of the soul searching they did on this course. I wonder how many divorces could be avoided if all couples underwent a counselling course like this *before* getting married, analysing their expectations and agreeing on the rules, rather than searching for help from a marriage guidance counsellor, or just giving up on their marriage, when their poorly thought-out and differing assumptions prove false, or things all go wrong under external pressure.

I tried to make our wedding a mix of Sicilian and English traditions. This proved to be difficult. In the end, we had a wedding unlike any other.

Valentino stayed with his mother the night before the wedding. My younger sister Josephine, who was also my bridesmaid, stayed at our house whilst my parents and my older sister Susy, with my little nephew, stayed in the hotel across the road.

"They have comfortable beds," explained my mother.

"And showers that actually work," added Susy.

On the big day, the appallingly enthusiastic Italian wedding photographers, all six of them, appeared at my house at seven in the morning, expecting to photograph me wandering about in an attractive negligée having my hair lovingly curled by a team of hairdressers, then doused in several cans of hairspray, prancing about my (very tidy) bedroom trying on various pearl necklaces and having a few finishing touches added to my already immaculate pancake make-up. Then I would loll about on the bed among some satiny, lacy cushions before posing some more in my wedding gown.

They had actually brought a collection of potted plants to pose around the house, just to make it look more.... more what? More like a jungle? I have no idea.

What they actually found was my sister and me running up and down the stairs past each other in bras that clashed with our knickers, shouting things like;

"Do you think if I eat cheese for breakfast I'll have bad breath?"

"I need the hairdryer *now*!"

"If you're making a third pot of espresso can you bring me one with six sugars in it?"

"My feet must have grown. These shoes are crippling me. Can I try on some of yours?"

"I can't answer the door in my knickers! YOU've got to open it, and WAIT TILL I'VE GOT UPSTAIRS!"

The situation was so desperate that we ordered them to go for a walk and photograph the beach and come back an hour later.

When they arrived for a second time, the rest of the family had also arrived, and we were all assembled in the sitting room trying to resolve a bit of a crisis. My younger sister is very voluptuous. Her bridesmaid's dress displayed her voluptuousness to its fullest extent.

I am afraid I inflicted this on her myself, although it was completely unintentional. I had personally tried the dress on, since I had to buy it in her absence, and I had thought it looked flattering yet modest. Unfortunately, by the time she flew down to Sicily and tried it on, we realised that, on her, the effect was very different. Most women with a cleavage like hers earn their living from it and have had to invest a small fortune in silicone to get the look. She, on the other hand, was given it all by nature, and spends every summer feeling sporadically upset, intimidated or furious at all the undesired attention she receives. The summer we holidayed in Sicily together and I met Valentino, she broke down in tears one day when it all became too much for her.

"It's not fair!" she wailed. "When you go to the beach you look like a girl in a bikini. When I go to the beach I look like pornography! It's not fair! Snot fair!"

It had been too late to exchange the dress, so now, on the morning of the wedding, our resourceful mother was experimenting with an attractive silk wrap. The idea was good but there was simply not enough fabric to go round.

"It looks like a hanky draped over two beach balls," I said.

"It's better than nothing," snapped Mother.

She studied the effect for a moment with one hand held over her mouth.

"Or maybe not," she concluded.

Next we found a large Pashmina shawl which matched the dress.

"She looks like an extra from *Les Miserables*," said our other sister Susy.

"Well, what the heck are we going to do?" wailed my Mother. She sounded desperate now. "How can she go to church like this?"

"It's a house of worship," said Josephine firmly. "Everyone's minds should be on higher things."

So we set off, trying to keep our minds on higher things although, in that dress, even I had difficulty looking my sister in the eye when I was talking to her.

The English guests, about forty friends and relatives who had flown down and all stayed in the hotel across the road, united outside my front door with about half the Sicilian guests, and any other villager who fancied joining in, waiting for me to emerge. I battled my way through the undergrowth, arranged artfully around my doorway by the photographers, to a chorus of shutter clicking. The English women wore frocks covered in pastel coloured flowers and large hats with fake roses on. The few Sicilian women who came to my house instead of waiting at the church were in black evening gowns dripping with black sequins, black shawls, black lace head coverings, black stockings, black shoes and dark, black, black, black, black, black sunglasses from Gucci's new Summer collection.

I spent a long time fiddling with the front door key which got jammed in the lock, while the photographers documented the whole fiasco with multiple views of my backside. Then I hooked my arm through my father's, and off we went. Our procession on foot through the village gave me the chance to greet all my new friends as we strode through the narrow streets. A gang of little boys ran along to join us, shouting excitedly. The Sicilian men following behind my father and me in their fabulously sharp black suits and dark sunglasses made the biggest racket they could, singing in Sicilian, shouting bawdy jokes, and shooing the village's resident stray dogs away cheerfully. The net-curtain lady pulled her curtains back and fully exposed her face to daylight to express her best wishes, Oxygen Man and his wife looked delighted to see me, and Giuseppe came out of the ice-cream parlour and stood on the pavement watching the whole procession go by with a grin of satisfaction, waving a pair of ice-cream cones at us all.

Italian brides favour the 'meringue' style of wedding dress, and I am sure the Sicilians all thought my English bias-cut satin looked like a nightie, but I did not care. At least my veil was very flouncy by way of compensation, rather like those netting balls you can use to make lots of lather in the shower. My father was so proud of me, and probably so relieved to be marrying my off at long last, that he had tears in his eyes at one point. Or perhaps it was the bracing wind blasting in from the sea.

The entrance to the little village church was decked out in white flowers, and the priest was hovering excitedly behind Valentino and The Godmother at the church door. The Godmother looked for a moment as if she disapproved of my attire, and I am sure she was thinking that I would have looked far better wearing an additional, say, eighty metres or so of fabric. To her credit, though, she rallied quickly when she realised Valentino was appreciating me eagerly. I suddenly wondered if the flimsy dress outlined my lower limbs in a way Catholics would find lascivious. Should I have worn my dressing gown over the top of it? What if I was making a *brutta figura* in front of the local priest? Maybe he would refuse to christen our future children.

Luckily, my little sister Josephine was there to steal my thunder.

Our priest allowed us to do the actual marriage vows in both Italian and in English as well, for the benefit of my family and friends. First he spoke the Italian part and then my sister, the only fluent Italian and English speaker present, stood beside him in all her glory and repeated the priest's part of the vows in English. Many Catholics commented to me that it was remarkably kind and liberal of a Catholic priest to allow this dual ceremony, as many would have refused such a deviation from the usual rigid formula. They said he may have been risking disapproval from the higher echelons of the Catholic hierarchy. Considering the way my sister was dressed, I think he may even have been risking excommunication.

I had coached Valentino to say his vows in English. He managed to recite almost everything quite well. His only hiccough came over the line 'I promise to love and honour you for the rest of my days.'

He mispronounced this, perhaps deliberately, as,

"I promise to love and annoy you for the rest of my days."

His brother Alberto regularly leant over in comic style to check with my little nephew Jim whether Valentino was really speaking English properly. I was so distracted by the enthusiastic exchange of 'thumbs up' signals that I actually fluffed one of my own lines, and provoked an exchange of 'thumbs down' signals between them instead.

The gradual progression through the vows, especially after the interminable wait through a Catholic-length sermon beforehand, felt like such an exciting climax that I developed a tight knot in my stomach. As we spoke each line, bringing me closer and closer to being Valentino's wife, his religious wife, I almost trembled with excitement and delight.

Meanwhile Josephine was dabbling in method acting, and so enjoying her role as a pulpit-thumping Catholic preacher that she started to develop a hint of an Irish accent. She was delivering her lines in the style of Ian Paisley. She stabbed the air with her index finger. She raised her voice to a volume that roared through the apse and echoed inside the cupola. She left heart-stopping dramatic pauses that could strike the holy fear of God into any living man.

We all felt her building up to a spectacular conclusion. Her hair had unravelled and taken on a life of its own. There were veins standing up on her temples. By the time she raised her arm and boomed out the immortal words,

"What God has joined, let no man cast asunder!"

my hair was being blasted backwards by her breath. The dramatic tension was so intense that I fully expected a streak of lightning to smash the stained glass window to smithereens, flash down through the nave of the church and rend the altar in two. She pronounced us man and wife to a spontaneous standing ovation and, as the thunderous applause died down, I noticed the Padre mouthing 'brava' to her. Even The Godmother looked satisfied with a job well done. As we left the church, I think my sister may actually have got more confetti chucked over her than I did.

Dear old Saint Rosalia was proving to be not only the most rapid and reliable wish-granter in the Catholic panoply of saints, but also the most thorough, since she had just granted my wish number two twice. What if she was doing this instead of granting wish number three, a baby, I suddenly thought?

The next stage of the wedding, for me and Valentino, was the photographic session. Italians leave their guests hanging around for at least two hours between the church ceremony and the reception, while they wander off to a range of arty-farty locations to have several million photographs taken in pretentious poses. Their guests are not entertained with nibbles and drinks. They are left with nothing, as it is considered rude to start eating or even drinking before welcoming the happy couple to the reception.

I had argued about this constantly before the wedding, employing and honing all my techniques of conflict resolution discussed at the pre-marital course, but to no avail.

"It's just rude," I said.

"Don't be silly, we have to have wedding photographs," said

Valentino.

"Yes, of us *at the wedding*," I retorted.

"Of course, and at other places as well," said Valentino.

"At least we should give the guests some drinks while they wait," I said.

"That's not the tradition," said Valentino.

I realised I would never win when the caterers laughed aloud at my suggestion that they served drinks to my guests while they awaited my arrival at the reception. They refused point blank to comply.

"Signora," they told me, "that's not how we do weddings here."

In the end I arranged with the hotel, where my guests were staying, that they would return there for a couple of hours and have a few simple nibbles and drinks before being taken by coach to the reception.

I envied them. I had to stand around being photographed on picturesque cliffs overlooking the sea in a howling wind, hoping my veil would not take flight and drag me over the edge in some dangerous parody of hang gliding; then lean elegantly against quaint fishing boats, posing for the cameras while hoping not to spend the rest of my wedding day with a green, slimy bottom; then drape myself languidly against some scratchy olive tree and kiss Valentino on the lips, but not really kiss him because that makes you look ugly in the photos, just touch his mouth with my lips, and put one hand exactly *there* and the other right *there*. No, *there*.

The reception was held in a seventeenth century villa in Palermo. Nearly all villas in Palermo date from the seventeenth century. This is because Palermo was rich at that time. Everything has been developing cracks since then.

So, there we were in our seventeenth century villa which, like most buildings in Palermo, looked crumbly yet stunningly beautiful. At Italian weddings the bride and groom sit on their own, at a cosy little table for two overlooking all their guests. This avoids the problem, at English weddings, of making the in-laws pretend to enjoy each other's company for an entire meal while sitting opposite an empty space and talking to each other sideways. In the case of our in-laws, the problem would have been compounded by the fact that my parents cannot speak a word of Italian and Valentino's parents cannot speak a word of English. Whenever my father meets foreigners he speaks a language of his own invention, called Foreign, which is a melange of any words he happens to know in French, Spanish, Portuguese, German, Arabic, Welsh and occasionally Japanese. He constructs whole sentences in this more global successor to Esperanto, but regrettably the only person who can understand him is me.

To overcome the language problem our parents would face, Valentino and I decided to sit them at a table with some cousins of Valentino's, who speak both Italian and English. Unfortunately, they were so confused by my father's way of speaking that the whole table ended up playing charades over dinner and not saying a word in any language at all. The waiters joined in and at their table there was more laughing than at any other.

Since all the tables were having a whale of a time, though, Valentino and I mingled like the Mad Hatter's tea party, sitting wherever we fancied and joining in our guests' conversations. The English guests thought that the seafood buffet, which was actually a kind of pre-starter before the main starter, was the entire meal.

"That was wonderful," said my aunt Felicity. "But I'm so full I can hardly move!"

"Muy delizioso, sharken fishen sushi essen," said my father.

"Same here," said my sister Susy. "I hope they'll leave a good long pause before the cake cutting so I can let it go down."

"Me too," said my nephew Jim. "I ate a whole righty-ho fish and some octopus suckers as well."

"Oh, is that what they were?" said my mother, leaning over to listen in from the next table. "I ate an awful lot of smoked salmon. I'm not sure I could manage any cake at all."

"That was a wonderful starter," I overheard The Godmother saying in Italian to Valentino. "Nice and light so as not to take our appetites away for the real starter. Ah, here it comes."

A squadron of waiters appeared with large plates of pasta.

"Who's that for?" asked my Mother in English.

"Buon appetito," said The Godmother, smiling back at her.

By the time the first part of the main course, a mouth-watering risotto, was served, the English guests were looking scared. When it came to a plate of steak and then another plate of fish, they had given up completely and did not even pretend to eat it. The Sicilians wolfed down the lot and immediately started looking out for the pudding buffet so they could plan their battle charge tactics carefully, to make sure they were in the vanguard. During this important strategic hiatus, the bilingual conversation at cross-purposes continued.

"It's nice to sit down to a sensible wedding dinner where a reasonable, eatable amount of food is served," said my new father-in-law in Italian, contentedly patting his tummy, "rather than these traditional weddings where they just show off by serving up more food than anyone can eat."

"Yes," agreed The Godmother, "and then you have to shove it down out of politeness, just to make a *bella figura*."

"Have they all got four stomachs like ruminants?" asked my mother. "I mean, where on earth do they put it?"

"They'll live on nothing but mineral water and fags for the next three days," I told her. "From a physiological point of view, I've no idea how they do it."

"Are there a lot of diabetics and people with thyroid problems?" asked my father.

"How did you know?" I asked. "They all have one or the other by the time they're middle aged."

"Exactamundo," he said, nodding to Valentino. "Tres mal, tres mal essen zu viel. Muy mal."

There were three puddings per person but the Sicilians all took six each, except the diabetic ones, who took ten. The English guests were polite, were elbowed out of the way, and were left with a few crumbs. I felt bad for them and instructed the waiters to make *absolutely* sure the English guests got at least three times as much champagne as any Sicilian. I calculated that, that way, everyone would go home happy.

After the meal, Valentino's friends organised the music for dancing. At normal Sicilian weddings the eating goes on all evening and then everyone staggers off to bed, but all our guests, Sicilian and English alike, agreed that the dancing idea was a fabulous way to burn off some of the thirty-thousand calories most guests had consumed at dinner. Valentino's cousin Calogero offered to teach the guests a Sicilian folk dance, so everyone gathered eagerly in a circle which filled the dance floor, arranged in couples. The music started up, a rollicking Sicilian tune with piano accordions, violins and other rowdy instruments. It sounded like English country music on cocaine.

Calogero called out directions into the microphone and we followed the instructions, weaving in and out of each other and changing partners, whirling each other around and generally laughing breathlessly. He told us he would start off with a tarantella and then move on to some other traditional dances. We were instructed to make bridges with our hands and all run under them. For another phase of the dance, the men had to go round in a figure of eight on their knees while the ladies skipped from side to side over their lower legs. The dance went on and on, and became more and more ridiculous. At one point, Calogero had us all walking in a circle, bent over with our left hands plunged down between our thighs holding our partners' hands, while our right hands were stretched out towards the buttocks of the person in front and grasping their left hands in turn.

My mother and several other older guests stood on chairs and tables to watch the whole proceedings properly. Eventually my mother was laughing so hard she fell off her chair.

At this stage my German friend Kerstin said,

"You know, I don't think this really is a traditional Sicilian folk dance."

As the dance went on and on, more and more people wanted to join in until we had all the waiters included, and five toddlers in the centre of the circle simply jumping up and down. The dance ended after forty-five minutes when Calogero noticed some of the older guests were suffering from heat exhaustion yet somehow, in the grip of dance mania, doggedly refusing to sit down.

"Was any of that a real Sicilian folk dance?" I asked Valentino as I collapsed into a seat.

"The first ten minutes or so were traditional moves, then it all became the inspiration of Calogero's brilliant mind," said Valentino. "But it was all pure Sicilian in the sense that it was very funny, and a bit mad."

Eventually the groups of guests started to melt away and I was kissed again by everyone.

"Wonderful English wedding," said the Godmother in Italian.

"That was so much fun to see a real Sicilian wedding," said my Mother in English, "though I'm afraid I need a lie down and a Rennie now."

"I'm surprised your sister didn't fall out of her dress doing that dance," said one of my new brothers-in-law. "Pity."

"Sayonara, everyone!" said my Father.

Everyone went home looking exhausted and happy, just the way Valentino and I felt.

When we reached our house, he swept me up in his strong arms, kissed me passionately, snagged my dress on the door catch and ripped a great hole in it as he carried me over the threshold into our home and the rest of our life together.

17

A BUN IN THE OVEN

For our honeymoon we chose to go on a cruise along the Nile, combining my passion for history and foreign culture with Valentino's love of water and floating vessels. The second week was to be spent in a hotel in Luxor, giving me the chance to indulge my nerdy fascination for ancient history to its fullest extent.

No sooner had we embarked aboard our small cruising vessel than I realised I was pregnant. I knew it for two reasons. Firstly, I could not even think about food without vomiting. Egyptian cuisine may not be the most distinguished in the world but, truly, it is not *that* bad. Secondly, I became so appallingly sentimental that I sometimes felt I might be losing my mind. I once caught sight of a puppy playing with some children on the riverbank and was moved to tears, blubbering about how sweet and vulnerable and innocent it was. When I saw some beautiful long-horned oxen dragging a wooden plough near Thebes, identical to the ones depicted in relief carvings inside the ancient temples, I felt an almost uncontrollable impulse to donate my life savings to allow the hapless beasts to retire in dignity, and to help the poor peasants catch up with some of the technological developments of the last six thousand years. Hormones have a sense of humour.

For every picture or statue of the Virgin Mary holding baby Jesus that you see in Sicily, you will see at least ten of Joseph proudly cuddling his new son. This emphasis on "The Virgin Father" is undoubtedly because Sicilian men are simply baby mad. I have yet to meet a single male Sicilian over the age of eighteen who does not go gooey-eyed at the sight of a young child and talk fondly of the marvellous day, hopefully in the near future, when he will become a father. Most young men in their late twenties who have remained single can be heard lamenting the fact that they still are not married and consequently, do not have any children. Have they missed the boat? They worry about these things.

Since my husband is definitely a keen contender for "most baby-mad man in Sicily", I had always anticipated a reaction of delight when the day came to inform him that I was expecting a baby. In the event, when I told Valentino my suspicions that we were expecting an additional family member for company at home in, say, about nine months, he became so excited I feared he may actually fall overboard. He tried to restrain himself in the absence of confirmation, but those magical eyes of his lit up and glowed. I am not sure how many of the sights of ancient Egypt he actually saw, because every time I looked at him his gaze was fixed upon my belly. The best thing about being pregnant - oh alright, I will be honest, the only good thing about being pregnant - is that suddenly you no longer feel obliged to suck your tummy in when being watched; you can let it hang out in all its rotund, flabby glory, and you get repeatedly congratulated on it, to boot. In fact, it tends to become public property, so that people you hardly know take it for granted they can fondle and caress it at will. I tend to suffer from colic, so I was quite pleased about this.

Despite my as yet undiagnosed affliction, the first week of the honeymoon was wonderful. We saw fabulous sights and achieved the requisite sense of romance, despite the unpleasant nature of showers on boats, which feel akin to squeezing into a vertical coffin and spitting all over yourself. The view of the Nile from the boat was beautiful, the ancient monuments were even more exciting and moving than I had hoped, and our camera did not work so we could not take pictures of any of it.

By the start of week two of our honeymoon, I had gone forty-eight hours not only without eating, but also without even being able to hold down water. After an intense discussion in a very swirly green marble hotel room with attached gold twiddles, which would have made anyone feel a bit sick but which made me feel as if I might die, we made the reluctant decision to cut the holiday short and fly home. Valentino kept me alive by purchasing miniature boiled sweets and making me practise holding them under my tongue, even when chundering, in the hopes that some of the sugar would diffuse into my blood stream.

Booking a flight out of Egypt at the last minute was so mind-curdlingly expensive that I realised the oxen and peasants would just have to wait. In fact, in my delicate condition, we were lucky the shock did not induce a miscarriage. We flew to England rather than Sicily, as it was cheaper and quicker. As we boarded the plane I caught a whiff of aeroplane fuel and started heaving as soon as I reached my seat. I had never experienced nausea-related problems on a plane before, so I was interested to find out that the first indication of an "I'm gonna hurl" expression on your face makes every single air hostess come running up to you with anti-emetic tablet. I politely declined it, explaining that I was pregnant, and was instead provided with a sheaf of about twenty sick bags, which I proceeded to fill up rapidly. A brief way into the flight, the air steward forced the person next to the toilet to exchange seats with me, reassuring everyone in the vicinity that it would be better for everyone since they had run out of bags.

We went straight from the airport to the hospital, where I told the triage nurse I was pregnant and explained how I knew. She looked as if she thought I may need the psychiatric ward. I think it was the bit about the oxen. After donating a cup of pee, the doctors looked fairly relieved to confirm that I was pregnant, and yet also concerned to inform me that I had gone into acidosis and dehydration. I was put on a glucose drip. Within a short space of time, I felt well enough to realise that the hospital was revolting and I wanted to go home to my mother's house.

When we got there, Valentino immediately got on the phone to notify every resident of Sicily and southern Italy that we were with child. Meanwhile I was raiding the fridge looking for peculiar things to gobble down as hastily as I could. Pregnancy-induced food cravings are a most peculiar experience. You yearn to eat foods you have hated your whole life, and feel sick at the thought of eating your favourite snack. I felt as if my body were possessed by an alien who was exercising ruthless mind control over my actions.

"You'll never guess what," said Valentino, looking delighted as he put the phone down. "Last month, Manfredi and Mirella went on a pilgrimage to the grotto of Santa Rosalia of Mount Pellegrino and prayed for you to get pregnant the very day we got married! That's why we've been so lucky."

"Oh, I see," I said. I was assembling a custard and broad bean sandwich which, I can assure anyone who has not yet tried it, is fairly advanced level cookery.

"Who would have thought it would work so well?" he said, literally bouncing up and down with excitement. I was more excited by the new delicacy I had invented.

I vividly remembered making a rash announcement during course seventeen of one of the family's twenty-course barbecues. I had said that I hoped to have a baby as soon as we were married, meaning that I was knocking on a bit and did not have many more fruitful years to squander. I felt my eggs may not all be of the highest quality, considering the trials I had put them through. I had become alarmed by a poster at my gynaecologist's surgery in London which said that, every time a woman gets drunk, all her future babies get drunk with her. Whilst I was never exactly a beer monster, I was nevertheless haunted by the idea that my future offspring may already be guilty of under-age drinking, and felt tormented to think what it may have done to their single-celled proto-livers. The dreaded poster also said that each time a woman gets flu, or takes a tablet, then the eggs have it too. This is why there is a progressively greater likelihood of genetic abnormalities in babies as the mother gets older. I concluded the best hope my eggs had was for them to get well away from my ovaries as fast as possible.

When I had expressed this wish, though, the words 'as soon as' had been intended to mean 'after about a year figuring out how to find my way round Palermo by car and fight for a parking space,' or at the very least 'after two weeks to enjoy a decent honeymoon and get the laundry done after returning home.' Little had I imagined that my brother- and sister-in-law would sprint off and appeal to the most diligent and prolific wish-granting saint in Catholic history, filing an application for my lifelong desire to be granted *precisely as uttered*, to the letter, on the very night we were conjoined in holy matrimony, upon our nuptial couch.

After puking up the broad bean and custard sandwich, which I still remember being delicious, by the way, I desired pickled things. I salivated with delighted anticipation as I mixed up a fabulous bowl of gherkins, pickled mushrooms, olives, capers, bell peppers and countless other delights in vinegar, rather like a fermented, savoury fruit salad. It was like the ambrosia of the gods and stayed down for a full twelve minutes.

Why don't you have something plain like boiled rice?" suggested Valentino as I was rummaging in the fridge for something else to scoff down, despite knowing I would puke it up again. It was like being bulimic.

"Rice! Euch!" I exclaimed, horrified. "How gross!"

I later overheard him worrying to my mother in the next room, while she explained a few of the basics of pregnancy to him. For those who have never had the experience of being pregnant, I shall explain briefly the medical background. Human gestation allegedly lasts nine months, although the afflicted woman frequently experiences perceptional distortion and feels that she is actually pregnant for nine years instead. Palliative care is the only resource available to manage this symptom, and this consists of making frequent and obsessive reference to a calendar. Doctors encourage this by asking the patient which day her last period began, and then writing it down, so frequently that she cannot forget it even when her child is about twenty years old. Ask any mother the date of her last period before each of her children was conceived and she will blurt it out instantly without hesitation, even when she is so senile she no longer remembers their birthdays or even their names. This treatment by the doctor encourages a kind of nostalgia for menstruation in the pregnancy-afflicted woman which may be mentally harmful.

The gestation period is divided by the medical profession into three trimesters. Each trimester, or three month period, has distinct symptoms. The first trimester closely resembles a severe hangover, with the relentless nausea that turns into copious vomiting at the first whiff of some pongy aftershave or a waft of car exhaust. It is a lot like one of those hangovers where you drift in and out of consciousness with your chin resting on the rim of the toilet bowl saying the Booze Abusers' Prayer: "Dear God, I swear I will never, ever, ever drink a drop of alcohol ever again if only you will please stop my brain rotating within my skull right now!" and then before you can say "Amen" you chunder once more and slump to the floor. The pregnancy hangover doesn't go away at all for three long months, unfortunately, no matter how long and hard you pray. Therefore, to experience the sensation of the first trimester for yourself, drink a full bottle of whisky each evening and then have some wobbly raw eggs on mouldy bread for breakfast, and then go out and sniff a tramp's armpit. Repeat daily for twelve weeks.

The sensation of the second trimester can easily be experienced by putting on about seven woollen jumpers in August and then stuffing a hot water bottle up the innermost one. Turn on your central heating to the highest setting and then add a backpack full of bricks, slung on the wrong way round, and go for a long jog, up and down the stairs, until your back feels as if several discs have slipped out of place and one of your hips is occasionally popping out of its socket. The colloquial expression "to have a bun in the oven" is derived from the fact that pregnant women do, indeed, feel so hot they can achieve the temperature of a normal domestic oven. Drink ten or twelve cups of espresso to ensure your heart nearly beats out of your throat each time you move and be sure to sleep with the backpack strapped on tightly, so you cannot breathe properly. Also, put on a pair of boots three sizes too small for you so that your feet are in excruciating pain every time you walk. You will need to tip itching powder into your clothes on a daily basis to simulate the uncontrollable itching you would feel if a genuine bun in the oven were stretching your abdominal skin to about twenty times its natural size.

For the third trimester, add a whalebone corset inside the hot water bottle, laced up so tightly you are almost fainting from suffocation, double the itching powder, and add a small wallaby to the bricks in the rucksack, so that you get kicked in the guts, hard enough to be winded, several times an hour. Have someone beat a mallet against the small of your back as soon as it stops hurting, to ensure the pain is relentless and intense. Replace the boots with a new pair five sizes too small, and sprinkle some gravel into them before putting them on to simulate the sensation of the newly forming bunions you would have forming on your feet if you were genuinely in the family way. If you are truly committed to feeling the experience of motherhood for yourself, you could try eating a handful of electric plugs because as they come out, this just might give you a faux sensation of what it feels like to get fourth degree haemorrhoids as a result of your pelvic floor collapsing under the weight of another person crouching on it day in, day out.

We stayed in England for a week until I felt ready to face the flight back to Palermo, which meant that Valentino had the unique honour of spending his honeymoon with his in-laws. Lesser men might have been broken by the experience, but my brave Valentino rose to the occasion like a hero. Whilst my mother was filling me in on the medical information outlined above, and other important facts regarding my life over the next nine months, Valentino carried out a Sicilian-style invasion of the kitchen single-handedly. He dedicated himself to ensuring the proper nutrition of his offspring.

"I can't even get into the kitchen to make a cup of tea," said my mother in a rather bemused voice one morning. "I don't understand how he fills the place up so extensively. It's quite a big room and there's only one of him."

"It's a genetic thing," I explained. "You should see them when they're working in packs. You can't even *look* into the room."

"Well, I suppose it doesn't matter," said Mother. "The rest of the family can dine like kings on your leftovers. In fact I think we'll all have to go on diets when you go home."

After a week I was feeling stronger, so we booked the flight back to Palermo. My sister Susy telephoned ahead to warn the budget airline to stock up on extra sick bags. They answered that I would be absolutely barred from boarding the plane if there was any chance whatsoever that I might be taken ill on it, and then they asked for my name. Susy told them I was called Penelope P. Knut, with a silent K. She spelled it out for them several times and they noted it down carefully.

At the airport, Valentino placed himself at the head of the throng and put up a heroic fight for the seats beside the toilet, which actually nobody wanted anyway because the engine noise is so bad you cannot hear what anyone is saying, even for several hours after landing. When we emerged from airport security, there was a welcoming committee of about three hundred of Valentino's closest relatives, waiting to greet the newest member of the family. I was given a pretty warm welcome myself, too, but it was my tummy that was greeted like a celebrity.

I discovered that Sicilian driving was another of the triggers that made my stomach decide to evict all its contents. So was the smell of Sicilian street stalls selling grilled innards. So was the smell of any other vehicle on the road. So was the smell of anyone who had eaten garlic lately. So was the smell of any house that had had its floor washed recently; in other words, all houses in Sicily.

When I got home I realised that my nasal sensitivities would shame a bloodhound. I would be sick each time the neighbour smoked a cigarette inside his own living room, even when my windows were closed. The fumes of petrol wafting off our car down in the garage smelled so strong to me in the living room, even though there were two doors between the garage and the house, that we had to park it outside instead. When Valentino arrived home from work, he had to hoot the horn of his motorbike loudly before approaching the house so I would have time to close the kitchen window. Otherwise, the fumes would waft upwards and.... well, I think the pattern is emerging quite clearly.

Because of these smell problems, I spent the first month of the pregnancy losing weight rather than gaining it. I was rushed off to hospital for blood tests. Lots of blood tests. Waiting in a hospital while you feel ill only makes you feel even worse.

The hospital Valentino took me to was called *Ospedale Buccheri La Ferla Fatebene Fratelli*. The Sicilians are good at coming up with catchy names that way. Buccheri and La Ferla are the names of the founders. The Fatebene Fratelli translates as The Do Good Brothers. Although they sound as if they should be wearing dark glasses and playing saxophones, they are actually an order of monks, who lurk in the corridors annoying the patients.

They mean well, but they all have medieval-looking skin diseases that make you desperately hope they won't come any closer. I'm sure they all have nothing worse than eczema or psoriasis, or maybe a few septic bedbug bites in the most severe cases, but there's something about seeing them in their full-length brown monks' habits and white cord belts, with knots all along them, that makes you think of leprosy, scrofula and smallpox. It's like an intensified form of how it feels to wait in a dermatologist's waiting room; nobody wants to handle the magazines, and everyone sits in a funny way to make sure no part of their bare skin comes into direct contact with the seats.

The Do Good Brothers dedicate their lives in Buccheri La Ferla hospital to trying to make patients join them in the hospital chapel for a brief spot of group prayer, Gregorian chanting and bible reading. I was approached by a rather desperate looking fellow, who guaranteed it would take no longer than ten minutes. He assured all the waiting patients around me that he would only do one prayer, and that he could recite it super fast. He promised that the bible reading would be so short it would seem like a Haiku poem. Eventually he offered to skip the Gregorian chanting altogether. Yet still nobody wanted to go.

Was it because the patients were scared their name would get called to have their X-ray taken while they were off saying the Lord's prayer, so they'd miss their turn and have to book another appointment in a month's time? Was it that they had already been on a pilgrimage to seek a cure for whatever disease they had, and reckoned some extra last-minute praying would be superfluous? Or was it the angry-red, peely exposed dermis on that Do Good Brother's hands, dotted with pustules, which may have recently come into direct contact with the prayer books in the chapel?

Finally the Do Good Brother gave up, failing to disguise the fact that he was exasperated and disappointed with the lot of us, and probably felt a bit sore and itchy inside his habit. He headed off for some solitary prayer, again. He probably consoled himself by fervently reciting prayers in Latin, whilst mortifying his flesh with a flagellant, an even scratchier hair shirt and some extremely stingy iodine lotion.

The outcome of my blood tests was that everything was fine, the pregnancy was proceeding normally and all I had to do was eat more. Therefore, for the second month of the pregnancy, Valentino took matters in hand and initiated a feeding campaign similar to that used in France for the production of paté *fois gras*. I started to gain weight despite the astounding frequency with which food persisted in moving in the wrong direction. I also discovered a charming habit of the Sicilians with pregnant women. If you have a pregnant belly and anyone is eating in public, the minute they lay eyes on you they offer you some of what they are eating. This is because you may suffer from a craving and feel desperate for whatever you have just seen.

This cultural habit of feeding up pregnant women arises from the traditional Sicilian belief that birthmarks are the imprint of an unsatisfied craving the mother suffered during pregnancy. People will say "My daughter Giusy was born with the desire for cherries" as they point out a red patch on the child's leg, meaning that their endless craving for cherries while pregnant literally stamped itself on the baby. Many people are fully convinced that the phenomenon is scientific fact, and believe that refusing a pregnant woman food might actually cause her baby to be born disfigured.

The gravity of this situation means that pregnant women are offered all kinds of foods utterly unsuited to their condition. Fishermen in the village would approach me as I walked past, wielding raw sea food. I was sometimes presented with lumps of unpasteurised cream cheese. Valentino soon trained me that I was never allowed to refuse anything. I was to accept it graciously and then slip it to him.

"We mustn't offend people," he grinned, as he surreptitiously slurped down the last of a tray of raw sea urchins.

It was shortly after we got back from our honeymoon that I realised I could not stay in the house while Mary Poppins was cleaning. The smell of absolutely any cleaning product made me throw up. I asked her to come two mornings a week instead of all day once a week, and I camped out in the ice-cream parlour with Giuseppe Ice-cream until the clouds of ammonia and perfumed toilet cleaner had wafted away. I used to take my computer with me to work on my translations, and sometimes taught English lessons there, too, to a doctor who could not manage any other time. I could not stomach ice-cream or coffee, so I left a stash of my own teabags with Giuseppe and he made me cups of tea at twenty minute intervals.

Valentino became suspicious when he continued to come home from work and find the house spotless, yet noticed I ran to the bathroom and made horrible sound effects every time he so much as sprayed a kitchen work surface with disinfectant. In the end I just had to confess.

He heaved out a sigh, and said nothing. A few minutes later I heard him on the phone telling his brother and laughing like a drain, so I knew it was no problem.

"Do you want me to tell her to stop coming?" I asked when he finished the phone call.

"What?" he asked me. "Are you mad?"

18

I GET CURED BY A WITCH DOCTOR

"We're going on an outing tomorrow," Valentino announced one Friday afternoon. "We'll have to get up early, as it's the other side of Sicily."

The next morning we set off early. We were going to Tindari, famous for its statue of a black Madonna with a black baby Jesus. Like most of the "black Madonna" statues from places where the majority of the population is white, she is carved out of wood, and so was originally light-skinned. Wood darkens over time so, eventually, she became black. This transformation meant she was not just another Madonna statue but, rather, something rare, precious and the product of a miracle; and so pilgrims visited her from far and wide.

She dates from around 800 AD, according to a guide book I sneakily read beside a souvenir stand without actually buying it; Valentino has said we had been spending rather too much, and ought to economise. This explained why he always offered to hold my handbag for me when I went to the toilet. He was worried I might get distracted by something for sale on the way.

The walk up to the sanctuary, which is actually a huge church, was lined with stalls selling souvenirs. There was a forest of black plastic madonnas in all sizes, ranging from the two euro pocket size all the way up to thirty euro whoppers as big as Sicilian grandmothers, beside mountains of rosary beads, and just in front of various black Madonna bumper stickers saying "My driver went all the way to the sanctuary of Tindari and all he bought me was this Black Madonna bumper sticker," or something along those lines. I could not read them properly as Valentino was nervously pulling me away. In among them was a most peculiar tourist souvenir; a collection of pirates' heads carved out of coconut shells, complete with red bandanas and gold earrings.

The Madonna of Tindari is carved from a rare type of cedar wood which comes from Turkey and the Middle East, according to the guide book I don't have, and was brought to Sicily by sailors in the Byzantine era. Legend has it that the ship upon which she was being transported – where to, nobody knows - was driven into the bay of Tindari by a ferocious storm. The sailors dumped most of the cargo on the beach to make the ship more manoeuvrable, and set out again. Another storm blew up, more violent than the previous one, and drove them back onto the beach once more. They deposited the statue as well, the last thing they had on board, and set sail with their fingers crossed. This time they got away safely and floated off into the sunset.

Meanwhile the small number of Sicilian bumpkins who eked out a living in the remains of the once grand city of Tyndaris, founded by the Ancient Greeks, were most excited by what they found on their gorgeous strip of beach. She was already a centuries old antique, from a far off land, and she was black skinned with a black baby; yet she was clearly the Madonna with baby Jesus. The locals took her up to their tiny church on the top of the high peak overlooking the bay of Tindari, and there they prayed to her. News spread of the miraculous way she had come to Tindari, and of her remarkable black skin, and pilgrims began arriving from distant places.

The Mediterranean was plagued by pirates in those days, and a gang of Algerian desperadoes under the command of a ruthless leader called Rais Dragut destroyed the original church in 1544, along with the entire town, so a new one was built as soon as possible. This made sense of the coconut pirate heads! They were Rais Dragut and his gang.

"Let's go inside the church," said Valentino.

"Of course," I agreed.

Our Lady of Tindari now stands in a completely modern church, finished in 1979. It was decorated with mosaics and stained glass windows in fairly traditional style, yet the modern touches were obvious in all the details.

"It's a bit of a Disney church, isn't it?" I commented.

"What a beautiful church," said Valentino, who had not heard me.

The Madonna statue was displayed up on high above the altar, and beneath her was a Bible quotation in Latin, from the Song of Songs: *Nigra sum sed Formosa*, 'I am black but I am beautiful.'

Despite the Disney touches, the decorations in the church were very beautiful. The interior walls are entirely decorated with mosaics depicting scenes from the life of the Madonna. The tesserae are exceptionally small, so they contain a great amount of detail. One showed Joseph, with Jesus as a young boy. Statues and images of Joseph with the young Jesus are so common in Sicily that you see them more often than images of the Madonna and child. In a culture where fathers are so involved with their children and such active parents, it was inevitable that a church dedicated to the Madonna had to have at least one image of the father and son. The inscription with the mosaic said 'Saint Joseph intervenes to help us.'

I sat on one of the pews, feeling appallingly heavy and hot, and said a little prayer to ask the Madonna to help me have a painless childbirth.

"Alright, if you cannot manage painless, at least bearable," I begged her. Valentino leaned over from behind, put his hand on my stomach and patted it lovingly as we looked at the mosaic of Joseph together.

From the piazza outside the church we saw a marvellous view over the bay. When the sea level is low, the beach forms a strange shape which looks like the black Madonna and her child viewed side-on. Story has it that a pilgrim in early Medieval times, who had a small baby, refused to pray to the Madonna because she was black. When she left the church she slipped and dropped her baby, who slid right down to the beach but was saved from drowning by the strange strip of sand which rose up to save him, and the miracle restored her faith, so she went back to the church to pray to the black Madonna in thanks.

A tragedy of Greek proportions took place during the third month of my pregnancy.

It all began when Valentino collected Mary Poppins and, after no more than five minutes of sanitising the light switches, she burst into tears. She explained that she had found out her son had joined the Mafia and was selling drugs, and she was desperate to buy him out. Joining the Mafia is like signing up for fifteen years in the army and joining a brainwashing cult like the Moonies, all rolled into one. New recruits are first made to perform some crime before Mafia witnesses so that they are unable to report anything to the police without risking imprisonment themselves. Then they are required to work their way up to a sufficient level to become a fully-fledged member by performing various tasks. At this point they are sent to brainwashing centres which last at least two weeks and during which they are told that their family no longer matters, the police and other authorities no longer matter, and that they are honoured members of the Mafia, which is their only family now: the Mafia is wonderful, the Mafia is great, the Mafia is their life from now on. The programme uses all the tried and tested techniques of established cults, including repetitive brain washing combined with dietary protein deprivation to increase impressionability, the presence of good guys and bad guys, to create deep feelings of personal allegiance to the leaders perceived as protective allies, and the imposition of unpleasant punishments, all of which ultimately create the effect of Stockholm Syndrome.

Mary Poppins was desperate to buy her son out of the Mafia and she asked if we needed her to do any more work. She would increase her hours as much as we were willing. Could we recommend her to any of the neighbours? She needed to earn as much money as she possibly could. I immediately started to go through all the neighbours in my head who might need a cleaning lady and promised to phone them all. Valentino fell quiet and slipped out of the room and, when I went looking for the phone, it was missing.

"Wait," he told me. "You can call them later. In fact it's better to talk to them in person."

He was out of the house for the rest of the day. That evening he told me, "That's the last time she enters this house."

I was bewildered by his attitude, and felt upset too.

"You mean you're penalising her for being honest?" I said. "She's not a crook. The whole reason she told us was because she is horrified, and she wants to get her son back on the straight and narrow. Why don't you want to help her?"

"I'm a lawyer," said Valentino. "If I have any demonstrable connection whatsoever with a member of the Mafia I can never work again. The fact that I know about her son means I can't talk to her again without reporting him to the police. In fact I ought to report what she has told us today to the police. I'll pretend I never heard it, but I can't let her come here again, and pretend again. Anyway, she wants to buy him out, but what about him? He may not have the same attitude as her, in fact I'm sure he doesn't. We don't even know her attitude for sure. What people say and what they truly think are rarely the same."

"So that's it? No more Mary Poppins?" I asked.

"No more Mary Poppins," he said, definitively. "I'm sorry. I'll look for another cleaning woman."

After two weeks, Valentino managed to find a new lady, who came highly recommended by Signor Bruno, the owner of the lemon orchard opposite our house where I once hallucinated. Her sister was his own cleaner. She was the wife of a fisherman in the village and they needed extra money because his back problems had become so severe that he needed a major operation, and was currently unable to work. Her name was Ninfa, which means nymph.

Ninfa, regrettably, did not have any form of obsessive compulsive disorder like Mary Poppins, but I liked her immediately. She asked me if we could talk to each other using the informal, friendly form of you instead of the formal, polite one. This led to asking each other's ages, as it is usually the older person who authorises the younger one to switch to the informal mode of speech, and so we found out that we were born on exactly the same day.

Ninfa's eyes looked maternal and kind, and she was very lively and extroverted without being overbearing. She gave me all kinds of advice about living in Sicily, whilst also filling me in on village gossip. Sometimes I used to drop in on her at home in the village just for a chat.

One day, I nearly got run over on my way out of the post office. As it turned out, the driver swerved in the nick of time, swore in Sicilian, and drove off, so essentially nothing actually happened, yet I was left in a state of utter agitation. Being pregnant made me feel a heightened sense of vulnerability, as if whatever happened to me had happened directly to my precious baby.

Instead of going straight home, I decided to drop in on Ninfa in order to let off steam by gibbering at her. She was having breakfast sitting just inside her front door - which meant she was in the middle of her kitchen - having a shouted chat with the neighbour across the road, who happened to be sitting in her kitchen, drinking coffee. Despite both being in their separate homes, they were not fifteen feet from each other, having breakfast together.

"I knew something was wrong," Ninfa said. "You're so pale and wiped out. You've got worms. I could see it."

"What did you say?" I asked, assuming I had misunderstood.

"You've got worms," she repeated, slowly.

"I definitely haven't," I said. "I just had a scare."

She laughed like a drain. "That's what I mean," she said. "In Sicilian, we say you've got worms if you've had a big scare and you can't calm down afterwards. It feels as if you've got worms in your tummy, creeping around and keeping you agitated. It's very bad to have worms when you're pregnant. I'll do the prayer to heal the worms for you. It's our thing, a kind of magic medicine."

A prayer? To heal metaphorical worms? I agreed, purely because I was curious to find out what this "prayer" would be like.

"Are you English?" asked Ninfa's neighbour, suddenly.

"Yes," I confirmed, "from London." She came out to have a better look at me. She was wearing a cerise velour tracksuit, with a sequinned motif all over the front, and a pair of golden trainers with a rhinestone decoration at the sides.

"It must be wonderful there," she said, her eyes drifting off dreamily.

"Yes, what on earth are you doing in this dump when you could be somewhere as wonderful as that?" asked Ninfa's mother from above us. I had not noticed her, up on her balcony. Ninfa's white-haired mother always wore black since her husband had died three years ago.

"Mamma, how would you know what London's like?" asked Ninfa, laughing.

"Well it's more famous than Aspra," her mother answered. "Do you take me for an idiot?"

Ninfa laughed, then stood up and led me into her kitchen.

"I'm closing the door now," said Ninfa. The lady across the road gave an understanding look, and glanced at me encouragingly. I was receiving medical treatment. Neighbours were not allowed to watch.

My newly self-appointed witch doctor poured some olive oil onto a plate and made me stand near it, by the table. She lifted up my top to expose my bare tummy, and told me to close my eyes and try to think only of the olive oil. Then she dipped her thumb into the oil, closed her eyes, and started to make a very tiny sign of the cross in the oil on my tummy, over and over again, while muttering a rhythmic poem too quietly for me to hear. Maybe it was the rubbing, which was quite relaxing. Maybe her voice was very soothing. Maybe the prayer really did have power and maybe olive oil actually does have magical properties. But it worked. I actually felt perfectly calm at the end of it. The worms were gone.

Olives and their oil have been central to all Mediterranean and Middle Eastern cultures for many thousands of years. Olive oil is packed with nutritious substances and it is literally impossible for bacteria to grow in it, so it became a central part of medicine in ancient times as it genuinely can cure many types of infection. Some oil was made specifically for medicinal purposes, and was pressed from bitter olives, either unripe ones or wild ones which taste far too awful to eat. For the ancient Greeks and Romans its cleansing qualities made it ideal for washing, in place of soap. This is almost certainly why it also took on a role in ritual purifications.

The oil was the mainstay of many economies, and such a source of wealth that it was used to anoint Kings. Oil that had gone rancid was never thrown away, but burnt in oil lamps to make light after the sun went down, and for this reason became part of many sacred rituals performed in dark, gloomy temples. Olive oil is still the only oil allowed to be used in certain sacred rites in the Jewish, Christian and Muslim faiths.

Perhaps I had been privy to a healing ritual used for hundreds of years?

Ninfa told me that the magic of the prayer can only be passed on to another person on Christmas Eve, at midnight. You teach the prayer to the person you have chosen to share it with, and they have to memorise it there and then. It must never be written down, and it must never be revealed to another person except in this way. If the person to whom you have passed on the magic casually reveals any part of the secret, not only do they lose the ability to do the magic, but so do you.

I spoke to Val about this afterwards.

"Oh, that's a big *cavolata*," he said immediately.

Cavolata means a "cabbagey thing" and Italians use it to mean a "load of nonsense."

He told me he once had sunstroke as a child. The Godmother frog-marched him off to an old woman who lived nearby for 'treatment.'

"What did she do?" I asked.

Valentino laughed. "She balanced a plate of olive oil on my head and set it on fire. There was cotton wool and cups and stuff. The fire's supposed to draw out the heat."

"Did it make you feel better?" I asked.

"I thought my hair was going to burst into flames," he answered, laughing even harder. "I only felt better afterwards out of relief that my hair hadn't been set alight."

"So you didn't get better at all?"

"Well, after a while I did. But that was because my mother made me have aspirin, sugar water, salt water, and orange juice and made my brothers and sister rub ice-packs on my wrists and ankles. She gave me any treatment she could possibly think of."

The fact that these olive oil rituals have survived shows how much the oil is still valued. Some Sicilians still think that accidentally spilling olive oil means someone has cast the evil eye on you and wishes you ill. If this disaster should occur, the only remedy is to scatter salt far and wide.

Spring had turned into summer and the cicadas were buzzing non-stop nowadays. The extraordinary heat generated by my growing offspring within me, added to the dizzying heat of a Sicilian summer all around me, made me start fainting regularly. As my epic pregnancy progressed and food continued leaking out of me ever more frequently, The Godmother started to offer me more genuine help. Although the critical comments continued, the help was genuine, and much appreciated.

Mr. Lucky Faeces the construction engineer turned up out of the blue one day while The Godmother was doing some ironing for me. He was looking for Mr. and Mrs. Muppet, who had not paid the last instalment of the house.

"Oh, they're out at the moment," The Godmother told him. "But they said they would be back shortly," she lied. "Why don't you wait here and I'll make you a cup of coffee?"

She filled his coffee with three sugars, and he grinned like a little boy whose mother had just given him ice-cream. How did she know he would like all that sugar?

She set about flattening my fluffy bath towels into paper tissues while she chatted about a new building being built in Brancaccio. She asked if the engineer knew who was managing the construction. Apparently he did, and this led to more chatting about people in the neighbourhood. She managed to steer him smoothly onto discussions about school, university, who had been his best man, who his various cousins were and who had been their best man, neighbour and childhood companion, all the while reducing a messy mountain of my laundry into flat squares with sharp corners. She seemed to know everyone he mentioned, and her memory for all the different names left me speechless. She steered him into speaking Sicilian and threw in some jokes to make him open up further.

I sat stroking my vast paunchy tummy, amazed at how smoothly she worked all the information out of him, all the while appearing to be loving his boring, cigarette-smelling anecdotes. I knew her well enough by now to realise she was acting, yet she did it so well! She casually raised the subject of various fittings that were still missing from my house.

"Oh, there are a few small sums of cash still missing," was the even more casual answer Mr. Faeces offered her.

"Not from this household," she replied, pressing the button on her iron which made it blast out a jet of steam at least three feet long, in the direction of Mr. Faeces' face.

He calmly lit a cigarette. The instant the smoke reached my nostrils I felt my stomach heave.

"Don't you know there's a five thousand euro fine for smoking in front of a pregnant woman?" asked the Godmother. "Get out on the balcony right now!"

She was using her face that made you feel as if you had been thoroughly spanked just to look at it. For the first time since meeting her, I think I felt love for this magnificent woman. The engineer sprang to his feet as if his legs had obeyed The Godmother before checking with his brain for permission, and The Godmother hastily shooed him out onto the balcony, holding her steam iron firmly in her hand. His hammer could not help him now!

He stumbled backwards to get away from her, and caught the ammonite fossil with his heel. He tripped back against the metal railings, yelling out in such pain that it was a moment before I realised the ammonite had slipped underneath the railings and fallen to the ground below. It would probably have broken. How was I going to tell poor Jim that his precious fossil was ruined?

The Godmother and Mr. Faeces were looking over the balcony railings, then both darted back into the kitchen together and made a dash for the stairs. When I say dashed, I mean the Godmother moved with the greatest speed that her bunions permitted. I glanced over the balcony and realised why. There was a man lying awkwardly on the ground below: the ammonite had knocked him out cold.

I waddled down the stairs behind them, supporting the weight of my abdomen with both hands. The Godmother had pulled her very large mobile phone from her pinny and was calling an ambulance. The man had surprisingly little blood coming from his head but he was definitively, extremely unconscious. The fossil was still in one piece, I noticed.

"Do you know anything about first aid?" the Godmother asked Mr. Faeces. Gradually a crowd of neighbours appeared. Mrs. Sterile took one look at him and started hyperventilating with panic. The others patted the man, they shouted at him, and Carmen brought cold water with sugar in just in case he came around. Mr. Faeces stood aloof, his eyes looking stunned like a rabbit in car headlights. They all looked immensely relieved when the ambulance arrived and, at last, there was someone present who knew about first aid.

They asked us so many times what had happened that I started to feel faint, so The Godmother ordered me inside to lie down. The ambulance men decided to take my blood pressure as well, just to be on the safe side.

"You've had a terrible shock," they told me, "it could be dangerous in your condition."

I'm not the one who got brained by a fossil, I thought, but said nothing.

"Luckily everything's alright," they reassured me a moment later. "But you must lie down." I decided now would probably not be the ideal moment to retrieve the fossil. Also, I was not able to bend down far enough to pick it up by myself. I would have to hope it was left there and send Valentino down for it later.

"I have to get on," said Mr. Faeces. "It's all under control now, isn't it?" He seemed in great haste to get away, even though he had not yet had his chat with the Muppets which was, after all, the purpose of his visit.

"Yes, off you go," the Godmother authorised him with a stare like a bolt of lightning. "I don't need you any more," she added, ominously. I knew she would initiate a major research campaign now she knew all his key contacts. And of course, she had God on her side, too.

When Valentino got home from work he moaned a great deal about the fossil, but eventually I convinced him to bring it inside.

"It's going inside a cupboard," he insisted. "It could have killed that man."

"How is he?" I asked, knowing Valentino would have been logged onto the Auntienet all day. "And who is he?"

"Some lowlife, who several people reckon is in the Mafia," he answered grimly. "And I'd like to know what he was doing under our balcony."

"Looking for Mr. Faeces?" I suggested.

"Yes obviously," said Valentino. "But why?"

19

OH, I DO LIKE TO BE BESIDE THE SEASIDE!

Valentino decided the best solution to my tendency to overheat and faint was for me to spend as much time as possible bobbing up and down neck-deep in the sea. This had the added bonus of justifying the fact that I wore nothing but flip-flops, ever, since I was unable to get my swollen feet into anything else.

One day on our local beach I realised that, despite being six months pregnant, I was the slimmest woman there. There were so many obese ladies in bikinis, standing in a group chatting, it looked like and emergency global summit meeting of Weightwatchers. Of course, I am not claiming that English people look glamorous or cool at the beach. The standard procedure at South End, my former "local" beach, was to roll your trousers up to mid-calf length or tuck you skirt into your knickers at the side, balance a hanky, knotted at each corner, on your head and paddle in the freezing water for five minutes, then have fish and chips in a deck chair with a mug of tea from your thermos flask.

One of the very voluptuous ladies suddenly made a beeline for the sea, and a group of five little boys tore down the beach after her to float in her slip stream as she launched herself into the water.

"Tsunami!" they screamed at the tops of their voices.

Meanwhile her friends were settling down for a light snack. They had packed a picnic of twenty-five sandwiches a yard long, eight cream cakes and several roasted chickens, seafood salad, biscuits and apparently everything else in their kitchens. They sat in the sun eating the lot, each smoked a cigarette, and lounged under the sun like sea lions for long enough to go as brown as hazelnuts. Then they charged down the beach and threw themselves at the water, creating a second tsunami that obliterated Sardinia.

Being on a beach packed with women who have terrible figures and simply do not care is far and away the best therapy an insecure woman could possibly undergo. I think if more people knew about my local beach, plastic surgery and indeed dieting would simply die out. I am certain the women of the world would be infinitely happier.

Sicilians make the most of their beach time. They set themselves up as if they live there for, over the summer, they almost do. Whilst most of them are impressively well equipped with furniture, food and any other comfort money can buy for use on the beach, it is also one of the ideal environments to observe the classic Sicilian art known as *l'arte dell'arrangiarsi*. This literally means "the art of arranging yourself," though perhaps in English we would call it improvisation. Perhaps we would call it making do. Perhaps we just could not imagine it.

Once, my father-in-law was in a shop in the village when a woman came in asking for a gazebo. Sicilians planning to spend their summer holiday on the beach put these up so they can eat their lunch in the shade and prevent their babies from getting skin cancer.

"They've all sold out, I'm afraid," this lady was told.

"Well in that case, give me seven packets of black bin liners, all those garden canes in that bin over there, and three rolls of sticky tape," she answered without hesitation. "I'll arrange myself."

Later that day, Daddy-in-law spotted a grandiose, black, plasticky erection on the beach. It was made out of an uncountable number of black bin liners, sticky tape and... yes indeed, the whole thing was supported by a framework of interlinked garden canes. It was... drumroll..... a gazebo!

"Was it fairly well made?" I asked him, incredulous.

"All the shop-bought ones were blowing away, and I saw the canvas tearing off a few of them because the Sirocco was blowing strongly," he answered, "but her one looked rock solid. She was under it with about twelve children and fourteen other adults. They were having pasta *al forno*."

That lady certainly knew how to arrange herself. She was a novice compared to a family who camped out on our local beach all that summer, though. They had a gazebo-and-tent complex, all interlinked. It included a dining room with their wooden dining table from home, and their dresser, complete with ketchup and a range of other condiments in it as well as all the family china. There were no less than three barbecues for cooking, two for meat and vegetables and one upon which they propped the coffee pot and saucepans of milk for the children. Next to this was the children's bedroom area, with curtains for privacy, and beside this they had a chemical toilet with an "occupied" sign for when they did not want to be disturbed.

Of course, people who holiday in five-star accommodation don't always want to bathe in the sea, sometimes they want their own private pool. The (paddling) pool was near the edge of the sea to maximise on the glamorous view. They had dug up some of the succulent plants that naturally grow out of the sand on some Sicilian beaches and re-planted them around the pool, to give it that touch of class and exclusivity.

The thing I found most impressive of all was the way they created their own pizza oven in a hole that happened to have occurred naturally in one of the cliffs to one side of the beach. They gathered driftwood, dried it in the sun, then lit a fire in the back of their "pizza oven" and slotted their pizzas in. I think they were even baking fresh bread each morning in there. They were certainly catching fish each day and cooking that up nicely.

Of course, an arrangement as grandiose as this could not possibly have just one storey. Oh no, they had an upstairs, accessible via the staircase from the car park to the beach. This was usually their delivery lorry. It opened amply on one side for them to get the bread out, but it was, for the duration of their summer vacation, the master bedroom area, stocked with mattresses, sheets and even a nightlight and music centre connected to the car battery.

One day, Val and I arrived on the beach very early and I spotted the mistress of The Buckingham Palace Summer Residence - Her Majesty, so to speak - having a shampoo in a little angle of sea sheltered by a rocky outcrop.

"Can ya give us the washing up liquid?" she bawled out at her husband, "I've run out of shampoo!"

Even with toiletries, she knew how to arrange herself.

I spent the whole of that day in the water, bobbing up and down with just my head and shoulders sticking out, observing the comings and goings around Buckingham Palace. I emerged from the water realising that my face and bosom were deeply tanned whilst the rest of me remained the usual translucent blueish white. The only way I could look good for the rest of the summer would be in an off-the-shoulder, ground length evening gown. As I emerged from the water I realised I had a throbbing headache, too. Valentino sat on the beach with his arms around me and we watched the sun sink in the sky, admiring the beauty of the reds and golden colours over the rippling deep blue waves as he caressed my tummy. I realised I was feeling sick; sicker than usual. In fact, I was feeling terrible. I had sunstroke.

I decided to visit my personal witch doctor.

I sat in Ninfa's dusty little alley on one of the neighbour's chairs. In Sicilian villages you often end up on other people's kitchen chairs, brought out onto the pavement for a shoutversation with the neighbours over the road. Wily pensioners in our village sometimes put out a guest chair to lure passers-by, who may still be there at sundown when all they popped out for was a loaf of bread to go with their lunch.

I reached out just to test the distance. I could almost touch Ninfa's house and the one across the road at the same time.

"How did you get so much sun on you?" Ninfa asked. "Did you stay out at lunch time?"

"Yes. Now I've got a terrible headache, and I've been sick a couple of times."

"Oh, that's terrible. Definitely sunstroke" said Ninfa.

"Very bad sunstroke," shouted Ninfa's mother from her balcony.

The neighbour came out of her front door with another chipped, purple chair which she shifted a couple of times until she could set it down nice and steady on the uneven pavement and watch the proceedings from a good vantage point. She must have been so absorbed that she had forgotten she still had her tea towel in her hand. Apparently treatment for the worms is private, but sunstroke therapy can be done with an audience. Or else it was just that she could not be sent away, since I was actually sitting on one of her chairs for treatment.

Ninfa popped inside and reappeared with a small plate, a tea cup, a bottle of olive oil and a piece of cotton wool. She balanced the plate on my head and instructed me to hold it steady. Then she poured olive oil onto the cotton wool until it was saturated and placed it on the plate. Then she produced a cigarette lighter from her pocket and bore down on me with the little flame flickering. My head throbbed and waves of nausea kept flooding through me.

"The flame draws the fire out of your head," her mother called out. "Don't worry, she'll make you better."

Ninfa set fire to the cotton wool and everyone let out a sigh of relief as it, evidently, burned merrily on top of my head. Ninfa started muttering a little poem in Sicilian under her breath with her eyes closed and then, the moment it finished, she clapped the teacup upside down on top of my head over the cotton wool, snuffing out the flame. Then everyone looked at me expectantly, wondering if I had really been cured.

I did not feel wonderful, but I did gradually start to feel a little better. Perhaps it was the huge jug of sugar water she made me drink, and the salty olives she gave me to eat afterwards.

I spent the evening lying in bed while Valentino very kindly rubbed my swollen legs. I took some paracetamol, hoping it would do no harm to my baby, and lay pondering on sunscreen and wrinkles. In Sicily, you have to make a direct choice between one or the other. To stay white, or to go brown? To apply cream, or to become creviced? That is the question.

In England, the government's panic-mongering warnings about skin cancer had apparently made people forget the meteorological reality that the sun only shines in England about three times a year, weakly. People were slathering on sunscreen every time the cloud cover cleared for a couple of hours. Many schools enforced a rule that sunscreen must be worn by all children at playtime, every day.

When I first moved to Sicily I had succumbed to the brainwashing, and coated myself daily with SPF 50. I walked about looking like a Geisha. I was not tanning at all. My face was absorbing the rays of the sun merely in order to re-release them at dusk in a phosphorescent haze. Confused moths fluttered around me in circles, I frightened the local fishermen, and the thick layer of grease permanently on my face made me re-live my teen years by sporting a steady crop of pimples. Meanwhile back home in England, the newly disseminated sunshine phobia was starting an epidemic of rickets among children. This government-inspired choice to become a nation deficient in vitamin D meant that, beyond bone deformity, the British were setting their children up for immune deficiency, increased risk of allergies, and obesity. There would be no risk of that for the Sicilians, not only because the sun beats so hard you probably get twenty times the recommended daily amount of vitamin D every time you look out of the window, but also because the Sicilians dedicate their lives, from March to October, to getting tanned as leather-brown as they possibly can. I believe they regard having overly white skin in summer as an embarrassing fashion gaffe.

On the occasions when I raised the topic of skin damage, people would laugh heartily. "I've got Sicilian skin!" They said. "It's tougher than cow hide!"

You would never catch a Sicilian sporting geisha-like sun-block, or risking a pimple. God forbid a pimple! Pimples are very much to be avoided in Italy. Forget going short-sighted, Italians say that acne is the inevitable result of indulging in prolonged sessions of frenzied masturbation. Whilst this is used by parents to discourage self-gratificatory behaviour, it also means that unfortunate teenagers with zits are not only called "pizza face", but also... well., something rather more embarrassing. It is easy to see why Sicilians choose to tan, and to hell with the crows' feet.

This leads to one of the major problems I had had since moving to Sicily: estimating people's age. Correctly guessing age is important in Sicily. In many situations, choosing the right word for "you" depends on whether the person you are addressing is older or younger than you. Beyond this, Italian culture in general is very age-conscious. Among my English language students I had already heard many a moan about Sicily's deeply-entrenched gerarchy. The young had to defer to the superior knowledge of the old in nearly all situations and, in the workplace, this resulted in some very uncompetitive businesses. In hospitals it had sometimes been downright dangerous.

Estimating the age of an English person is fairly straightforward. It depends merely on assessing the degree of facial wrinkle perfusion and then cross-referencing this to the frumpiness of their clothes as a double-check. In Sicily the procedure is infinitely more complex. There are so many more input-factors that the necessary calculation relies on a lengthy algorithm.

The first problem is that the wrinkliness-to-age correlation is not linear. People who spend large amounts of their time sunbathing or engaged in outdoor work under Sicily's relentless, baking sun develop a wrinkle-quotient that far exceeds that which an English person can achieve over a normal lifespan. Thus, to make the initial calculation, it is necessary to assess the quantity of crevices per facial square centimetre, and then divide this wrinkle-quotient by the depth of skin tone, a measurement which, again, has to be adjusted by the ethnic multiplier.

Sicily was conquered and occupied in the past by North Africans of Arab descent, Vikings, Germans, French, Spanish and others. This is why there is no such thing as a 'typical' looking Sicilian; they are completely assorted, often within the same family. A person with a slightly Moorish or Arab look, featuring black hair and eyes, will start off with far darker skin than someone who looks like a genetic heir of the Norman invaders with blue eyes and fair hair. The Sicilians who start off with fairer skin will progressively develop far more wrinkles than those who have a genetic head start in the melanin stakes.

Sicilians take great interest in skin tone when a baby is born. Everyone crowds around and discusses what type of *carnagione*, or skin tone, the baby has. Dark like Daddy? Pale like Mummy? Super-dark like Granny Pina? They hardly have time to get onto whose nose the baby has got.

Once you have calculated the wrinkle-quotient-to-skin-tone-ratio, this needs to be cross referenced to dress sense. Here again, many of the Sicilian women in my town cheated outrageously. I met a woman as old as sixty, with a nine-month-gestation size paunch, wearing a skin-tight luminous yellow Lycra vest top and shorts, proudly displaying her deeply tanned, cellulite-lined midriff, criss-crossed with stretch marks. I saw a grandmother in a transparent black lace blouse and a pair of shiny red leggings, replete with visible labels, and silver and diamante stilettos to accessorize. This rendered the clothing cross-reference factor unreliable or, at best, very tricky to estimate.

The upshot of all this was that a great many Sicilians I met assumed I was barely out of my teens, and spoke to me very patronisingly as a consequence. They assumed a didactic attitude while imparting facile information. Meanwhile I assumed they were about the age of my mother, and therefore anticipated forgetfulness and the inability to throw away junk mail without reading it first. When we discovered we were about the same age, I could not tell which of us was more embarrassed.

"Are you asleep?" Valentino whispered to me when he had finished the leg rub.

"No, just thinking," I answered.

"Thinking what?"

"Thinking I must buy a big sun hat tomorrow."

He lay down beside me, covered me in kisses, and fell asleep with his arm draped around me and our baby.

The Godmother announced one day that she would like to drop in and have lunch with Valentino and me.

"I know you're feeling sick all the time," she said, considerately. "Don't worry about cooking anything fancy."

Did she seriously think I would fall for that one? I realised by now that I would be assessed, and silently awarded points for all aspects of my performance, so I planned ahead. Step one was to invite my sister-in-law Mirella and brother-in-law Manfredi as well, for The Godmother never made her most cutting remarks to me in front of witnesses. The more people present, the less chance she would have of getting me alone. Next, I needed to plan the food.

I must first explain that there are two bakeries in our village. One is known as the Seafront Bakery, and the other is universally called the Big Bum Bakery. The Big Bum Bakery is named for the baker's wife, whose derriere is roughly the size of France. These are not the official names, I must add, but I have never heard either of them referred to by the name painted above the door.

The baker's wife, who handles the till at the Big Bum Bakery – Mrs. Big Bum herself – took a real shine to me from the first. I knew her well enough to make peculiar requests by this time, so I went down to the bakery with two of my own baking trays, which had been gifts from The Godmother, and asked if her husband could bake me a loaf of bread in one, and his best ever *sfincione* in the other. *Sfincione* is a Sicilian speciality, something like a very, very thick spongy-based pizza. I have simply no idea how to make *sfincione* so I asked the baker's wife how to talk as if I did. She could hardly speak for laughing when I explained what I was up to, but eventually she coached me to sound like a master baker.

"I wish you could tape record the whole thing for me," she said, wistfully.

Next I dropped in on Vampire Angela's supermarket for ten jars of ready-made *ragù*, for the pasta. Once I had decanted everything into a saucepan, I went and put all the jars in my neighbour Carmen's bin, so there would be no risk whatsoever of getting caught out. She was wearing a pair of lilac satin baby-doll pyjamas with high-heeled feathery slippers and had just had new hair extensions, in aubergine, and longer than ever before.

"Slosh a bit of wine in," Carmen advised. "It makes everything taste better and you never taste wine in ready-made things. It will seem more home-made."

I cooked prawns in the oven, exactly as my favourite fisherman had instructed me. I also roasted some fish in foil, which he had cleaned, gutted and seasoned for me down on the beach.

I had it all nice and ready as Valentino returned from work, and the Godmother arrived with my father-in-law, at the same time. I had carefully sprinkled flour around the kitchen and dirtied a few utensils to leave lying around the sink. I was wearing my pinny, the one which I had made to save two euros. The battle was on!

When Manfredi and Mirella arrived, we sat down to eat. Everyone wolfed the food down with undeniable gusto and enjoyment. Valentino and my father-in-law, my dear sweet father-in-law, praised everything so sincerely that it was impossible for The Godmother to criticise. This time, the victory was mine.

After everyone had gone, as I cleared up, Valentino asked me how much the food had cost.

"Erm, not sure," I answered.

I suddenly filled with guilt. I admitted I had cheated, and told him how.

"Oh I knew that," he said. "I appreciate that you want to make everything perfect for me, "but you don't have to resort to this kind of thing. I love you because you're intelligent, interesting and exciting. If I wanted a hand maiden I could have chosen from thousands of Sicilian girls. I fell in love with you because you're different."

That was it. That was when I realized that, as far as my husband was concerned, it did not matter what the Godmother might do; I had won, and would always win.

"But do keep trying to get better at cooking," he added with a wink. "We can't afford to replace the saucepans every time you burn the bottoms black."

20

PRIVACY

The day after I suffered a second bout of sunstroke, Valentino insisted on taking a day off work to take me to the doctor. While I was in the doctor's waiting room, I got chatting to the old man sitting beside me. I had seen him a few times with the ex ex postman, so we already knew each other by sight. He told me his son had broken both legs, his pelvis, a collar bone and one arm when a balcony landed on him.

"He was very lucky," said the old man. He wasn't being sarcastic. In Italy, people die every year from derelict balconies landing on them as they walk out of their front door.

His son had spent a very long time stuck at home and was getting serious cabin fever. He couldn't even sit up, as he was set rigid in plaster and metal bars. After some months, when he still had both arms and both legs set in plaster but was healing nicely, his best friend came over with his Fiat Uno, opened the boot, put the back seat down and slotted his friend into the car from behind.

"I'm taking you to the pub," he said cheerfully.

Then his friend got into the driving seat, shut the car door, and the sudden noise made the balcony he was parked under collapse completely and crash down onto the car.

"My son would have died if he had been sitting up instead of lying flat," the old man told me. "His friend got a broken neck. They're in hospital together now. My son's happy to have company this time! They're both so lucky. God was looking out for them."

I asked the doctor about this when I got to see him. He likes to practise his English with me, and I always enjoy seeing him.

"We're half African here," was his comment.

"What do you mean?" I asked.

"We Sicilians are only about two to four percent North African, genetically, but culturally we're about half and half. Most Europeans would mend a balcony before it got to that state, but we only mend it after it's fallen down. We Sicilians are in constant conflict between our African side and our European side, you know. We hate following rules and tend to admire people who are skilled at cheating. That's our North African side, from the Arabs.

"Sicily's mid-way between Europe and Africa. The people of the two continents have been fighting over it since the dawn of time." He started counting on his fingers. "It has two weather systems, a North African desert climate and a European, Mediterranean temperate climate which do battle in the air, when the Sirocco blows. It has two cultures, a European culture and an African culture which have taken turns ruling us and which we'are still trying to mingle successfully. It has a racial mix of Europeans and Africans, who've successively invaded from the north and the south over the centuries and produced families of blue eyed blonde people with frizzy-haired, black-eyed relatives. It has a mixed cuisine of European foods like pizza, which are typical further north in Italy, and all our nut-laden sweets and elaborate spicy dishes from the North African Arabs. That's why everything in Sicily is unstable and in constant conflict. It never manages to decide whether it's European or African, because the two identities are incompatible."

"A geologist would tell you that Sicily's currently moving in the direction of Africa at the rate of almost one centimetre a year," I suggested, "so perhaps it's made its choice and is voting with its feet."

"But very slowly!" laughed the doctor. "You know northern Italians call us Sicilians *Africani*, meaning it as an insult?"

I did know. I had heard Sicilians being called this when I lived in Milan.

"We Sicilians don't take it as an insult. Those *Milanesi* are just ignorant about history. The Arab-speaking Moors of Africa brought us Sicilians pasta and ice-cream, our beautiful majolica ceramics, our precious citrus trees and our first irrigation systems, hundreds of our towns, our street markets which have been flourishing for over a thousand years, lots of our language and surnames and place names, and some of our most beautiful buildings, including churches built while the Normals ruled. Most of the Africans' culture and technology diffused northwards and entered the rest of Europe in the Renaissance, but the continentals don't know it, apparently."

"So the Sicilians are proud to be called 'African'?" I aked.

"I'm very proud of it," the doctor said. "I think any Sicilian who knows about history is."

When we got around to talking about my health, the doctor said he wanted me to have blood tests very frequently. He advised me to go to "the Johnny Depp clinic" in the local town.

"Is there seriously a clinic called The Johnny Depp Clinic? I asked, incredulous. I had been in Sicily long enough to realise that here, anything is possible.

"No," he answered, and laughed. He handed me a card with an address on it. "Just go there and you'll understand."

When we emerged from the doctor's, Valentino looked worried. Any sign that our baby could be at risk made his stomach gnarl up with anxiety.

"Everything's fine," I tried to reassure him. "I feel fine and so does the baby."

In reality, I had fainted three times in the last couple of weeks and my platitudes were unconvincing.

When we arrived at the Clinic, we queued for several days (Oh alright, it was only several hours) whilst old people queue-hopped in front of us. Eventually my paperwork was processed and I was ushered into the room behind the reception area, which smelled of disinfecty alcohol. Out came Johnny Depp with a syringe in one hand and a fist full of glass test tubes in the other, and a rubber tourniquet in the breast pocket of his white coat.

Who would have thought Johnny Depp had an identical twin, adopted at birth by Sicilians?

Having a needle jabbed into your arm at weekly intervals for months on end is not fun, but I can definitely say that having it done by Johnny Depp certainly makes it more tolerable than it might otherwise be. After he had taken my blood, he gave me a little slip of paper and told me that whoever came to collect the results must hand over this piece of paper.

"We can't give the results to anyone else but you, unless they have this," he explained, "because of privacy."

I think the Sicilian concept of privacy may be one of their "African things". It bears no resemblance to any concept of privacy I had ever heard of before. Not only Sicilians, but Italians in general, do not understand privacy. The Italian language has no word for it. In an Italian-English dictionary, you are offered words which mean intimacy, isolation, or solitude as a translation for privacy. The Italian solution to this linguistic shortfall is simply to use the English word, pronounced very badly with an Italian accent: praaaivasee. It is a trendy buzz word in Sicily these days. This is probably because of *La Legge Sulla Privacy*, or 'The Law About Privacy,' which is what the Italians call their version of the Data

Protection Act.

Sicilians seem to love this law, I believe because it gives them a universal, infallible excuse for laziness and incompetence. "No I can't give you your blood test results because of the Legge sulla privacy." "No I can't give you any money out of your bank account because of the Legge sulla privacy." "No I can't move my car out of the way of your garage door because of the Legge sulla privacy."

One of my neighbours, Mrs. Greenfingers, had planted a row of luscious leafy plants along her railings, which created a bit of dappled shade and reduced the x-ray view passers-by had into her living room by about ten percent. Everyone in the street used to praise her on this wonderful idea for obtaining a bit of privacy. Sorry, I mean praaaivasee.

The Godmother liked it more than anyone. Every time she came to visit us, she would stop, bend over and peer through it, looking for a suitable hole through which to check whether the neighbour was at home. The Godmother wanted a good look at her privacy. Mrs. Greenfingers was usually in her garden, peering back out. If not, The Godmother would push some leaves aside and shout out at the top of her voice until she emerged, and responded to The Godmother's friendly greetings and enquiries into her private life. Indeed, the Godmother asked her for gardening advice on cultivating such a succulent screen, as she had decided she thought her newly installed privacy was so enviable they would like to have some praaaaivaseee of her own. Do not run away with the idea my mother-in-law is a particularly prying person. Oh no, everybody peered through that plant screen, all the time. Mrs. Greenfingers was too polite to comment on the fact that, every time she visited, The Godmother snapped a few leaves off her Praivaseeee.

Once, I heard The Godmother carefully explain privacy to one of her neighbours. Now that privacy was so trendy, she was certainly not going to pass up her chance to show off a bit.

"My daughter-in-law is English, and they think privacy is very important," she boasted from her balcony, her tea-towel fluttering in the breeze. "They have a terrace outside for doing barbecues, but there's a solid wall between them and the neighbours, so they can eat in privacy. That's the new way of doing it," she explained, switching into Sicilian conspiratorially. "*Capisci?*"

She pronounces *capisci* as capeesh, and it means "do you understand?" Sicilians only use this word at the end of a detailed explanation of something precious, a titbit of information for the select few. Getting "capeeshed" is a priviledge that The Godmother has bestowed on me several times.

The day after we met Johnny Depp, I had further reason to ponder on praaaaivasseeee. The Godmother turned up unexpectedly at my house with a special kind of Sicilian sausage that is about three yards long and all coiled up into a spiral. If you've ever been on one of those up-the-jungle holidays in Thailand and tried to avoid malarial encephalitis by taking a rucksack full of mosquito coils with you, you'll be able to visualise it quite well. You usually slap it onto a barbecue, but The Godmother did the other great Sicilian thing, frying it in orange juice.

"This sausage tastes simply divine!" I exclaimed as I chewed on it merrily. It was truly the processed pork product of the gods.

"I'll give some to Mr. and Mrs. Sterile," Valentino decided. Sicilians do this whenever they cook something that turns out particularly delicious. We regularly ate dishes handed to us from balcony to balcony.

"Good idea," said the Godmother.

We happened to be up on the roof terrace: the one with solid walls that gives us our wonderfully trendy privacy. Hubby hammered on The Wall of Privacy till he established with disappointment that our immediate neighbours, Mr. and Mrs. Sterile, were out. Then he climbed up onto the wall, so he could peer past their roof terrace, and into the terrace of the neighbours beyond them, Mr. and Mrs. Greenfingers, to find out if they were at home.

The Wall of Privacy has a slippery marble top, which slopes downwards towards the outer wall of the house. After springing up onto it, with his bum hovering over a sheer drop of at least thirty feet, Valentino spotted Mr. Greenfingers and started telling him in Sicilian about sausages. Actually, he had to attract his attention by shouting rather loudly, at an estimated 700 decibels - another Sicilian cultural tradition. I am pretty sure, by this time, they even knew about that sausage as far away as Catania and maybe even Naples.

Mr. Greenfingers was so excited about tasting the porcine ambrosia that Hubby grabbed some and climbed over The Wall of Privacy, the one that looks like a chute made for whooshing you off the terrace and down thirty feet to a splattery death, all the while holding the plate of sausage in the air like a silver service waiter. His legs flailed over the precipice, his buttocks dared to defy gravity, and finally he plopped to safety on the other side. He walked across the immediate neighbour's roof terrace, commenting that their new barbecue looked nice, and handed some sausage to Mr. Greenfingers, who ate it on the spot.

"Oh my God! It's the best sausage I've ever tasted in my life!" he exclaimed, most satisfyingly. "Where did you get it?"

"Our local butcher," shouted the Godmother from behind me. "It's black pork from the Nebrodes."

"Every bite is a mouthful of heaven!" shouted Mr. Greenfingers, with his mouth full. Of heaven.

Whilst Mr. Greenfingers continued his poetic eulogies about The Godmother's culinary talents, I was having a hyperventilation attack. I had almost been widowed. While Valentino climbed back (my head was in my hands by now, I could not look), The Godmother and Mr. Greenfingers engaged in a chat about the wonders of praaaaivaseee.

I think all this makes it abundantly clear that Sicilians just don't comprehend privacy in the English sense of the word. They know how to keep secrets, though. One of the harshest criticisms a Sicilian can make of anyone is *"Da troppo confidenza!"* This means, "He confides too much", or "He is too open". You're supposed to keep your personal stuff personal, no blabbing. *Capeesh*?

A week later, The Godmother arrived with sparkling eyes. She was bearing news hot from the Auntienet, and *praivaseee* clearly was out of fashion today.

"I've been asking discreetly about the *Stronzo*," she told Valentino and me. She meant the construction engineer, Fortunato Mastronzo.

"What's happened?" asked Valentino.

"His son went missing over three weeks ago," said The Godmother, "and four days ago his brother and a cousin of theirs disappeared, too. That man whose head got hit by the fossil is still in hospital," said the Godmother, "and his relatives are telling everyone that Mr. Faeces tried to kill him."

"Where is Mr. Faeces anyway?" asked Valentino.

"Not at his house. Nobody's seen him lately."

"Oh," said Valentino.

"Oh," I repeated.

"Yes, oh indeed," agreed The Godmother.

21

A FIRST COMMUNION

When our good friends Roberto and Muriel invited us to join their daughter's first communion, I was excited. Not only did it give us a chance to spend a day with them and for me to wear my new silk dress before my baby tummy got too large for it, but it would also give me the chance to attend a first communion for the first time ever.

It was the height of summer and I had been pleased to find a very light matching silk wrap, to cover my shoulders in church without making me feel too hot. I had bought some fake suntan cream, so that my legs matched them when I took it off. I do not know how Valentino managed to put up with wearing a suit with a jacket and tie but, outside the church, there was already a vast throng of other men, all of them in black suits and dark, dark black sunglasses. Valentino, who is not like a real Italian in many ways, never wears hair gel and has only one pair of sunglasses, chosen because they go right round the outside of his normal glasses.

"They make you look like a hoodlum," The Godmother often says to him.

"Rambo! Rambo! Here comes Rambo!" grubby children, the type who pat stray dogs, sometimes say to him.

"You look like a welder in goggles," I said to him the first time I saw them. "Why don't you buy some prescription sunglasses?"

He got hot under the collar. It turned out he had once bought a very expensive pair of prescription sunnies and worn them for exactly half an hour, to go sailing. While he was fiddling with the rigging, a gust of wind made them plop into the sea, never to be seen again. Ever since then, he goes into a huff whenever prescription sunglasses are mentioned.

Various children, aged about ten, started to gather, dressed in white robes like miniature monks' habits. This was the first time I discovered that First Communions are done in groups, like those Moonie weddings where thirty couples are married off all at once. The girls all carried little bouquets of flowers and all the children, boys and girls alike, wore a colossal wooden crucifix pendant around their necks, literally seven inches in length, as if about to initiate some form of juvenile inquisition. Everyone was milling about, asking the children if they were nervous or excited, and looking out for friends and relatives as new clusters of people arrived. I experienced a wave of dizziness and pregnant nausea, and lurked near a wall in a small patch of shade.

"Did I tell you they've arrested Mr. Faeces?" mentioned Valentino casually, as I leant against the wall and he held his arm around me.

"What?" I asked. "No you have not! How could you forget to mention that?"

"Well I've mentioned it now," he said.

"I thought he was already on trial," I said.

"He was supposed to be," said Valentino. "Apparently he didn't present himself at court, so they had the police track him down and take him in."

"I kind of hoped he was dead," I admitted.

"It would be much harder to sort out all the documents for our house if he was," said Val.

Roberto and Muriel's little girl stood out from the other children. Muriel is French and blonde and their children, Lea and her little brother Mirko, have inherited their mother's platinum blonde hair and their father's huge, dark Sicilian eyes. They are so beautiful they look too good to be real. Lea was chasing a butterfly and holding her little brother's hand as they scampered around the churchyard, a glimpse of her lavender, flowery party dress sometimes visible beneath the sleeves of her communion robe. She laughed and played with the other children awaiting their big moment. All the mothers fussily reminded their children to be careful not to get dirt on their shoes.

All of a sudden, a very thickly varnished horse-drawn carriage pulled up outside the church accompanied by loud shouting and several car horns hooting, to attract as much attention as possible. The door of the carriage slowly swung open. It was lined with deeply buttoned red satin, rather like Count Dracula's coffin. Slowly and awkwardly, a podgy little girl stepped out. She was wearing a miniature wedding dress with an immense crinoline skirt, held out by a multi-layered, hooped petticoat. Her coiffure was embellished with masses of false locks of hair, which hung down to her knees in a cascade of very rigid ringlets deeply encrusted with at least three cans of hairspray. More hair stuck up nearly six inches on top of her head, and the astounding do was peppered throughout with red roses and rhinestones inserted into the mass of nylon. Her shoes were encrusted with diamanté embellishments and her hands were a mass of jewellery. She was fully made up with foundation, mascara and eye-shadow as well as scarlet lipstick.

Various guests around me were muttering things under their breath about "*tasci*", a Sicilian word which means "nouveau riché and appallingly vulgar."

"Oh, now the show's really starting" whispered Valentino with relish, from behind his welding goggles.

"There's always one," said Roberto gleefully.

Next the little girl's mother emerged from the carriage. She was wearing a stiff, boned bodice encrusted with embroidery and a full-length matching skirt with a train which trailed about a foot behind her on the ground. Without wishing to use unduly harsh vocabulary to describe the family, I shall simply say that they were of below average stature, and that they clearly liked their food. The mother was very possibly a perfect sphere. The train of the skirt would certainly not have been a train on a woman of the height for whom it was intended. The shoes may not have been over-sized and evocative of Minnie-Mouse on another woman. And the bleached white, fleecy hair would certainly not have been particularly out of place on a sheep.

She paused as she touched ground beside the carriage and waited like a film star for her assembled family acolytes to photograph her as she stood proudly by her daughter. She looked about the rest of the families, as we stood speechless, mouths gaping like goldfish, staring at her. She and her maroon lipstick were fully satisfied that the family had made a huge impact upon the crowd. She felt magnificent. Magnificent.

She summoned her husband to stand the other side of their daughter as she posed for photographs; no doubt the photographer was using the widest angle lens he could muster. The would-be communionee's big brother followed, evidently primed to assist with his mother's train and other accoutrements. He sported a black satin shirt and a sparkly suit made from some kind of synthetic and metal thread which twinkled like slate-grey chain mail in the heat. He looked as if he were slowly being boiled-in-the-bag.

I thought I had now seen it all but – Oh! How wrong I was! The older sister came out last, and she stole everyone's thunder. Not only was her sheer physical bulk guaranteed to command attention wherever she went, but her dress was made from some type of ultra reflective, bronze-toned metallic fabric with a permanent pleat feature, though her voluptuous form had successfully flattened out all the pleats wherever it was in contact with her formidable body. It was backless, but she was not. She actually had so much back that there was a spare pair of breasts hanging down each side, ruthlessly bisected by her black bra strap in a way I thought looked painful, and which transformed the two extra breasts into four, like dorsal udders. Why someone would choose to wear a black bra under a backless dress was a conundrum rapidly supplanted in my mind by the further mystery of why on earth she had chosen to wear black tights with the highest-heeled, flimsiest pair of slip-on backless sandals I had ever seen. Her efforts to avoid stepping out of them in her slippery hosiery were so desperate that she ended up literally dragging her feet forwards across the floor, one at a time, as if they were on rails, thus avoiding the risk of stepping out of her shoes by never actually letting either of them lose full contact with the ground at any time.

"First communions would be so boring if people like these didn't come to them," said Valentino, very quietly.

When the priest started into the service, the first communion was indeed very boring. I had another dizzy spell which I realised was one of my pregnancy-induced low-blood sugar crises, and caused a fluster of rustling and whispering and handbag-rummaging as all the women around me looked for a sweet to give me. A remarkably thin woman had about seven different packets of sweets in her bag and very generously gave me handfuls of every type.

Mrs. Magnificent was instructing her husband to take lots of photographs of the whole proceedings. Then she decided to take more herself. This enabled her to parade up and down the church aisle and produce echoing heel-noises to make sure we had all noticed her shiny shoes, and how swishy the train of her skirt was.

The children were lined up and the priest asked them various questions about the bible and the meaning of certain lessons they had learned during their first communion course. I was surprised at how superficial and brief the priest's questions were. When I was a child, starting at primary school and continuing at secondary school, my teachers gradually worked their way through the whole bible, reading out excerpts and making sure we not only knew the story by heart, but were able to explain the lesson it taught. When some detail slips my mind and I ask Catholics in Sicily about a character from the bible and what they did, they never seem to know what I am talking about.

"Didn't you study any of this?" I ask them.

"Nope," they answer.

"What did you learn in Religious Instruction at school?" I ask them. "What does the priest talk about in church?"

"Er, other stuff," they answer, vaguely.

"How do you know what Christianity really is," I ask them, "if you don't know the bible? How can you believe, when you don't know specifically what you believe in?"

"It's called faith," they say, confidently.

When the priest deemed the children ready to take their first communion, he popped a small biscuit into their mouths. Having thus been orally suffused with a higher degree of holiness and closeness to the divine, they were allowed to stand up, complete their participation in the service and sit through a long talk about... well, I could not say precisely, but it was long. It did involve the usual sessions of Gregorian chanting, or should I say Gregorian caterwauling, by a Cats' Chorus of elderly women accompanying themselves on an electric organ and a guitar that badly needed tuning.

When the service was over, we took wistful leave of the Magnificent Family and the other children, and headed to Roberto and Muriel's house for a buffet meal. This was held in their vast, jungly garden and was very enjoyable, though I did sit silently for part of the time, not feeling particularly well.

"What's up?" Valentino asked me, putting his arm around me.

"Oh, I'm just wondering what type of spread Mr. and Mrs. Magnificent have laid out for their daughter's guests," I answered him.

22

A VEHICULAR FUNERAL

The olive harvest came early the year I was pregnant. Normally it is in November, but that year it was still late October when friends of ours started taking a week off from their work as lawyers, doctors or university professors to help their parents with the olive harvesting on their family smallholding. Any Sicilian family who can afford a small plot of land grows a few olives.

The olives receive the kid-glove treatment from start to finish. They are picked by hand, as mechanical pickers would bruise them. Picking them by hand means going up ladders and agitating tree branches to make the olives fall onto clean white sheets carefully laid out on the ground. Once you have started picking your olives, you have to finish as soon as possible and get them to the *frantoio*, the oil press, immediately. If they sit about for a few days they will start to oxidize. At the *frantoio* they are crushed mechanically between stone wheels, then the pulp is spread onto thin mats which are stacked in a stainless steel press. As pressure is applied, oil and water-based juice seep out. No heat is used, so this oil is called "first cold pressed."

People who have taken their own crop of olives to the *frantoio* usually take it home like this, with the sediment still in it, as this imparts fantastic flavour. This kind of oil is distinctly green and, when it is very fresh, it can burn your mouth like chilli. Any oil sold commercially has the sediment, and with it the flavour, filtered out to reduce the acidity to below one percent and to increase the shelf-life. This oil is called "extra virgin" and Sicilians sneer at it.

Valentino bought a year's supply of good, green oil from some neighbours of ours who produced enough to sell a little. Valentino's idea of a year's supply of olive oil was thirty litres. For two people. We had already used up his previous year's stock and he had been coming very close to a panic attack over it.

Sicilians call natural, Sicilian olive oil *l'olio buono*, "the good oil," to distinguish it from vegetable oil or supermarket olive oil.

"Don't fry in olive oil," they say, "It' a terrible waste of the *good* oil."

This is why Sicilians grill their meat. Then they douse it in so much olive oil it floats about on the plate.

I have a friend who used to work in a *frantoio*. Strictly speaking, she not simply a friend, but I am saying that out of laziness. To be honest, she is my husband's sister's husband's brother's wife. I think that means she is my sister-in-law-in-law-in-law. Of course, in England you would never get to meet someone so tenuously connected to you, but in Sicily you spend Christmas and Easter and birthdays with them and stay in their houses for entire weekends, along with thirty-five other relatives so bizarrely connected that you don't know what to call them. This, by the way, is the reason why Italians all seem to have about three thousand cousins. They just call everyone a cousin as they do not know what else to call them.

Anyway, my sister-in-law-in-law-in-law had to give up working in the *frantoio* as she developed a serious allergy to all types of olive oil other than first cold pressed.

"When they heat the lower grades of oil to purify it," she told me, "it gives off a vapour that smells appalling and coats every part of you. You get so greasy and stinky! They use hydrochloric acid to clean the machinery and the floor of the *frantoio*, otherwise you'd slip over in grease as you walk about. Drops of it constantly contaminate the oil, but nobody cares."

If she eats any grade of oil that has been processed or heated, or indeed cold pressed oil that has been cooked with, she swells up like the Michelin man and struggles to breathe. Yet raw, pure extra virgin olive oil has no effect on her at all.

Perhaps there is an olive oil prayer that could cure her.

Just after the olive harvest, in the early autumn, I attended a vehicular funeral.

I went out for a walk whenever the weather was decent, hoping to keep myself in reasonable shape and just a tiny bit fit for the forthcoming childbirth. I had taken to fainting every few days, and became very breathless when walking upstairs. My gynaecologist seemed strangely disinterested, but Johnny Depp had checked my blood and told me I was in need of exercise and less sugar. Since Johnny Depp is not the kind of man you can dismiss easily, I was therefore often to be seen waddling about the village like Humpty

Dumpty. My friend from the council, Totò Cuffaro, was most gentlemanly and always offered me a lift if he passed me in his car. One day I was caught out in an unexpected shower of light rain. My hero Signor Totò came to the rescue.

By now Totò's maroon Alfa Romeo was, basically, made of brown sticky parcel tape. As I had watched his car enter the final, declining phase of its life, that brown parcel tape was holding the doors on, it was fixing the windscreen in (which was made of transparent polythene), it was wound all round the middle of the car going over the roof and under the undercarriage, it was holding the rear bumper on (at one side, anyway) and it was even securing the hubcaps.

Once the car became afflicted with 'failure to thrive', the driver's seat was upholstered in a solid sheet of sticky tape strips, patchwork style, with no trace of the original leather to be seen. The vehicle had no number plates near the tragic end, I think because Totò must have run out of tape before he got to them.

I draped the loose seatbelt as far around my vast pregnant tummy as it would stretch and left the end dangling by my side, as usual. We exchanged the usual pleasantries while we rolled along, chillaxing at twelve miles per hour. A car approached which was rather like a go-kart, in that it had no bodywork other than the absolute essentials. I think it was composed of pieces from at least five different types of Fiat, judging by the range of colours and the fact that the parts did not fit together particularly well. It was at least eighty percent rust.

"Cor, look at that heap of junk!" laughed Signor Totò, stepping on the accelerator and shooting up to almost 20 mph in a sudden surge of confidence. "How embarrassing to be seen in such an old banger!"

As we passed the x-ray go-kart, we realised its exhaust pipe was scraping along the road releasing sparks like a firework. It made a tinny noise, as if the driver and passenger were newlyweds and the scrap metal they were towing behind them had been tied on at their wedding by their scallywag friends.

And that was the fateful moment.

There was a dire 'clonk' noise from somewhere down below us, and Signor Totò and I exchanged glances. We both knew something terrible had happened to his vintage Alfa Romeo. Totò pulled over and we jumped out: His exhaust pipe was lying in the road, several metres behind us, trailing probably not less than 20 miles of tangled, sticky brown tape in its wake. Smoke was billowing out from under the bonnet. Finally, there was a decisive 'Poff' noise, and the engine cut out. That was when we both realised the end had come.

"My dear old Alfa Romeo," said Totò, like a priest delivering the last rites, "you have served me well these past twenty-three years, but henceforth I will save a fortune in sticky tape. We must now part company for ever. *Che liberazione*! Good riddance!"

Since my first lesson in 'Aggressive Driving,' which Valentino decreed a resounding success, he had taken to placing me behind the wheel at sporadic intervals and insisting that I drove. I liked my walks in the village but, as he rightly pointed out, I sometimes had to go further afield and, once our baby was born, driving confidently would be essential. He was currently driving me to the Johnny Depp clinic every time I needed a blood test, but he could not keep on doing this forever. Sooner or later I would have to figure out how to get myself there, and arrive without such severely elevated levels of adrenaline that Johnny Depp would forcefully detain me there pending the arrival of an ambulance.

As I drove, Valentino gave me a constant stream of advice and instructions, which saved us from turning upside-down or becoming a write-off, at regular intervals. The following is a summary of the guidelines I learnt during these invaluable hours risking my life to get from one side of Palermo to the other. Apart from the obvious piece of advice on driving in Sicily, which is 'Don't!', there are some key skills to master if one wishes to become a Sicilian road user.

Before all else can be tackled, appropriate use of the horn must be mastered. Once you see a car approaching you at several times the legal speed limit, on your side of the road, your instinct will be to pull as far into the kerb as possible and apply the brakes. As we already know, this approach is wrong. If you do this he will not even realise you are there, and will peel the whole side of your car. However, it is also absolutely critical that you do not deploy the horn in this situation under any circumstances. Doing so will make the other driver think that you are one of his 345,098,990 cousins saying hello to him, causing him to squint ferociously as he tries to identify you through his grimy windscreen, and to press out a reply to your friendly greeting on his own car horn, in Morse code.

One essential habit for surviving driving in Sicily is the same as the key habit to make a marriage work: constant communication. When in a car, you communicate with other road users using the horn. It is used for friendly greetings, telling other drivers what you intend to do (so much more practical than the indicators, which are usually broken anyway) and telling other drivers what they should do. Any time you see a car appearing in a side road, give one sharp hoot on your car horn. If you fail to do this, they will assume you are inviting them to pull out in front of you, and will do so even if you are at a distance of ten centimetres from them and travelling at three hundred miles per hour. The friendly little toot tells them: "My foot is on the accelerator, and it is staying there."

As we were leaving the village one morning I saw a car upside down, lying diagonally across my path by a side road, surrounded by glass sparkling prettily in the sunshine, and black plastic things which presumably were once bits of car. The driver of that deceased vehicle clearly invited someone to pull out of the side road in front of him without realising it.

When you see someone you know, deliver two greeting hoots if you have no sense of rhythm, or else tap out a little tune if you are musically inclined. You could hoot along to the 1950's dance music you are listening to and wave a little hand jive to them as well. Be sure to stop and talk to them for a few minutes, but remember that road placement is essential in this situation. You must position your car precisely in the middle of the road so that no other vehicle travelling in either direction is able to pass until you have finished chatting. The driver of one of the vehicles just might be a mutual friend and it would be a tragedy if he were to drive on by and miss the opportunity to join in the conversation.

It is essential to hoot at any car as you overtake it. Otherwise it may swerve suddenly and unpredictably into you, leading to a side impact which could drive you off the road. Under such circumstances the driver is normally avoiding a cluster of run-over dogs or cats (once there is one dead feline in the road, others cannot resist sniffing their decomposing companion as part of the mourning process, thus terminating their own lives prematurely and creating the phenomenon of dead cat 'art installations'.) Alternatively, he may be avoiding a pile of broken glass and some vehicle components shed in an earlier accident. Certainly do not expect the driver to look out for you in his rear view mirror before dealing with these obstacles. Who do you think you are? That mirror is for him to hang his rosary beads and picture of Saint Rosalia off.

Traffic lights are regarded as decorations in Sicily. Sicilians love multi-coloured lights so much that in many towns and villages they leave up what look exactly like Christmas lights all year round. Like traffic lights throughout Italy, the red light is more than twice the size of the amber and green ones. North of Rome this is a strong hint to pay attention to it. In Sicily, it is assumed that the red light is larger because it is a pretty colour. Red is regarded as the classic summer colour in Sicily and all men own several pairs of red trousers for the summer months, yet it is also epitomises Christmas. This makes it simply ideal for year-round street illumination.

Car parking is a uniquely challenging activity. Finding a space for your Fiat can take more time than actually driving across Palermo to your destination. Smarter drivers than you will budge in front, drive the wrong way down one way streets, and mow down toddlers in their quest to get into that tiny gap before you do. I recently underwent the astonishing experience of waiting, indicator a-flashing, for a car to pull out of a space outside the bakery and then pulling forward only to find that I was beaten to the spot by a Fiat Cinquecento in red (weird individualist freak) which had raced along the pavement behind seven parked cars, all the way from the crossroads, to insert itself into the space from the other side.

Finding your parking spot is only the first part of the ordeal. Now you have to obtain a "scratch and win" type parking ticket to put on the dashboard. You must wander round asking pedestrians or shopkeepers if they know the whereabouts of the nearest cafe or tobacconist which happens to stock the relevant tickets. But woe betide you if you buy the wrong type of ticket! You need to tell the bar tender precisely where your car is parked. Then you search for your silver Fiat Punto among all the other silver Fiat Puntos, and scrape off the relevant numbers to display the time and date you parked. It is more of a "scratch and lose" activity to be honest.

When you do finally discover a space, figure out which type of parking ticket you must display on your dashboard and even hike to a bar which sells the tickets, you will only return to find that you have been boxed in by someone double parking. In many districts of Palermo, double parking is for the goody-two-shoes whilst triple-parking is *de rigeur* for the more relaxed motorists.

Sicilians often lament the fact that they are highly strung and fly off the handle at the drop of a hat, wishing they had more of what they perceive as our Anglo-Saxon self-control. Yet I am continually astounded at the phlegm they display when finding their car boxed in by a melee of about twenty vehicles. They will patiently sit in their car or stand near it, giving the occasional laid-back hoot on the horn for simply ages, waiting for the owners of the other vehicles to come out of the bank, pharmacy or some other establishment. Then everyone rearranges their cars to let one out, double parking them again and slowly dispersing back into the various shops they were perusing. If someone found themselves boxed in by a double-parker in England we would call the police without waiting ten seconds, and some impulsive types would possibly succumb to road rage and vandalise the offending vehicle.

On the subject of hazard lights, please note that it is mandatory to turn them on whenever you are parked dangerously in a strictly no parking zone, such as blocking the entrance to an ambulance bay. The hazard lights tell people you are only there briefly and for a critically important purpose, such as to get some coffee in a nearby bar or to grab a quick deep-fried spleen sandwich. Such use of the hazard lights has become standard in London too nowadays, so perhaps it was too obvious for me to mention.

Sicilians are deeply attached to their cars but they are also in love with their motorbikes. With the kind of traffic one encounters in rush hour, the vast majority of men travel to and from work by motorbike every day, taking their wife on the back and leaving her at her place of work first. Unlike mainland Italians, it is unusual to see a Sicilian man on a Vespa scooter or a farty little motorbike. These are for the teenage boys, who cannot afford anything else (including a crash helmet), and for the girls - that is, the ones who haven't got boyfriends or husbands to give them a lift. Sicilian men travel on serious motorbikes with large, fast engines, Honda or BMW being regarded as the elite. Be careful not to kill them! They are very prone to speeding and will overtake you to the left or the right, or even by driving up over the roof of your car and down your bonnet. Maybe that was an exaggeration. But they would love to buy a motorbike to do that with, if one existed.

If you still believe that Concorde was the fastest motorised means of transport created by man, you clearly have never witnessed Sicilian men on their motorbikes trying to get home before a thunder storm begins. I should explain that, when it rains in Sicily, it buckets down like a tropical monsoon. The sky is capable of depositing so much water in so little time that, not only do the poor motorcyclists get drenched through their waterproof jackets and trousers and even get their hair wet inside their helmet, but also the sewers cannot cope and half the roads in the city get flooded to a depth of up to four feet. This means that the man on the motorcycle cannot get home to eat his pasta. He may have to travel four times his normal commuting distance to find usable roads. Therefore, when the sky turns black and you start to get blinded by flashes of lightning and hear thunder which makes the car windows vibrate, think of the poor people on their Honda bikes desperate to get home, drop all their sopping wet clothes into the shower tray, hair-dryer their chest hair and finally eat their plate of pasta. Slow down, keep to the kerb, and give them room to pass. You won't actually see them, as they will be about as fast as the speed of light, but believe me, they are there.

Car rental in Sicily is quite a surprising experience for most people the first time around. Firstly, it is blood-curdlingly expensive. The insurance will be exorbitant but heaven help you if you opt out of that! If you book online, or even if you pre-pay, you will find that when you arrive you have to pay a lot more, "for extras". These "extras" will be different every time. The rep at the sales desk will not take you to the car to inspect it for any existing damage. You will just be given the key and the number plate and sent off to search round the car park full of five hundred silver Fiat Puntos. When you do finally discover your own Fiat Punto, you will find that it has a fairly impressive selection of dents and scratches. These are not regarded as "damage" in Sicily and will not, therefore, be marked on the rental contract. A dent is regarded as 'normal wear and tear' unless it exceeds a depth of at least three inches or has actually breached the body of the vehicle and reveals what lies beneath.

Sicilians drive three types of cars. The first type of car is an "old car". If you have an old car, it is a white Fiat Uno. The second type of car is a "new car". People with a new car have a silver Fiat Punto. The third type of car is the girlie car. This will be a white Fiat Cinquecento. Sicilians don't bother with other types of car because they cannot get the parts. There are few foreign car factories in Sicily, and few authorised dealers, so you have to order the parts from Rome or some other far flung place and possibly wait weeks. And pay a fortune. Sicilians don't have a fortune (unless they have "earned" it in creative ways, but we won't talk about that just now.)

Outside the category of car is the commercial vehicle, the *Ape*, which means "bee". This is a microscopic van-type vehicle, consisting of a *Vespa* type Scooter (*Vespa*, for those of you who don't know, means "Wasp") with a miniscule cab encasing the front wheel and handlebars for steering, and an outsized baked bean can wrapped round the back wheel, wherein to store one's wares such as vegetables, fruit, bread, or anything one might be able to sell at the roadside. These vehicles exist exclusively in the colour light blue. I believe other hues are illegal. The bee and wasp names are, I presume, inspired by the fact that these vehicles are powered by something like suped-up lawnmower engines which make the same loud, persistent buzzing noise as an oversized stinging insect. If you find yourself stuck behind one, you may discover you have developed tinnitus after they eventually disappear down a side road, in exactly the same way as you hear deafening static after emerging from an overly loud nightclub.

Sicilians spend a great deal of money on their cars. Firstly, to insure any car for a year you have to pay about twice what you paid to buy the car in the first place, and that's only for third party cover. I have never met anyone in Italy who had anything more than third party cover for a vehicle. Then there's petrol. A litre of petrol in Sicily costs more than a litre of champagne (OK, I'm not talking about Moet Chandon here). Then you have road tax. Then you have speeding fines. These can be hundreds of Euros and often include confiscation of the driving license for a month or more. They are particularly costly as they are graded depending on the margin by which you exceeded the speed limit. In Sicily, a favourite of the Italian traffic police, the *Vigili Urbani*, is to denote a section of motorway or a major state road as having a speed limit of thirty kilometres an hour. This is less than twenty miles per hour. It's about the speed at which your granny can tow her tartan shopping trolley on wheels. They put up lots of notices saying the speed limit is seventy just before the go-slow section, then lie in wait with their radars, ticketing every vehicle that comes past.

Motorway driving in Sicily is completely different from motorway driving in the rest of Europe. The motorways only have two lanes, which many people find so frustrating that they drive along the hard shoulder instead. There are the problems of finding cars travelling up the slip road in the wrong direction. There is the fact that the 'I'm pulling out if you don't hoot' rule means they *always* pull out of slip roads in front of you, because they have already built up so much speed that no matter how much you hoot, the Doppler effect means they think it was a rare bird cooing to its love in a distant nest. Above all, there is the fact that there are never any warning notices or road cones set up to close a lane when there are road works going on. You just find yourself screaming at seventy miles an hour towards a dead-end, demarcated by a sign embellished with diagonal red stripes and a row of bum cleavages, getting sunburnt and sweaty while their owners mess about with tarmac (yes, some things are just like home). There is no hard shoulder and there is a ten ton lorry overtaking you in the next lane. Here is where you test the emergency braking powers of your silver Fiat Punto and hope that the driver of the white Fiat Cinquecento behind you has got fast enough reactions to go from seventy to nought in five seconds while conducting the Emperor Waltz with both arms and one leg.

Road holes are a major hazard in Sicily. They are literally

everywhere. You will never find twenty feet of road free of a significant hole. They can be as much as two feet deep. Look out for puddles! They may contain far more water than you estimated! When driving along in a particularly holy area, you can adopt one of two tactics. One is to look for a hump before the hole, accelerate towards it and thus lift your vehicle up into the air enabling it to fly over the hole and land gently the other side. This is clearly a technique for advanced drivers. The other is simply to swerve around all holes to avoid thumping down into them. Fiats have fairly rigid suspension, so some form of hole avoidance is to be recommended. Extreme hole avoidance can become addictive, however, and as cars overtaking you may not have got round to hooting yet, it would clearly be dangerous if you were to take a huge and sudden swerve in front of them.

Pedestrians are the final road hazard to be aware of in Sicily. They are often sensible enough to realise that they should keep well out of your way, yet you will find that there is a steady but reliable supply of fools just waiting to leap in front of you as you rocket towards them. They will often be daredevil young lads who like to feel they can outrun any Fiat Uno that may dare to defy them as they cross the road. They may be lardy little kids in jumpsuits drawn towards the cake shop. Most often of all, however, they will be a little, old, round-shouldered granddad, about three feet tall, carrying a colossal crate of oranges or bread or artichokes from his delivery van to his shop. He is seventy-five years old, he has been doing this backbreaking work full-time since he was nine, and frankly he does not care if somebody takes him off now. Or does he? Perhaps he feels his time on this earth is running out and he simply cannot afford to waste precious minutes of his remaining life waiting for all the Fiats to get out of his way. Perhaps it is because he has a picture of Padre Pio and another of the Baby Jesus of Naples pinned up in his shop and he knows they are looking out for him. Or else perhaps he knows that his six foot tall son Totò is in the Fiat behind you and, if you touch a whisker on his body, you will find yourself going swimming with concrete boots on.

This brings me to the single most important rule for road safety, not only in Sicily but throughout Italy. That is, always have a religious icon dangling from your rear view mirror. You can touch it and say a little prayer before crossing a particularly ropey looking road bridge which has not been restored since Ancient Roman times. You can also look at it for inspiration and safe guidance throughout performing any particularly tricky manoeuvre, such as a three-point turn on a motorway. Sicilians will often go on a pilgrimage somewhere and bring a dangly icon or at least a rear window sticker back for their car. The Godmother always takes two suitcases when she travels on pilgrimages, one for luggage and a second, empty, one to fill with sacred relics to distribute among her loved ones on her return. Sicilians also usually have the local priest come and bless their new car or motorbike before they drive it, dousing it with holy water and saying potent prayers over it. At the very least, furnish yourself with some rosary beads. They will help you defy all the odds and survive driving the streets of Palermo and the motorways of Sicily. Do not expect divine protection without them.

23

SOME OUTINGS AND A TRIP TO THE OPERA

By this time, the baby was due to pop out at any moment and the waiting was torment. I was still fainting, still vomiting and, additionally, struggling to breathe; I was literally counting the seconds till I could have my own body all to myself again.

At least it took my mind off Mr. Lucky Faeces. Our steady trickle of information about Mr. Faeces seemed to have dried up. His trial was still pending, whilst our application to have the house registered as a human residence rather than a slaughterhouse had ground to a halt, because nobody could find him. Our appeal to get running water had ground to a halt for the same reason. Apparently, for the process to move forward, we needed him to pay a large amount of fees and to sign various documents, which would then have to be decorated with red ribbons, ceiling wax and other fancy stickers to make them look Christmassy, and more important, after queueing for an aggregated three months in public offices with grey walls and lots of mosquitoes. I would have been hopping mad about this, if it had not been for the fact that I was instead focused on cultivating a steadily increasing sense of dread and trepidation about going into labour.

Valentino spoke with glassy eyes about the possibility of a water birth, drug free because we would meditate together and light candles. Apparently he anticipated that my breasts would spontaneously flow like the Trevi Fountain with nourishing Earth Mother milk. He was learning how to massage pressure points to help me handle the pain of labour contractions. He had heard that aromatherapy with lavender and peppermint essential oils can be used with great success to control pain during childbirth. He could do all of this, but I had heard epidurals work pretty well and was planning to ask for one of those, too.

Valentino was so excited about the imminent arrival of tiny

company that he could hardly bear to go to work each morning. He would give me a quick peck on the cheek and then bend down and say a long, lingering farewell to my colossal stomach that sometimes lasted several minutes.

To pass the days in anticipation of the excruciating pain of labour contractions, Valentino took me on some excursions into the mountains. This helped get me away from the unbearable heat, and also gave him a good excuse to take a few random days off work. To his credit, he also took on board most attentively my complaints about the fact that the only times I had actually left the house for the last few weeks was to go and see Johnny Depp. Under different circumstances, dropping in to visit Johnny Depp would have been fine by me, but he did have this damned annoying habit of stabbing needles in my arm every time I saw him. He managed to do it while staring at me with his bedroom eyes, but lately he had started asking me for cups of piddle as well. It was starting to seem a bit kinky.

One of my favourite places which Valentino took me to visit, with our unborn baby, was the eighteenth century hunting lodge of King Ferdinando Borbone, in the village of Ficuzza. It lies in a mixed forest of cork oaks and other trees, up in the mountains surrounding the small town of Corleone, famous worldwide for its fountains. Oh, alright, I am just toying with you. It does have lots of beautiful fountains, but I know Corleone is really far more famous for its Medieval churches. Ha! Got you again! Actually Corleone is in reality renowned for being a town where the locals are very skilled at making their own unique blends of flavoured liquers. What? You didn't know that? Well, now you do.

We reached Corleone before Ficuzza, cruising into the town in the blazing heat of the afternoon. Valentino parked, as instructed, directly outside an ice-cream parlour. I had already observed, from our moving vehicle, that the heat was making the tarmac sticky and melty, so I was planning to make a dash straight into the café and stuff down enough ice-cream for two people, in order to lower my core temperature to a comfortable level and possibly save my half-cooked baby's life. I did take the "eating for two" principle very seriously during my pregnancy.

Once I had opened the car door, I realized that the heat was so intense I would certainly die before reaching the safety of the ice-cream counter. Uncharacteristically quick-thinking, I slammed the door shut, and turned the air conditioning up to maximum force to compensate for the twenty-degree increase in temperature that had taken place during the seven seconds the car door had been open.

Whilst doing so, I also screamed at Valentino,

"Shut the door! Shut the door! Shut the door NOW!!!!!"

Once the air-conditioning had had a chance to cool the car down to about fourteen degrees centigrade, at which temperature I felt comfortable, and once Valentino had memorised a very complex set of instructions which he swore to follow to the letter, I allowed him to exit the vehicle. He did so in such a way as to leave the car door open no more than three seconds, as previously negotiated, and rushed to the ice-cream counter, barging the other customers aside as per my directions, explaining apologetically that his wife was pregnant and it was an emergency; this detail constituted reckless ad-libbing on his part. Having obtained the ice-cream I had requested, I opened the window exactly seven inches, as per specifications, giving him just enough space to slot it into the car, and then hastily closed the window again. At this point I ate my ice-cream in comfort, while Valentino ate his outside the car. Perhaps he felt eating ice-cream in heat high enough to make rocks spontaneously split in half was preferable to sitting in a car cooled down to the temperature of England in late Autumn.

Once he had leapt back inside the car at record speed, being careful to minimise a mixing of internal and external air, I asked him to drive away from this crazy oven of a town and take me up to a cooler altitude. That was all I ever saw of Corleone. Sorry to disappoint you.

We reached the mountain village of Ficuzza, beside the forest of Ficuzza, in a very light mist at early dusk, as the sun was sinking in the sky and illuminating the rocks of the bare mountains and the leaves of the cork trees in pink. The village is dominated by a huge palace at its centre, with a fairly simple façade with clock towers at either end, but an extravagant and huge writing mass of nude figures carved over the main entrance.

"Tell me about this place," I asked Valentino.

"It was the hunting lodge of King Ferdinando I of the Two Sicilies. I don't know much else."

Luckily there was a local guide to show us around. She was young and lively, and told us her grandparents had taught her most of the history of the palace and the town. She also had two young children, she told us, and she advised Valentino to pick up her chair at the entrance, so I could sit on it in each room as we toured around.

"It's terrible standing up when the baby's that big. Though actually," she added, smiling down at my vast tummy, "I don't think either of mine ever were quite as big as that."

We began walking up a beautiful marble staircase, with different colours of stone used for the steps and the handrail.

"King Ferdinando was such a lecher," the guide told us, "that he had this palace constructed full of secret passageways. He used them to escape from angry husbands whenever he needed to. Local legend tells that he had sex with every single woman in the village. He was the king so it was almost impossible for them to refuse him."

"So are those nudes over the doorway his favourite conquests?" asked Valentino.

"Just warning visitors what to expect!" laughed the guide.

The wood surrounding the hunting lodge – which was more of a palace really - was full of wild animals, and hunting was very popular in those parts. The husbands had weapons and a good aim. Sneaking around in tunnels probably saved King Ferdinando's life many a time.

The Hunting lodge was completed in the early years of the nineteenth century, and its design was based on the English halls of this period. The parts of the palace we saw were lovely, but sadly stripped of most of their original interior decoration and furniture by fascist soldiers during the Second World War. They used the antique furniture as firewood. This was an act of pure spite; being in the middle of a forest, they can hardly have suffered from a lack of available wood to burn. They also wrote on the walls, painted fascist slogans and military instructions on antique frescoes, and stole paintings, alabaster sculptures and anything else of value they could carry away. Much of the palace has been modestly restored but, with all the antique furniture destroyed and the original features ripped out, the past grandeur can never truly be recreated. The walls, which were once covered in beautiful paintings, were just plain white.

"My grandfather remembers how beautiful this place was before the war," the guide told me, "and he hates coming here to see these blank white walls and empty rooms. The last time he came here he cried, and said he never wanted to step inside again."

Our guide told us that the cruel abuses the area had suffered continued, at the hands of Sicilians, after the war. People would come in hordes from the surrounding areas and strip the cork trees bare to sell all the cork, or even fell them to get the bark off easily, instead of harvesting the correct amount of bark and letting them renew themselves. The locals in the village were so concerned at the devastation of the forest, and the failure of the government to do anything about it, that they decided to take the matter into their own hands.

"The old people invented a story that the cork trees were

possessed by demons," our guide told us as I sat on my wooden chair, and she and Valentino sat on a bench opposite me. "When cork bark is stripped away from the tree, the inner bark and the sap is a bright, intense orangey-red. This red sap tends to ooze down the tree if too much bark is taken away at once. The locals put the word out that this sap was the devil's blood."

"And I bet people believed it," said Valentino.

"Were they really that naïve?" I asked.

"Oh yes, the kind of people ignorant enough to destroy cork trees would definitely fall for *cavolate* like that," said Valentino. I like it when he calls things 'cabbegey nonsense.'

The guide nodded in agreement. "They made the tale even better when some local children happened to find a colossal fungus growing on one of the trees. By sheer chance, it had the form of a grotesque face. So their parents led some outsiders to see it, telling them it was a demon unmasked. They knew word would spread. The cork thieves were terrified and kept well away. So the cork forest survived intact. Nowadays it's flourishing and makes a charming place for a country walk."

"Except for those who are great with child and have legs that look and feel like tree trunks themselves," I said.

"And it's getting dark now anyway," said Valentino.

We thanked the guide and set off, admiring the beautiful forest from the car.

A few days later, Valentino told me he had to go out for a couple of hours "to get something really important."

"What?" I asked.

"A surprise," he told me.

I waited impatiently until I heard the car entering the garage. He came upstairs carrying two suitcases, followed by my mother and father. I was so happy to see them I cried. He had taken the week off work to take us wherever we wanted to go.

"Once the baby is born, you'll never get the same quality of conversation and attention again," he said. "This is your last chance to spend time together focused on each other."

He spent the week taking us on outings to beautiful places I had never seen yet. This was also the first chance my parents had had to explore Sicily properly.

We loved the castle at Caccamo. My parents both have heart conditions and, since I had tree-trunk legs and an abdomen like the front end of a missile, we were as slow as each other walking up the long cobbled slope to the entrance. In the Medieval castle, there is a carved wooden altar opposite the long dining table, with an antique rug upon which visitors could kneel while praying. But – Aha! – the rug hides a trap door, operated by a lever the other side of the room. The wicked count who owned this castle would lure his enemies into his home with the offer of lavish dinners, feigned friendship and terribly expensive imported wines; wait till they were inspired by the urge to pray (they were Medieval, after all); and then pull the lever to send them crashing down the chute directly into his pitch dark rocky dungeon, which had no exit. Then he would sit back down, thump his fist on the dining table and shout "More capons and a flagon of wine, wench!" as he listened to his victim howling about having two broken legs, probably.

One of the most exciting places Val took us to was a town called Castelbuono. If you speak Italian you will know that this means "good castle". The place is well named because there is a castle there, and it is pretty good actually. It was medieval, huge, had a scary portcullis and a massive dungeon, a secret underground tunnel leading you to the church, and there were countless places with no handrail where a clumsy pregnant woman with frequent dizzy spells could fall about thirty feet onto a solid slab of rock. The walls around and inside the castle complex are a mix of stone blocks and actual pieces of the cliff that the castle was built upon. The chapel was particularly astonishing, with scores of sculpted cherubs appearing to emerge out of the walls rather like ghosts.

The town of Castelbuono turned out to be a wonderful place to spend a day. It had bars on every corner which sold mouth-watering sorbet ice cream, home-made from fruits such as mandarins and mulberries and watermelons. I know they all sold good sorbets because my mother and I tested every single flavour.

"You'll ruin your appetite for lunch," Valentino told her, as he watched her tucking into her fourth ice-cream at about twelve noon.

"No, I'm having ice-cream for lunch," she replied.

"You have to eat something sensible and nutritious," he told her.

"No, I don't," she retorted like a naughty school girl. "My mother's dead. I can do what I like now."

After our ice-creams, we found a cavernous and jaw-dropping antique shop, crammed with *pietra dura* inlaid stone table tops, magnificently carved wooden furniture, ceramics, gold figurines and even an eighteenth century toilet. There was also a food emporium with organic meat, eggs and cheeses from surrounding farms, exotic sausages and salami and other meat dishes. Yet even this was not what made Castelbuono really exciting. In Castelbuono, we ate manna.

As we strolled along the road from the castle (actually Valentino strolled, my parents dawdled and I waddled and moaned), we passed a woman with a stall in the street laden with cellophane packets of off-white sticks of manna. This is the miracle food that falls from the sky in the bible and feeds the Israelies. The bible describes it terribly badly, in my opinion. Whoever wrote this section of the bible needs to work on their descriptive prose:

"And when the dew that lay was gone up, behold, upon the face of the wilderness there lay a small round thing, as small as the hoar frost on the ground. And when the children of Israel saw it, they said one to another, It is manna: for they wist not what it was. And Moses said unto them, This is the bread which the Lord hath given you to eat. This is the thing which the Lord hath commanded, Gather of it every man according to his eating." (Exodus 16:14-16)

The lady at the stall had various leaflets explaining it, but I felt too lazy to read them and just asked her to tell me about it. Apparently concerned about the extraordinary weight my pelvic floor was supporting by then, she let me sit on her own chair, and also fed me some free manna for good measure. It tasted like something between honey and maple syrup, but it was a little less sweet than either of them, so I noticed the heavenly flavour, and its lovely crystalline texture as it melted in my mouth. My mother asked my father to buy a little stash of it to take home.

The lady showed us a lot of interesting photographs as she talked, many of which were of her father and other family members harvesting manna. Manna is the sap of the manna tree, a type of narrow-leaf ash called *fraxinus angustifolia*. The manna trees have grown wild around Castelbuono for many centuries. They were once indigenous throughout the Central and Western Mediterranean, but they have gradually died out and recently began to become rare in the mountains around Castelbuono, too, so they are now carefully cultivated as well.

In July and August, the creamy white sap flows so abundantly that a little of it drips out of the branches and gradually crystallises, so it looks like icicles hanging off the tree. Local experts (generally, very small, very old men who look a lot like Getafix The Druid) know how to cut slits in the bark to create far more of these stalactites than occur naturally, and they monitor the trees over about two weeks as they extend ever downwards. The sticks of manna are cut from the tree when they reach the ground and are fully dry. Once it is harvested, the manna is broken up into short sticks to be sold.

It takes a lot of dedication to monitor the precious crop and protect it from the elements. If it rains or gets too humid during these days, the manna just dissolves and is lost. Very occasionally, when the weather conditions are absolutely perfect, it pours out of the trees and falls to the ground without having to be tended; the manna in the bible story refers to one of these gift harvests.

Manna only contains about three percent glucose, which makes it very useful for diabetics. In Sicily, if you flick a cupcake into a crowd, it has a seven-in-ten probability of landing on someone diabetic. The sweet taste of Manna comes mainly from mannitol, a type of sugar that is absorbed very slowly and which has laxative effects if you eat too much of it. Being constipated is the Italian national sport (serves them right for eating pasta all the time), so this is touted as its other great medicinal property. As we walked around castelbouno, we heard some ludicrously extravagant claims made for the magical medicinal properties of manna. Manna does contain various useful nutrients such as zinc but, frankly, the main reason for eating it is just that it tastes delicious.

"Manna can cure any allergy," we were told by various vendors in Castelbuono.

"It will cure any liver disease," said another.

"It can prevent death," said one woman. Honestly, she said that.

"For how long?" asked my Father.

The woman was taken aback when I translated his question into Italian, and Valentino turned away, laughing.

"Maybe we had better buy some more, to be on the safe side," Dad suggested with a cheerful grin.

When it was time for my parents to leave, my mother and I cried a little. I was afraid of going through the birth without her, even though I knew Valentino would be there.

"This has been the best holiday I've ever had," said my father. "Thank you for everything, Valentino."

"Me too," said my mother. "I enjoyed it more than our honeymoon."

"Yes," agreed Dad. "Me too."

I spent a week feeling despondent after my parents had left, and also worrying. Our baby was supposed to have emerged by now. Mini-Me was overdue. Valentino has a friend who is a politician, and who can get free tickets to just about anything, any time Valentino asks him. The day after a scan which confirmed the baby was fine, just not showing any signs of leaving home, Val came home with a special question.

"Would you like to spend an evening in a private box at the *Teatro Massimo* seeing an opera?"

Palermo's baroque opera house happens to have the second largest stage of any theatre in Europe, and also paintings of cherubs' bottoms all over the ceiling. And I love opera.

"Of course yes," I answered. I was thrilled.

When he came home from work the next day he excitedly showed me two tickets. It turned out that we were going to see *I Vespri Siciliani*, or *The Sicilian Vespers*, by Giuseppe Verdi. This meant I had the chance to learn some Sicilian history as well as hearing something new by my all-time favourite composer of opera.

"Have you seen this one before?" I asked him.

"No!" he laughed. "I've never seen any opera!"

My mouth fell open. Was he teasing me? Italians love opera. It is in their blood. It is their national thing. The funeral of Giuseppe Verdi in 1901 was the largest public gathering of human beings that has ever taken place in Italian history. Almost all the orchestras and choirs of Italy came together to play as a combined musical mass at his funeral service in Milan. Afterwards, the thousands of members of the public who had gathered to mourn their national hero in the streets spontaneously broke into singing the *Chorus of the Hebrew Slaves* from *Nabucco*. If you do not know it, you should. It is perhaps the most beautiful and moving of all operatic arias ever written. And thousands of Italians sang it in time and in tune and with heavenly voices, with no conductor. It must have been the best flash mobbing in the history of the world.

"But Valentino, I thought you liked music," I objected. I was still not entirely sure whether to believe him. "Whenever I play my opera CD's in the car, you sing along passionately."

"Yes," he agreed.

"And you like them, don't you?" I asked.

"Of courrrrrrse," he said in English, his eyes sparkling.

"So *why* have you never been to the opera?" I asked.

"I was waiting for you," he answered with a grin.

Bizarrely, then, it transpired I actually had married the only man in Italy who knew nothing about opera.

"The Sicilian Vespers" was an episode in Sicilian history that has become legend. On the evening of Easter Monday in 1282, when Sicily was ruled oppressively by the French, a large crowd was gathered outside the Church of the Holy Spirit in Palermo - a church which still stands, incidentally - waiting to hear vespers. As a group of noble women approached the church, some French soldiers stopped them. On the pretext of searching them for hidden weapons, the soldiers groped the women in front of their husbands and families. One Sicilian custom, which I believe everyone in the world is aware of, is that you do not tamper with a Sicilian woman. You do not touch, fondle, or fumble your way about the physical presence of any female who belongs to a Sicilian male, if you value your life.

The infuriated husbands and fathers let out a cry of "Death to the French" and, with the help of the whole crowd, set about fulfilling their battle cry in a vast massacre. Blood flowed outside the church, as the church bells rang out the call to evening vespers on Easter Day, the most holy event in the Christian calendar.

This triggered a six-week revolt in which anyone French was massacred, regardless of gender or age. Corleone joined Palermo and both cities gained independence. The revolt triggered a war that lasted exactly twenty years and spread to most of the Western Mediterranean. If you include countries drawn in diplomatically, it involved the whole of Europe.

Verdi was born in the north of Italy which, at that time, was part of Napoleon's French Empire. It would have been too risky to set the story in Sicily, so when the opera premiered he presented it as a story set in Portugal in 1640 while Portugal was under Spanish control. Nowadays, it is normally relocated to its original time and place – Sicily in 1282 – and this was the version that we saw.

I decided to download a summary of the opera's plot from the Internet. I found a very interesting Italian website for opera lovers, and printed the plot out in haste just before leaving the house. Valentino was chivvying me to hurry, because I had already spent an extraordinarily long time trying to improve my appearance. I enjoy dressing up a bit for the opera. Most women say they develop a fabulous healthy glow during pregnancy and radiate natural beauty. I was still being sick many times a day and looked pasty. I was also, by this time, wearing dresses in sizes so large I had, until this point, regarded them purely as a potential camping trip solution should one prove unable to find an affordable tent. In the end I applied and removed my make-up three times, and gave up. I consoled myself with the thought that it is dark inside theatres most of the time anyway.

The Teatro Massimo was built to celebrate Sicily's becoming part of Italy. What better way to celebrate becoming Italian than by building an opera house? It is not only beautiful and magnificent, it is also still the third largest theatre in Europe and has the second largest stage.

The size is less important than the decoration, though. The domed roof is painted with a vast fresco, embellished with celestial characters floating on clouds, hovering cherubs with bare bottoms, and gold leaf ornamentation everywhere. Each row of seats and private boxes has a different type of decorative light set below it. The twiddliness and magnificence are like that of a baroque church – though I do mean a *Sicilian* baroque church, not just any old baroque church. Most Baroque churches look functional and austere compared to Sicilian ones.

Once I had settled into our private box and admired the surroundings, I read my plot summary.

ACT I

In Palermo, French troops carouse about and live it large in the square as Siciliani hostilely observe them. Duchess Elena mourns her brother Frederick of Austria, done in by the French for treason. A drunken French officer commands her to sing about a storm tossed ship and thusslywise she riles up the populace to attack the Frenchmans.

A young patriot, Arrigo, is released by his guards and tells Duchess Elena he latterly has been acquitted of treason. Commander Monforte asks of the young man his name, for he seems to be a bastard, and Monforte offers the Sicilian youth fame and fortune in the service of France. Arrigo indignantly sends the Commander packing, whereupon the ruler warns him to henceforthlywise avoid the rebel Elena. But Arrigo enters her palace.

I dropped the sheet on the floor when the curtain went up, for there on the massive stage was a perfect reproduction of Palermo's Church of the Holy Spirit, outside which the actual rebellion took place in 1282. Let me tell you, when it comes to doing art and being historical, the Sicilians lead the world.

Act One was much more entertaining than the plot summary made it sound, and the storm tossed ship song was very catchy. The opera was wonderful, and the quality of the singers was world class. The singers walked in and out of the church door, the stained glass windows lit up and darkened according to the time of day, the sky changed colour as the sun set in glowing orange and red, and all of this was merely the backdrop to the best music written ever, anywhere in the world. This was why I had fallen in love with Italy in the first place.

Arrigo fell in love with Elena and a budding romance blossomed. It was an opera, so of course there was romance. In act three, Arrigo discovered that he was indeed a bastard, and his father was none other than Commander Monforte the Frenchman himself, who had defiled his mother. This put a spanner in the works as far as his courtship of Elena was concerned, indeed they both got riled up, but in the end she forgave him and agreed to marry him. Henceforthlywise they lived happily ever after.

When Valentino went back to work the next day, his colleagues eagerly asked him about the performance at Palermo's most splendid theatre. One of them mentioned the most famous aria from *The Sicilian Vespers*. What had he thought of it?

Aria means a chorus from an opera in English, but in Italian it means also just means "air".

"Well, I think they may have had air conditioning in the theatre," said Valentino, baffled by the question. "Honestly, I didn't really notice."

24

THE BIRTH OF OUR SON

A week after going to the opera, when I had still felt not one single contraction and the baby had not even descended into the launching position, the gynecologist decided I should be taken into hospital to induce the birth. While I was being admitted, a junior doctor filled out the cover of the cardboard folder that was to hold my medical notes. He asked me my name, date of birth and blood group and then said,

"Are your parents related to each other?"

I screamed with laughter so raucously that I almost rolled off my trolley. The doctor looked bewildered. He showed me that there really was a box printed on the form, for him to tick YES or NO, and to write alongside it the specific details of exactly how inbred I was.

"A lot of Sicilians do marry their cousins," the doctor told me. He seemed a little defensive, I thought.

"Oh," I said. "When you get admitted to a hospital in England, they fill out that folder by writing how many units of alcohol you consume each week - or is it each day? - to the nearest dozen. So you see, whilst you Sicilians are a bunch of incestuous teetotallers, we British are genetically diverse beer monsters."

He was not amused.

Sicily contains enclaves of people who are so pathologically distrustful of outsiders that they only ever get to socialize with their own family. Sicilians do not trust people from the next village. One of their favourite insults is "They're all inbred in THAT village." Yet actually, they're all inbred in ALL the villages.

Ninfa once told me she used to work in one of the local fish factories, stuffing anchovies into jars and pouring oil over them, and handling various other fishy products. Then she told me her heart's deepest secret: she had dated the love of her life when she was eighteen years old, and they were engaged, but his mother refused to let them marry. She insisted a girl who worked in a fish factory could not possibly be a virgin.

"What did she think we were doing in those fish factories?" she exclaimed shrilly. "You have a foreman breathing over you, watching you work hard every second. You don't even have time to take a pee, never mind get romantic with anyone. It's so loud you can't even hear what anyone is saying. And anyway, it's all women working there, except the factory owner and the engineer who mends the machines, and they're always the wrong side of sixty."

Whilst she sat at home broken-hearted, her handsome beau's mother forced him to marry his own cousin.

"She was fat. I mean vast," Ninfa told me in distress, at the climax of her story. "She was a great mattress of a woman! His mother thought that lump was better than me, because she just sat at home every day doing absolutely nothing, and because she was family."

So, what are the consequences of all this Sicilian inbreeding? Apart from a physique that resembles bedding? Albert Einstein is the Poster Boy for cousin marriage. Not only were his parents cousins, but he also went ahead and married his own cousin. His wife was not only his first cousin, but also his second cousin, since you can trace the relationship through both parents. This clearly proves that inbreeding does not always produce genetic defects. On the other hand, I think we also know that Sicily is not completely full of people like Albert Einstein.

"Veronica, are you alright?" said Valentino loudly.

"Signora?" said the doctor at the same time. I do dislike being dragged out of an interesting train of daydreaming.

"I'm fine," I reassured them both.

"My parents are cousins," said Valentino to the doctor.

"What?!" I spluttered.

"Yes," he said calmly.

Valentino then went on to tell the doctor that The Godmother and Don Ciccio are second cousins. I lay on my narrow, hard trolley in flabbergasted silence.

Having been formally admitted to the hospital, established that I was not inbred (though my foetus was slightly) and having also established that I was two weeks overdue, I was further informed by the Ward Matron that I had the largest belly she had seen in sixteen years' working as a midwife.

"And we had triplets here last week," she added, just to make me feel even better about it.

After that, the waiting started. They applied a type of gel to my pudenda that was supposed to induce labour. It induced an excruciating burning pain instead. By this time I had decided to name the place Hell Hospital. Then they applied more gel twelve hours later, which hurt even more. Then a junior doctor, at one o'clock in the morning, wanted to apply a third dose. I donkey-kicked him in the genitals but he managed to get some of it on me anyway. It hurt so much by that time that I cried audibly and did not care. I howled till my nose ran. In true Sicilian style, the doctor showed no empathy and attempted to reproach me for displaying cowardice.

"You haven't even got a vagina!" I informed him, using a raised voice. "What would you know about it?"

"Yeah, OK," he agreed, suddenly snapping out of doctor mode and becoming human. "This isn't working. We could either try dynamite to get this baby out, or just do a caesarean in the morning."

I authorised the caesarean and then lay awake all night, in a noisy room full of snoring mothers, feeling alone, scared and extremely abroad. I wanted to go home and I wanted my Mummy. If I had known what I was actually in for, I *would* have gone home.

In the morning, I was allowed nothing to eat or drink, not even a drop of water, and finally at one o'clock I was wheeled off down a corridor into the operating theatre. There, I was informed I would be having a general anaesthetic, instead of an epidural, because I have a heart condition.

"What?" I asked.

"There's not time to explain, lie down," I was told brusquely by a nurse wielding a tube that had twice the diameter of a garden hose, who then yanked my knees apart. When you are pregnant, your tummy becomes public property and anyone who feels like touching it goes right ahead and does so. Once you are giving birth, simply anyone who comes near you feels the right to do anything they want to your genital area. This woman was going for the bladder with her giant catheter tube. She stabbed at me excruciatingly about seven times, I almost bit my arm off in pain, then she picked up the glasses that were hanging around her neck and put them on, and got it in with just three more tries. The pain did not subside.

Next I was stripped off completely naked, all attempts at maintaining dignity having been utterly abandoned. My lower abdomen and groin were painted with iodine, which *stings*, I would like to remind you. Then three surgeons in face masks, holding scalpels and other sharp instruments, approached. At this point, silently but firmly, a mask was held over my face and I fell unconscious.

I woke up utterly paralysed. When I say paralysed, I mean that I could not even inhale. I was in this condition for almost a whole minute, unable to scream or tell anyone anything, as I could not open my eyes either. I realised I was going to get brain damage, then die of oxygen deficiency, and nobody would realise I had been awake and never got the chance to sue the pants off them all. There is absolutely no way to describe the level of terror you feel when you are wide awake and literally unable to breathe.

Then eventually, mercifully, something was yanked out of my arm and I could inhale, though just a tiny bit. I felt the seasick swaying motion of being wheeled along a corridor, and was then parked in the corridor for a few minutes before being put in a separate room, all alone.

"It hurts," I managed to whisper to the nurse who was wheeling me.

"You've just had a healthy baby boy, you should be grateful," she snapped, glaring at me disapprovingly, then she turned her back and left me alone, for a very long time. So I had had a boy. Thanks for telling me that exciting piece of news with such sensitivity.

I closed my eyes and bit hard on my own tongue trying to bear the pain. I realised that I was wet. My whole back and legs and all of me from the armpits down was wet. Had I peed myself? I could hear dripping, and in my delirious state I imagined a leaking pipe dripping water onto the floor. I could not raise my head or turn at all, so I touched the wetness with my hand and then raised it to my face: my fingers were red with blood.

At that moment two nurses came in, and indicated that I must lift up by bottom so they could change whatever was underneath me. They pulled out a huge disposable absorbent sheet, about three feet by three feet, sodden with blood, and inserted a new one. They replaced the now red sheet that had been on top of me with a clean one. They did not speak to me at all.

"Get someone to come in here and mop the floor a bit," said one of them. "There's a huge puddle."

I tipped my head over at that moment and caught sight of a large pool of red beside the trolley. So I had not imagined the dripping sound.

Once the floor was clean, they allowed Valentino to enter.

"They said you're haemorrhaging," he told me. "Do you feel OK?"

"It hurts so much. Why can't I have painkillers?"

"I'm not sure," he answered, "but they said you can't."

So there I was, lying on a trolley, having had a massive hole cut deep into my body, with my precious blood dripping onto the floor, and without so much as a junior aspirin to help me bear the pain. This is the Catholic way. The Vatican decrees that pain is sent by God, and it is His will that we are use the opportunity to prove our faith by bearing it. This is the reason Italian doctors deny painkillers to people dying of cancer.

After two hours I was wheeled to the ward, still haemorrhaging but with a more efficient irrigation system. I cried, but very quietly because I could not breathe properly, and Valentino laid baby Matteo on my chest. He was ivory white and big and perfect, and so beautiful that I felt just a tiny bit better.

Just a tiny bit.

If I could have had some morphine, or even a junior aspirin, I might have felt better still. Half a pint of single malt whisky might have helped, too.

25

THREE HOLD-UPS

New born babies are not particularly attractive on their first day of life. They tend to be a livid maroon color and many of them are strangely hairy. Squeezing down the birth canal squashes their heads into a bullet shape and it can take days for them to return to normal. Sicilian babies are generally born very small as well, with masses of black hair. The babies I saw around me in Hell Hospital were all nappy, with a huge pair of eyes peeping out of the top. They were adorable, but they looked like bush babies.

At almost ten pounds, Matteo was so colossal by Sicilian standards that some nurses debated whether to notify the press. He did not fit into the hospital cot, and had to keep his legs bent up all the time. Since he had escaped the traumas of a natural birth, he was ivory white with perfect features and a beautifully rounded head. His hair was blonde fluff and his eyes were blue and about nine doctors from different wards came to see him because, apparently, the whole hospital was talking about this child who looked like a porcelain doll. They all told me he was the most beautiful baby they had ever seen, and their kind words gave me a tiny bit of encouragement as I lay there in my pool of blood.

The Godmother stayed with me in hospital and took care of me and Matteo. She got almost no sleep day or night and only had a folding deck chair in which to snatch the occasional uncomfortable nap. She washed me and cared for me in every detail, including a lot of the care I personally think I should have received from the nurses, and she never complained once. She was so excited and delighted with little Matteo she sang Sicilian lullabies to him constantly. At the top of her voice. I believe this is the only correct way to sing lullabies among Italians.

Italian hospital wards do not have curtains around the beds, so when a doctor came around to conduct an internal examination, everyone on the ward got a full view. This included anyone who happened to be walking past outside, as Hell Hospital did not have curtains at the windows, either. For this reason, men folk were only allowed on the ward when they managed to sneak in under cover. For the other women who had their mothers with them, this may have been tolerable, but for me it was torment.

They kept me in hospital for four days with no painkillers whatsoever. They asked me every day if I had done a poo: apparently this was the required hurdle one must surmount to gain release from Hell Hospital. On the fourth day, I realised I may be set to beat the Guinness World Record for constipation, which is currently held by an Indian woman called Anusha who did not poo for 45 days. I understand Indian toilets are discouraging. I have been told some of them smell so bad they can make your brain melt, but frankly the toilet in Hell Hospital was not far behind. After four days I decided lying was the best policy, so next time a doctor asked me if I had done a poo, I assured him I had just dropped an absolute corker. I was duly discharged.

I was unable to stand up from a chair at this point, and needed Valentino to pull me up. The Godmother came to our house and continued to help a great deal with looking after her grandson. Her main way of looking after him was to keep tidying away the things that I needed within reach, since I could not get up and walk about, and also washing him till his skin peeled off. She also dressed him in so many clothes I was worried he would go into heat-induced convulsions, refusing to see the logic that he only needed to be as wrapped up as we were. We were wearing t-shirts. He was wearing two jumpers, a woollen cardigan buttoned up to the roll of fat where his neck would one day be, and a hat. Indoors.

The Godmother showed absolutely no sympathy for my pain. I never spoke about it, but I was white as a sheet and sometimes cried out involuntarily when I felt sudden pangs of agony. Valentino was understandably excited about our baby, but under his mother's influence he made me feel like the ripped up wrapping paper that got trodden on and kicked into a corner under the Christmas tree. I felt completely alone and my only consolation at this point was holding Matteo in my arms. I realised how many other new mothers go through the same pain when I received parcels of luxury chocolates and toiletries in the post, accompanied by loving messages from friends with young children of their own.

"You wanted a bicycle, so now pedal," The Godmother once said to me, out of the blue, after I had been home from hospital for six days.

This is the Italian equivalent of saying "You've made you bed, so now you've got to lie in it."

"What do you mean?" I asked her.

"I mean what I say," she answered.

The Godmother specialised in making 'serves you right' type comments, though she made them ambiguously so I could never challenge her. She was also extremely careful to say them only when we were alone. Valentino thought I was being paranoid when I told him things she had said.

The family doctor came to see me several times to check on the gradually decreasing haemorrhage and the cesarian scar, which was healing horribly and in slow motion. He has five children of his own, and he gave Valentino a detailed lecture on *exactly how* painful it is being physically cut in half, *exactly how* traumatic it is being unable to stand up, and *exactly how* important it is to receive empathy from the man whose fault it is. My dear old Val stopped listening to his mother at that point, and our marriage was saved.

By the time Matteo was two months old, I was able to stand up and walk about unaided, albeit unsteadily. Despite this, I still felt as if all my entrails were about to spill onto the floor. It was an unpleasant feeling which could only be ameliorated by wearing a modern, high-tech equivalent of a whalebone corset both day and night.

Planning to get to know the next town properly at last, and simultaneously to work off my seven-pound paunch by walking all over Aspra and Bagheria, I enthusiastically bought a baby sling. This looked rather like a rucksack with two leg-holes in the bottom, for carrying Matteo around strapped to my tummy. I planned a two-pronged attack on my pot belly. My son had created the bulge in the first place by kicking it repeatedly from the inside: now he could help to reverse the process and resolve the problem by kicking it back in, from the outside.

I took it for a trial run by taking a walk in Aspra, and realised that, firstly, you cannot see the ground in front of you when you are wearing a baby and, secondly, there were almost no pavements in the village. The inability to see the ground I was stepping on resulted in my turning up at home with a shoe coated in brown smelly stuff. The lack of pavements had previously been a minor inconvenience but, when you have a baby attached to yourself, *your* baby, a baby you nearly died to bring into this world, suddenly the effect of cars repeatedly clipping your elbows or straggling wing mirrors slapping your buttocks has a totally new effect. You start to view every vehicle as a lethal weapon, out to kill your precious progeny, and every driver deserving of a quick roadside strangulation. After that one walk with Matteo, I took another lone stroll and established that there were, indeed, no pavements anywhere in the village that spanned more than about twenty yards at a time. In between were the bad-lands, the no man's land where motorised vehicles regarded anything on two legs as fair game.

The upshot of this was that I gave up on my mission to walk the streets of Sicily and just used the baby sling for shopping trips in carefully selected, well-pavemented locations. In this setting, it served the dual purpose of stopping Matteo from crying, which he often did when not being held, and also disguising my paunch, which had so far shown no signs of deflating even though Matteo was no longer inside it. Also, the weather was getting cold, and he made a great substitute for a hot water bottle. I developed the habit of holding onto his little dangling feet as I walked about, to make sure they did not get cold.

One afternoon, Valentino and I decided to go and do the shopping together. I successfully negotiated to go to the large supermarket about half an hour from our house. This was an attractive, modern-looking supermarket, at least by Sicilian standards. It had housewares, and automatic conveyor belts at the till, and staff with uniforms. It had an aisle of stationery and a man in the car park to round up stray trolleys. It had a car park, for goodness sake! It was a *de-luxe* supermarket.

I must admit I still had mixed feelings about it. You could call it a love-hate relationship. This was because the employees were all spectacularly rude and unhelpful. If you asked them where anything was, they either told you it was out of stock, had never been in stock even when this was a blatant lie ("No, we've never sold spaghetti in this supermarket") or simply pretended not to hear you and walked away at high speed. It was worth putting up with this, though, because of their superior and extensive selection of fattening junk foods. They also had gerbil dung sachets far more concentrated that those of any other supermarket.

When Valentino went shopping alone, he tended to buy the same old boring healthy food every time. I wanted to peruse the new, exciting things appearing for the Christmas period and load the trolley with fancy types of novelty panettone, that Italian Christmas bread with fruit pieces in it, *torrone* and other Italian sweets, gorgeous boxes of coffee-filled chocolates and simply delicious Italian pastries. After all, I had the ideal belly hider, so why not take advantage?

As I cruised around the Aisles of Temptation, I realised that my cravings were not just simple sugar addiction or an overhang from pregnancy cravings. I had actually been though such a terribly traumatic and painful experience that I needed comfort food like a sick man needs medicine. Each fondant chocolate, or lump of nougat, or sensational pastry that melted in my mouth, wiped out just a little bit of that crippling pain that had made me nearly lose my mind, that unspeakable misery, that sincere desire to be dead that I could never tell Valentino about. Weight loss would have to come later; first, I needed to heal my soul.

This supermarket had an upstairs, accessible via two lifts which stood side by side. As we headed towards them, Valentino burdened with a trolley, and I burdened with Matteo, the set of lift doors on the left opened. One of the assistants approached from behind us and sprang into the enormous and empty lift. She stood in it flicking her long black hair from side to side, vainly looking in the mirror. She looked admiringly at her nails, which were two inches long and varnished in several colours, with glittery patterns on. Just as I reached the doorway and was about to waddle in after her, she pressed the button to go upstairs and left me standing there while the doors slammed shut in my face, almost clipping the end of my nose.

We waited for the other lift to arrive and empty out. I instructed Valentino to be ready with the trolley to break the ankles of any shop "assistant" who dared to try the same trick on us again. I was also planning to pick up a couple of cans of pineapple chunks and throw them at the lift-hog once I was upstairs. My across-the-board absence of competence in any sport is legendary, yet you would be amazed to witness how much my eye-hand coordination can improve inexplicably when I am out for revenge. This supermarket may be snazzy by Sicilian standards, but they did not have security cameras. My plan was to execute my vendetta fully, then deny everything, admit nothing, and if necessary make counter-allegations.

Once we emerged from the lift upstairs, I lost focus. There were just so many different types of chocolate! I succeeded in sneaking a great many fattening items into the trolley while Valentino was busy calculating the most economical brand of toilet paper. My precious little Matteo slept soundly the whole time, using my bosom for a pillow: surely the best pillow any of us ever sleeps on. Feeling his warm little body pressed against my heart, hearing his tiny, quiet little snore, and smelling his divine baby skin was the other great healer for me. Every time I looked at him, or felt him, or thought of him, it reinforced my conviction that the pain had been worth it.

"Ciao!" Valentino suddenly shouted, through me. His voice went in one of my ears and right out of the other one. Italians are good at voice projection that way. "Look who it is!" he instructed me, with a nudge.

A young man was filling shelves with chocolate bars.

"Do I know him?" I asked.

The young man left his chocolates to greet Valentino and me with a kiss each. He beamed with smiles, he petted Matteo, he congratulated us and I tried all the while to disguise the fact that I had no idea who he was.

"So, what brings you here?" asked Valentino, finally. "No *stigghiola* any more?"

That was when it clicked. He was Gianfortuna the Stigghiolaro! He told us that the council had revoked his license because they thought his Small Intestine Kebab stall was lowering the tone of the neighbourhood and, unable to find a new pitch elsewhere, he had had to take a job in this supermarket. The locals still lamented the disappearance of Signor Gianfortuna the *Stigghiolaro*, apparently, but his wife's laundry burden had plummeted and so had his weight. It was hardly any wonder I had failed to recognise him. He had wasted away beyond all recognition. I mean, he even had a *neck*.

At the tills, there was chaos. Careful examination of the situation revealed that only one till was open, despite the vast crowds, and it was manned by Lift Hog. Eventually we reached the front of the queue and Valentino and I split the work up in our usual way. I unloaded the trolley while he packed the bags at the other end.

"What's this for?" he asked, as a chocolate and hazelnut panettone was shoved towards him by the cashier.

"My breakfast," I answered boldly.

"What about these?" he enquired after a neat stack of three nougat bars came his way.

"Erm, just in case your mother visits," I replied. "You know she likes them."

Lift Hog looked at me and sneered. I looked at her straight back in the eye, regretting the fact I had not got any canned pineapple chunks in my trolley. All the assistants in this particular supermarket generally never made eye contact, except if they were telling you your debit card had been rejected and your store-card loyalty points had expired, in which case they wanted to watch and fully enjoy the expression of impotent frustration spreading across your face. She realised her gaffe, and hastily examined her nails:

yes, they were still false. She was a young girl, not more than twenty.

She was one of the very dark Sicilian types, with straight black hair almost to her waist and deep olive skin, and her face would have been beautiful if it had not been disfigured by her obsessive-compulsive sneering disorder.

"And this?" Valentino asked, holding a large box of almond biscuits in the air.

"In case I get peckish between meals."

At this point he stopped querying things and just crammed them industriously into an ever-growing mountain of bulging carrier bags. At the sound of rustling plastic bags Matteo was beginning to wake up and fidget with his legs. I do not know what it is about that sound that makes all new-born babies freak out, but I think it may be because it sounds so much like a crackling forest fire, which taps into an animalistic safety instinct.

"How old is your baby?" Lift Hog asked. I noticed a ruby engagement ring on her finger as she slid five bags of sweets across the scanner and a family pack of crisps.

"Exactly two months," I answered. Matteo had fully woken up and was turning his head and making little croaking sounds.

"I thought he was older than that," she said. "He's big for his age. He's got such chunky thighs!"

She continued shovelling food across the scanner; eggs by the dozen, vast slabs of delicious Pecorino cheese, carefully parcelled up bags of delicatessen meat, oranges and squishy orange sharon fruit, and freshly baked pastries. Little did she know I was silently plotting her doom.

"How many children have you got?" she asked, glancing over her shoulder: Valentino's eyebrows were just visible over the top of the heap of food she had piled up behind her.

"Oh, just this one," I answered.

She rang up the total, deftly using the ends of her sloth-length claws, which came to just over three hundred euros.

She stood up from her seat to lean over and take a better look at Matteo. "He's got blonde hair," she commented as she sat back down and pushed her long, glossy hair behind her shoulders. This comment needed no further explanation, as it is always regarded as a compliment in Sicily, where blonde hair is unusual. She was looking a little less snooty now, and I was almost toying with the idea of forgiving her.

"And blue eyes," said Valentino, his head bent down as he frantically crammed bags of sweets and a huge selection of teabags

225

into yet another plastic bag.

"I wish I could have a blue-eyed baby, but my fiancé's got brown eyes like me, so I don't think there's a chance."

"Why do you think I married an English girl?" joked Valentino. He held out three crisp, one-hundred euro notes to me, which I passed to Lift Hog. As she opened the till, I unclipped the sling at one side so I could pull it away from me and let her see Matteo's face. I lifted his tiny hand and waved it at her.

"Say ciao!" I cooed at him, and tipped my head right down to kiss the top of his head.

When I looked up again, there was a young man standing behind Lift Hog. Maybe he was just eighteen; he could not have been more than twenty. He grasped a large swathe of her black hair in one hand, and was digging the barrel of a gun into the back of her neck with the other as she winced. A second young man with black stubble like a toilet brush stood very close beside the boy with the gun. He swiped my three hundred euros out of her hand in an instant and grinned as he pocketed it, revealing a missing tooth.

"Hurry up!" the man with the gun shouted into Lift Hog's ear, so loudly that she flinched.

I stood frozen, in disbelief. It seemed utterly unreal. My mind started wandering to the spud gun I used to play with in the garden with my sisters. The pistol held to the girl's head looked very similar. We used to dig the barrel of the spud gun into a potato to make a "bullet" and then fire it at each other at close range. My sister was far better at it than I was, and always scored multiple direct hits. In under a minute she could turn a potato into a filigree sculpture and blast all the pieces at me so rapidly my dress would end up damp all over from the barrage. My mind wandered back and forth, from irrelevant memories floating in unbidden, to the scene before me which I had seen countless times in films and televisions dramas. Perhaps all that acting was what made it seem unreal now that I was seeing it happen in front of me?

The young man fidgeted with impatience as the girl pulled the banknotes out of the till, one sheaf at a time. His hands were grubby, I noticed, and his fingernails were dirty and broken. She showed no signs of panic; she just concentrated on pulling the money out systematically with her pink plastic nails.

"Hurry up!" he shouted at her again, twisting his grip more tightly around her hair. He jerked her head each time he spoke.

He was tall, surprisingly tall for a Sicilian and also remarkably good-looking. I found myself reflecting on how sad it was that a potentially fine young man should be engaged in such inglorious activities, and wondered if his mother would be saddened to know he had come to such a useless end, or whether perhaps she knew and did not care. I also wondered if he had a girlfriend, and whether she was also good looking but dirty. I wondered if he had bad breath. I also scrutinised his hair for signs of dandruff.

"Have you got a two-cent coin," asked Valentino suddenly, his head bowed down as he rummaged in the depths of his wallet. "I haven't quite got the right change."

"Er, Valentino," I said.

"Yes, what?" he asked, his head still buried deep in a plastic bag of packs of pasta in every shape that has ever been manufactured.

"Look," I said. He glanced up, and instantly reacted as if an electric current had been passed through him.

"What the hell are you doing standing there?" he squawked, his voice strangulated with panic. "Come on!"

He reached out and grabbed my arm, jerking me towards him so hard that Matteo almost slipped sideways out of the sling. I wrapped my arms around my precious bundle and shuffled as fast as I could towards the exit. Valentino came behind, chivvying me along but, I noticed, frugally making sure he towed our trolley with him.

"Run!" he shouted. "Don't wait for me!"

At this point I finally put on a spurt of speed, realising that a dramatic exodus of the supermarket was taking place. There were trolleys left all over the place and people were streaming through the exit. In the car park, Valentino made an Olympic-standard dash to the car and started throwing shopping into the boot in the hastiest, most reckless manner imaginable. As I was about to open the car door, I turned and saw the two young men, the one with dirty fingernails still brandishing his gun, sprinting straight towards us across the now almost empty car park at spectacular speed. Their faces were flushed red with excitement and bore expressions of triumph.

I ran around the car and hid behind it, crouching down between a low wall and the car's bonnet. The smell of hot engine oil filled my nostrils. By this time I was furious. I was fully ready to rip their heads off if either of them tried to touch my baby. Valentino, meanwhile, had snatched the car keys out of the ignition and stuffed them into his pocket.

The ugly toothless one ran around the back of our car whilst the handsome, dirty one scrambled over the bonnet. His muddy boots flew not six inches in front of my face. I thought they planned to use our car as their getaway vehicle. Maybe they would shoot Valentino to get the keys? Then in a split second, to my inexpressible relief, I realised that they were heading towards a scooter, parked beyond our car. They leapt on it and headed off, in a cloud of choking black exhaust fumes and the roar of a motor in dire need of re-tuning.

As they turned out of the car park and disappeared out of sight, Valentino and I instinctively dashed towards each other and hugged. By this time, at long last, I felt fully hyped up for a crisis, exactly when it was over. Valentino, on the other hand, was already filled with so much adrenaline that not only were his hands shaking, but his entire body. His eyes were opened as wide as a rabbit in car headlights. He was so hyped up I think he may even have been hovering a few inches above the ground.

"Sit down in the back seat of the car and have some chocolate," I told him firmly. "That's what you need to help you feel better."

He finished off a whole bar of it and sat for twenty minutes before he felt calm enough to drive us home.

The next day Ninfa came round to do the cleaning and was shocked when I told her about the hold-up at the supermarket. I may be slow to react in a crisis, but after twenty-four hours my nervous system had gone into a kind of turbo-charged nervous breakdown mode. She did the prayer for worms for me.

Shortly after the supermarket raid, we started to hear updates from friends and neighbours. The two young men struck again a week later, choosing the same cashier. This time, apparently, the one with dirty nails beat the butt of his handgun into the nape of her neck as he was leaving, making her fall to the ground and leaving her with whiplash injuries. No pineapple chunks were involved, and by this time I had fully let go of my desire to launch a vendetta against her: apparently someone else was doing so already. This second raid was witnessed by a colleague of Valentino's, who was immensely thankful he had gone alone and left his wife at home with the children.

The supermarket rapidly installed security cameras and hired a team of security guards from a private security company. Men from these security companies, called the *Guardia Giurata*, are ubiquitous in mainland Italy, but fairly rare in Sicily. Presumably there are fewer volunteers in the homelands of the Mafia, where the job is so much more dangerous. These guards are wannabe policemen, notorious in Italy for being the men who were rejected both by the Polizia, the civil police, and the Carabinieri, the military police. To be rejected by both of these organisations means that you have an IQ lower than that of a marmot and that you could not fire a bullet into an elephant at a distance of six inches. You are also likely to be a midget, struggle wretchedly with the art of controlling motorised vehicles, and have a streak of lunatic bad temper.

When I had briefly lived in Como, many years ago, I unintentionally befriended a group of these guards. It was rather like being buddies with Laurel and Hardy, Norman Wisdom and Mister Bean. I would have liked to become chummy with George Clooney instead, but you can't have everything. They were full of amazing stories about their colleagues. One of them had driven his car into a river while attempting to light a cigarette as he chased a "suspect"; another had once set fire to his own trousers while wearing them; one of my friends shot himself in the leg trying to clean his gun which was still loaded with bullets; and, worst of all, one man in their barracks shot his wife dead because he found a man's trousers in his bedroom, later realising that the trousers were in fact his own. Many of these men were armed to the teeth, not only with hand guns but also with rifles. One of them, who had three strategically placed missing teeth and one gold crown which made him look like a Mexican bandit, once opened the boot of his car and, with an unhinged look in his eyes, showed me a small machine gun which he set up on a tripod, and about eight long strips of ammunition for it, of the sort Rambo wears. He also had five hand grenades. I asked him what type of training they received to use this stuff.

He shrugged. "None."

When I heard the news that a *Guardia Giurata* had been hired, I banned Valentino from going shopping at that supermarket ever again. If he did not get shot by the thieves, he most certainly would by them. Presumably, many wives did the same because the car park was usually half deserted when we drove past. Word spread that the pair of armed raiders had struck again and that, this time, the ugly one was armed too. We were also notified via the Auntienet that our friend Gianfortuna no longer worked there. His wife had decided she would prefer he sold potatoes from the boot of the car by the roadside rather than risk going back there again. Apparently he had not put up much of a protest because he hated all his colleagues anyway.

One day Valentino went shopping alone and, as he was unloading the shopping I saw the bags were from the dreaded supermarket. I was furious.

"If you go there again your son could grow up an orphan!" I yelled at him. "I am serious! Do the shopping somewhere else! Anywhere!"

A few weeks later, we received an exciting update from a friend whose wife had also banned him from going there. Another renegade husband, he just could not stay away. He had gone there and realised that none of the usual staff were to be seen. The *Guardia Giurata* had vanished, too. Everyone stacking the shelves was new, and they all looked more interested in the customers than the stock. Everyone at the tills was new as well, and there were three people at every open till; one working, one watching, and a third helping customers pack their shopping into carrier bags. Almost all the staff were men.

"They've never had such good customer service there before," he enthused. Valentino listened to him, uncharacteristically tight-lipped.

Before he had got to the till, the two infamous young men appeared. No sooner had the first gun been produced than two of the three men at the till whipped out hand guns of their own and aimed them at the dirty boy's head. While the third wrestled him to the ground and handcuffed him, the men from the next till leapt in a very athletic manner across the aisle, and disarmed and cuffed the stubbly one. They all revealed their identification as Carabinieri and told the men their rights as they led them away.

"I suppose the Carabinieri will go away now and we'll get the usual *vastasi* working there again," commented our friend forlornly as he concluded his story. *Vastaso* is Palermo slang which, in the seventeenth century, meant a porter who would carry posh people from one side of a sewage-sloshed street to the other for a small tip. Nowadays it means "a potty-mouthed, bad mannered slob of the lowest social order."

"If they do bring the *vastasi* back, I won't bother going there any more," said Valentino. He shot me a guilty glance. "oops."

The next day, Valentino came home from work buzzing with excitement.

"Everyone at the law courts today was talking about a major Mafia *pentito,*" he said. *Pentito* means supergrass. Apparently he had revealed evidence relating to several dozen Mafia suspects to the police.

"Why would he do that?" I asked.

"*Mafiosi* do that when they've run out of other options," he said. "He's obviously pissed off too many Mafia associates, and it would only be a matter of time before one of them finished him off."

"Will they start to arrest people now?" I asked.

"If we've heard this news, they already have," replied Valentino.

26

THE GODMOTHER STRIKES AGAIN

We decided to have Matteo christened when he was three months old. Naturally, the Godmother was going to be my son's godmother. Who else could it be?

By this time I could lie down on the bed, and then get myself up again without needing help from a crane. I had also had time to compare my caesarean scar with some other recently chopped-up mothers. Theirs were about three inches long, whilst mine wrapped almost the whole way around my abdomen. I could not see my rear, but the ends may well have joined up at the back. Basically the surgeon, or rather apprentice butcher, who had delivered my baby had decided to extract him using the Matrioshka Method. Under this pioneering Russian surgical technique, you cut the top off the mother like a Russian nesting doll and – behold! – there is a smaller one inside which you can lift out. Then all you have to do is stick the top back on the outer doll and forget about her.

I went to a different gynaecologist and learned that the one who had overseen my pregnancy and Matteo's delivery was, indeed, not a real surgeon. He was registered, but he had never qualified to practise medicine. This explained why he did not know how to interpret blood test results as accurately as I did after five minutes of in-depth research on Wikipedia. This also explained why he wanted to physically examine my innermost crevices every time he saw me, when real gynaecologists do not even look up there while you are pregnant as it can provoke a miscarriage. This also explained why he seemed to think I should bow down and worship him each time I saw him, like a supplicant before an altar to Jesus the Light of the World. Mafiosi think they are more important than everyone else and they want everyone else to treat them accordingly. The fact that he gained his position by being in the Mafia explained why nobody had sued him, even though it is fairly easy to sue most bad doctors in Italy: the Mafia are still, in some contexts, the untouchables.

The upshot of having been bisected and then vaguely stuck together was not only indescribable pain. I also had to contend with the fact that, three months after giving birth, I still looked nine months pregnant. For the christening I had managed to acquire a pretty and flattering outfit in a dress size so vast it was only just shy of triple digits. Now all I needed to get myself into it was a corset strong enough to resist an outward pressure in excess 2,000,000 Newtons per square centimetre.

Accompanied by The Godmother, I went to one of Italy's notorious, massive out-of-town underwear emporiums and tried to buy an elastic corset to help my lacerated abdominal muscles keep my innards from sloshing about inside me, or, worse, spilling out of me.

"These are for wearing *after* giving birth," the shop assistant said, looking a little concerned. The Godmother looked at my poor, painful tummy and sneered.

"I was back in perfect shape and looking after my baby with no help at this stage," she said, smiling, to the shop assistant.

"It's easy to 'get back into shape' after a pregnancy if your original shape was spherical," I said. I really did say that, but I was scared of The Godmother, so I said it in English.

"Why make post-partum recovery into a competition?" was what I said in Italian. The shop assistant agreed with me, though not too vociferously. She glanced nervously at The Godmother. I added, "...especially when comparing a nineteen-year-old who had a natural birth with a thirty-five year old who had a caesarean performed by someone imitating the MO of Jack the Ripper."

I said most of this to myself while wandering away to fume over some tiny thong knickers made of pure nylon. They would have been great in a power cut, because you could just run around the room in them and generate your own sparks of electricity. Why did the Godmother claim to have looked after her children with no help? Manfredi had lived with Nonna full time until he was eighteen. She had taken the other children to spend every day with Big Nonna, who cooked all their food. As usual, trying not to inflame the situation because I loved Valentino too much to hurt him, I said nothing about this.

Armed with a military grade corset and fancy outfit, I was as ready for this christening as I was ever going to be. Having been brought up in a household so atheist that what we called "the bible" was a bookshelf containing the Merck Manual of Diagnosis and

Therapy, the British Medical Formulary, the Encyclopedia Britannica and seven years' copies of New Scientist magazine, I was not too sure of the procedure. I mean, I knew it would be done in church. I knew the priest puts water on the baby's head at some point. I had been in a Catholic country long enough to have a pretty good idea it would all take so long that my buttocks would become paralysed. The one thing I was absolutely sure about was that the baby should wear an extremely long, white, lacy, frilly beautiful little dress.

As I think we have established, the only domestic activity for which I have any propensity whatsoever is sewing. Let's make no bones about it, I am brilliant at sewing. I made my first dress when I was nine years old, and wore it to school, and was widely admired (until Philip Doye kicked me and left a muddy footprint on my backside, but we won't talk about that). I spent weeks working on a little dress for Matteo. I bought ribbons and lace and I embroidered it too. I sewed tiny pin tucks down the front, I put frills round the cuffs, and I embroidered a tiny pair of satin slippers to match. I knew he would grow into a strapping thug of a boy in no time, who would rub his cheek where I had kissed him and refuse to hold my hand in public, so I went all out to make him look like an utterly gorgeous little china doll whilst I still could. The outfit was fabulous.

My family flew out to Sicily for the Christening. My father was getting older and weaker and the low-oxygen conditions on the aeroplane had put his heart under great strain. His already bad hearing had become drastically was worse, his breathing was laboured, and he looked exhausted.

"Are you alright, Dad?" I asked him, very loudly, trying not to look worried.

"Course I bloody well am," he told me and my sisters. "I'm not about to croak yet!"

The photographers came to my house to take photographs in advance of the church service. They were the same photographers who had directed and stage managed my wedding, but this time, my family and I were ready for them. Everyone was done up to the nines in rhinestones and cloth of gold, with thoroughly sprayed, wind-resistant hair. Matteo looked absolutely adorable in his christening gown, and smiled or lay serenely to pose for photographs in everyone's arms, in turn.

Suddenly the Godmother arrived, with a different gown. It was nice but nowhere near as pretty as the one I had made. It was clearly very old, and had been "restored." It was about the right size for a Barbie doll.

"Let's get him dressed in this lovely gown and pose for some photos," she announced loudly.

"What?" asked my sister.

"This was the gown all my babies were christened in," she said. "Valentino was christened in it."

Matteo was born big, and had been eating for England ever since. It was already clear he was going to grow up to be a rugby player. The Godmother pulled my gown off him, then tried to dress him in the tiny gown she had produced. She draped it over the front part of his body, wedging his arms in so he was trussed up and unable to move, and sat posing for photographs while he cried.

She sat on the dress I had made. By the time I managed to make her get off it, which I only did by pushing her repeatedly in the side, it looked like a screwed up, desiccated old dishcloth that has been forgotten for months in the cupboard under the sink.

"At least we got some photographs of Matteo in it before she ruined it" said my mother sadly in English.

"Has the baby done a poo?" asked my father. "I think I can smell something."

He had indeed done a poo. It was the fourth one of the day.

The church service involved three christenings. We all sat happily listening to the service. It began normally enough, and then, when it got fully underway, there was a bible reading about lepers and how they are being punished for their sins, and that is why they are ill. The priest went on to explain, after various leprosy-related quotations, that diseases and all general sufferings are punishments that we deserve because we have sinned and merit punishment to teach us a lesson. The Godmother threw me a meaningful glance. Christened though he was, I decided to bring my son up with the New Scientist as his bible.

I was relieved that, at this point, Matteo did another poo. This one appeared marginally "unhealthy", let me say, and leave it at that. I do not wish to dwell on gross details, but you will realise the importance of this information later on.

The sermon continued. The priest was elaborating on the theme of disease as a holy yardstick of how bad we are, and how much we need punishing. The Godmother looked delighted. Matteo did another poo. Usually, when your baby does a smelly poo, you groan and at this point both parents mentally tot up how many nappies they have each changed over the last twenty-four hours, and whose turn it is. Tense negotiations and mental arithmetic sometimes ensue. This time, I was delighted to sneak out of the church into the hall at the back and do all the changes myself. I made them take far longer than necessary. They seemed to be growing more frequent. His diarrhoea served him right, of course. He was being punished by God for some sin or other. Maybe it was that time he had tried to use my left nipple as chewing gum.

The time for putting water of the baby's head came and went. I had feared it might be a big slosh, but it was just a dab. We posed for photographs and The Godmother did not let me hold Matteo in any of the pictures. She held him proudly herself, bursting out of his tiny gown as he was.

Finally we went to the restaurant at which Valentino and I were feeding the entire extended family at great expense. When we reached the restaurant, we realised one of the other christening families from the church was also eating there.

"We're being stalked by an enormous Sicilian family," shouted my father. Now he was losing his hearing, he always spoke too loudly.

"Shush!" said my mother.

"They don't understand English," said Dad. "You can say anything you like. Happy Christmas!" he called out to them, waving and smiling.

"Auguri!" they called back, waving and smiling and looking very happy.

My father sat beside my sister Susy. He did not like the fish menu. I had left Valentino to choose the dishes as I was still not well, and did not have the stamina to get involved. I knew it would feature fish, but I thought he had worked out by now that English people chop all anatomical parts off their fish, remove fins and other swimming-related paraphernalia, cover it in batter and deep fry it. I thought he realised they would not be keen to find swim bladders, eyeballs or scales in with their lunch. I was wrong.

"This looks like the entire contents of a rock pool, ladled into a bowl," said my sister as the first course, called *brodo di pesce*, 'fish broth', was brought out. She was right, of course. It was watery soup with a few mussels, clams, pieces of spiny fish and other marine life drifting in it. There were shells. There was a strand of seaweed. There was an eyeball gazing at her.

"I think I'll wait till the next course," said my mother, trying to look courageous. "I'm not that hungry." As she pushed the bowl away, her stomach rumbled louder than an earthquake.

The next course was pasta with prawns. I realised this would upset my father too much, so I asked the waiter to make him a risotto with sausage. When this was duly brought to the table, my father started protesting.

"I can't eat this," he said decisively. "There's fish in this. It smells awful."

"It's a risotto with sausage," said Susy patiently. "There's no fish."

"It's got fish in it," said my father.

"No, it's sausage," insisted my sister.

"Look, that's a fish," said Dad.

"No, it's a sausage," said my sister.

"What?" said Dad.

"Sausage," said my sister.

"What?" said Dad.

"IT'S A SAUSAGE!!!!!" screamed my sister at the top of her lungs. She happened to scream this just when every single conversation going on around the table, just at that very instant, had by sheer coincidence fallen into a momentary lull. She howled "It's a sausage" into a vast room of silent diners, every single one of whom stopped chewing and stared at her. Her face turned crimson.

"I think it's fish," said Dad calmly, oblivious to the audience.

"Shut up and eat it," hissed my mother, seated the other side of him, as the hubbub of conversation gradually resumed.

When we came to the toasts, my father turned around to hold his glass up to the family the other side of the restaurant, also celebrating their christening.

"Happy Easter!" he called out, holding up his glass.

"Auguri!" they called out, beaming smiles. "Appy Ister!" a couple of them called back.

While there was food on the table, the Godmother ignored Matteo, which meant I had to eat with him on my lap as he cried when left alone. After the meal was finished, the cameras returned and we were required to pose for more photographs.

"Let me help you," offered The Godmother generously, lifting Matteo out of my arms and holding onto him as she beamed at the cameras.

Just at that moment, he dropped a bomb on her. I do not mean any kind of bomb. I mean a brown, runny, leaky, absolutely stinking baby bomb which seeped through his microscopic swaddling-clothes style christening gown and spread out on The Godmother's skirt. That was the moment I realised I did not have to worry what the Godmother said or did any more. She could give me her worst and I did not care.

Now, for the rest of my life, I had an ally.

This brought the festivities to a slightly more abrupt ending than might otherwise have happened. I was pleased, as I was tired and wanted to give Matteo a bath and then put him down for a nap. On the way out of the restaurant the other family said goodbye to my father in a most friendly fashion.

"Happy Chanukka!" he called out, waving at them as he walked out.

The Auntienet was buzzing a week later. Thirty-two *mafiosi* had been arrested in our little backwater of a town. They were not small-fry, either. Each one of them was a major boss running his own international drug- and arms-dealing, extortion and protection racket operation. I think it would be an understatement to say I was amazed. Our town is honestly a one-horse town with a tiny population, so forgive me for being rather gobsmacked to find out that we had such a lot of Mafia bigshots here.

We rushed out to buy the *Giornale di Sicila*, Sicily's leading newspaper. It confirmed that the arrests had been made as a result of information and evidence provided by a single Mafia *pentito* – a supergrass who had revealed all to the police. Along with the thirty-two arrests, the newspaper revealed, the police had recovered thirty million euros in cash, buildings, businesses, supermarkets, and other varied loot. The money had been accumulated through drug trafficking, extortion, kidnap, illegal arms dealing and rigging elections.

One of the men arrested was the mayor of a nearby town. He was a member of the political party called the Lega Nord, which would never get elected in Sicily unless the elections were rigged, because their main policy is to cut Sicily loose and create a new Italy *without* the primitive peoples of Italy's incompetent south. Their politicians are regularly to be seen on Italian TV, railing against the Mafia of the south who are "dragging the whole country down". The idea that any Sicilian would vote for this party in a free election was ludicrous.

The newspaper page was peppered with hideously ugly mugshots. Two of them were neighbours of ours, and one lived up at the top of the road, on the corner. We recognised several others from nearby. When members of the Japanese Mafia mess up, I have been told, they are punished by being forced to cut off one of their own fingers. The Sicilian Mafia, on the other hand, apparently punish mistakes with a ferocious eyebrow plucking. (They don't really. I'm just kidding about that. At least I think I am.) In picture after picture, alarmingly dense men glared into the vacant middle distance, looking stressed or angry. Some of them were evocative of shaven gibbons. I checked every photo carefully, but could not recognise Fortunato Mastronzo in any of them.

"Just because he's not in the Mafia doesn't mean he's not a criminal," said Valentino. "I've heard on good authority that he's definitely going to prison."

"Good. He deserves it," I said.

I worked through all the information slowly, having to ask Valentino the definition of at least two words in every sentence. Valentino is appallingly bad at providing the definition of any word. The best definition he ever gave me was when I asked him the meaning of *lenticchie*.

"They're small red elliptical objects, for making soup," he explained. This was enough to convey the concept of lentils. If only he could achieve this level of precision most of the time I would understand perfectly, but usually I end up telephoning The Godmother to ask her, even when my husband is standing in the room right in front of me.

Valentino had already moved onto the second article and was repeatedly stabbing lines on the adjacent page with his finger, and making noisy and distracting exclamations in Sicilian.

"Mizzichina!" he shouted.

Poke, rustle rustle.

"Addirittura!"

The paper nearly ripped.

"Shush!" I shouted. "I'm trying to concentrate!"

In the end I just made Valentino read the article and then give me a summary.

"There was a massive shoot-out at the local city rubbish dump, including hand grenades and possibly landmines. The police found two bodies left there, one containing thirty-five bullet holes and the other with fifty-two of them. Apart from all the perforations, they were both charred and burnt to crisps as well, and one of the bodies had its head cut off. The other had its genitals lying about twenty feet away from the torso." Valentino winced as he said this.

"Mizzichina!" I shouted.

"It says the police could tell explosives had been used, because there were big areas of the dump that were just ash-filled circles of empty ground. So far, the forensics team has found signs there were at least fourteen people involved in the gunfight."

"Addiritura!" I exclaimed.

"They think there were other deaths there, though so far they haven't found any other bodies. And I bet they never will, either. They've identified the two bodies at the dump with DNA samples. Guess who they were."

"No idea," I gasped, "just tell me!"

"Mauro De Simone and Michele Calò, those old friends of Engineer Mastronzo."

"Mamma Mia!" I shouted, thumping the newspaper. "So does that mean he got some Mafia cronies to kill them? Was he the *pentito?*"

"It doesn't name the *pentito*," said Valentino. "The newspaper just says they were targeted for arrest and tracked all the way from Canada. They'd tried to rip off the local bosses." Valentino raised his eyebrows.

"So we don't know if Mr. Faeces was the pentito," I said.

"Nope," said Val.

"But if he's not named, that either means it *was* him, or that he was never in the Mafia at all," I reasoned.

"Yes," said Valentino.

"And we'll never know," I concluded, frustrated.

"Probably," agreed Valentino, turning back to the newspaper.

The Canadian arm of Cosa Nostra had a massive war going on now, the newspaper reported in a little separate article. Murders were taking place in Canada in blockbuster quantities, like an Arnold Schwarzenegger movie, apparently, in the struggle for new leadership.

One interesting snippet that came out of the whole monitoring and sting operation was the revelation of the Cosa Nostra membership initiation rites. It has long been known that joining the Mafia is rather like joining the Freemasons or the Moonies or maybe a US university frat society: they demand utter loyalty and have weird initiation rituals.

New initiates to the Sicilian Mafia have to do the following: firstly, prick their trigger-pulling finger with a thorn from a bitter orange tree (in case you've never foolishly tried to climb an orange tree, you'll have to take it from me that these thorns are two inches long and can pierce human bones); some clans of the Mafia use a golden thorn instead; secondly, bleed onto a religious picture; thirdly, set the bloody picture on fire whilst holding it in both hands; and, finally, whilst *not* screaming like a girl because their fingers are getting barbecued, recite an oath of loyalty until death to the Mafia.

The newspaper report went into gleeful detail on all this information. The police had learned from one bugged conversation, we read, that the new initiates who make mistakes are punished by having their legs thrashed with horsewhips.

"Well, next time I see a bloke limping along with blood seeping out of his trouser legs and with savagely plucked eyebrows, I shall NOT offer to help him across the road!" I told Valentino decisively. "So where will they all go now?"

"Probably the five star Mafia prison in Palermo," said Valentino.

The Five Star de Luxe Prison, which is really called the Ucciardone, is a large building in a fairly posh district of Palermo with a great many *mafiosi* in it, and a forest of satellite dishes on its roof. It has air conditioning, which most Sicilian homes do not, because they cannot afford it. Apparently the bosses in there are the only people who can eat fresh strawberries in winter, as they have them airlifted in and specially delivered to their cells. There have been cases of bosses commanding operations from inside, using their wives at visiting time as messengers. They communicated using an extraordinarily complex secret code. Asking "How is uncle Pino?" while scratching their right ear, for example, meant one thing, whereas posing the same question while touching the nose had an entirely different meaning, and so on. In some cases the police have monitored films taken at prison visiting time, and managed to crack the code after a year or even two years of careful observation. It is difficult to stop a crime organisation when you put members in prison yet still cannot remove them from power.

Even so, they do live behind a wall which is topped with a reassuringly large mass of barbed wire.

"You know you said about Engineer Mastronzo?" I said. "If he's going to prison, does that mean our house will be a slaughterhouse forever?"

"Oh, no, we'll have to apply for countless documents and bits of paper and it will probably take ten years or more, but eventually we'll get it registered as a house."

I breathed a sigh of relief.

"I hope," added Valentino.

"You hope? What if we don't?"

"Oh don't worry. It doesn't matter."

Valentino smiled one of his magic smiles that makes me stop worrying about anything, and then I felt alright.

EPILOGUE

A TRIP UP MONTE PELLEGRINO

I told Valentino I wanted to go up Monte Pellegrino as soon as my tummy had healed properly. I wanted to thank Rosalia for granting my three wishes. She had, as requested, sent me a man to love me, a wedding, and a baby. I also wanted to thank her for all those arrests and for making the engineer end up in prison, where he deserved to be. Finally, of course, I wanted to thank her for that marvellous poo.

"We're going in the car," said Valentino emphatically. "I am *not* running up there again at your speed. My legs still hurt from the first time."

When we walked through the Baroque church doorway and into the damp cave, there was my dear old friend Rosalia holding her arms out, to receive crash helmets, silver organs and limbs, and prayers on little paper scrolls. I took my own offering out of my handbag and placed it at her feet.

"What?" exclaimed Valentino in disbelief. "What are you leaving that great fossil here for?"

"The saints have mysterious ways of answering our prayers," I said. "Rosalia lived in caves, so I think that's why she used a rock."

Valentino rolled those big dark eyes of his.

"So long as you're happy," he said, putting his arm around me. "You *are* happy here, aren't you?"

"Yes, I am," I answered, looking at baby Matteo. "Yes of course I am."

DID YOU ENJOY THIS?

If you enjoyed this book, please go to Amazon and write a glowing review or, better still, persuade some of your friends to buy more copies of it.

The author is skint and would be so grateful.

MY THANKS

My thanks to Mike Doyle for designing a cover (which I didn't use), to Louse Dean for all her help with designing my blog, to Hubby for cooking all the meals, to The Godmother for keeping me on my toes, to my sister Isabelle Hughes and to Michaela Longo for conspiring to get me to fall in love with a Sicilian in the first place, and to the makers of Yorkshire tea, without whom I'd never have had the energy to write this book.

If you would like to read more of my pontificating, visit my blog.

 **SicilianGodmother.com**

Alternatively, you could try my other books.....

Available in paperback and Kindle on Amazon websites worldwide

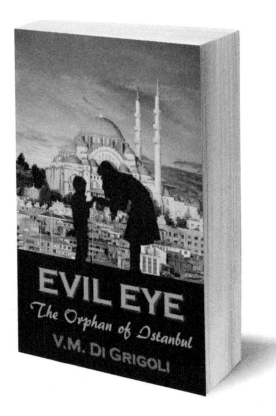

EVIL EYE
THE ORPHAN OF ISTANBUL

One orphan desperately tries to save another, lost in a city of ten million

Freshly graduated and orphaned at the same time, day-dreamy Celeste is hypnotised by the ethereal mosques and dazzling bazaars of Istanbul as an escape from all that hurts her. Yet running away from her problems only leads her into new ones.

Her students at the swanky language school seem more interested in their manicures than her English lessons. The morose caretaker of the orphanage where she volunteers stares at her boys like a vulture sizing up its next meal. Worst of all, her landlady lets slip sinister comments that don't make sense, leaves spine-chilling mystic charms around the house, and puts magic spells in places she should not be going.

When Celeste's favourite orphan vanishes, she embarks on a frantic search through crowded bazaars and dangerous alleys, desperate to find one small boy lost in a city of ten million. But can innocent Celeste save the child, and herself, before someone destroys them?

FRIENDS WITH SECRETS

*Two ordinary women caught between a Colombian drug
cartel and the Soviet Mafia*

New York, 1993: Mistry thinks she has a safe job in a bank, but
when she realises a client is using her to launder money, someone
tries to kill her. How can she outwit a criminal who has already
outwitted the police?

London, England: College teacher Crystal befriends a teenage
language student from war-torn Georgia as he confides in her how
his brother was kidnapped and held to ransom. A Colombian
student, realising she has spotted him receiving a huge sum of
cash, threatens to kill her if she tells the police. When another
student vanishes, Crystal realises she has stumbled into a deadly

conflict between a Colombian drug cartel and the Soviet Mafia. She already knows too much. Who can help her now?

As the net tightens around Crystal, and Mistry's assassin tries to kill her again, they cross paths and realise their only hope is to unite forces. Two scared young women discover just how resourceful danger can make them.

But are they in time to save each other's lives?

HOW TO PROTCT YOURSELF AGAINST THE EVIL EYE

Since Neolithic times people have feared the evil eye – the potent stare of an envious person, believed to cause sickness, suffering or even death. This intriguing book explains where the Bible, the Koran and most religions warn of its dangers and offer defences against it, as well as revealing the more ancient secrets of amulets, purifying rituals and protective gestures still used across the world to this day. After reading this book, you will never see the world in quite the same way again.

The author, who studied Classical History at Cambridge University, interviewed shamans and believers in the evil eye around the world to research this highly entertaining book, which has over 80 illustrations.

SICILIAN CARD GAMES
AN EASY-TO-FOLLOW GUIDE

'SICILIAN CARD GAMES an easy-to-follow guide' gives very clear instructions for twelve Sicilian card games, with photographic illustrations. It is the ONLY book of Sicilian card games in print worldwide. Sicily has its own unique deck of playing cards, and a wealth of games exclusive to the island. PACKS OF SICILIAN PLAYING CARDS CAN BE ORDERED ON AMAZON.COM Card games are central to festivities at Christmas, Easter and other family gatherings. Some games are hilarious, and simple enough to be enjoyed by young children yet a great way to make them practise mental arithmetic. Other games are quite challenging. Most village squares have a full-time squadron of old men who play outdoors, smacking their winning cards down like a butcher with a meat cleaver. The games in the book are: Buona sera Signorina, Cavalli, Cu cu!, Camicia, Asino, Sette e Mezzo, Trentuno, Centocinque, Brìscula, Tresette, Terziglio, Scopa.

'SICILIAN CARD GAMES an easy-to-follow guide' includes an interesting explanation of the origins of Sicilian playing cards. This book makes an entertaining and economical gift for all ages.

FULL COLOUR LARGE FORMAT EDITION

With 3 bonus games and full-colour photographic illustrations.

GIOCHI DI CARTE SICILIANE
GUIDA FACILE AI GIOCHI CLASSICI

Italian language edition written with Fabio Sirchia.